8 13ø
J
1
9 18

Acknowledgements

Illustrations by courtesy of the following:

American Spice Trade Association: Black and white photograph accompanying Recipe 484.

The Bacon Information Council Ltd: Colour pictures nos. 1, 7, 11. Black and white photographs accompanying Recipes 128, 227.

Batchelors Foods Ltd: Colour pictures no. 4. Black and white photographs accompanying Recipe 16, 70, 134, 187, 264, 273, 299, 339, 434.

Alfred Bird & Sons Ltd: Colour picture no. 28. Black and white photographs accompanying Recipes 580, 590, 607, 612, 640, 644, 645, 652.

Bird's Eye Frozen Foods: Black and white photographs accompanying Recipes 15, 132, 179, 223-4, 234.

Blue Band Luxury Margarine: Black and white photographs accompanying Recipes 386, 398, 445.

British Egg Information Service: Black and white photograph accompanying Recipes 281, 536.

The British Electrical Development Association: Colour picture no. 12.

California Raisin Bureau: Black and white photographs accompanying Recipes 176, 183, 210, 408, 427, 433, 495−6.

Campbell's Soups Ltd: Black and white photographs accompanying Recipe 127, 259.

Canned Foods Advisory Bureau: Black and white photograph accompanying Recipe 43.

The Cheese Bureau: Black and white photographs accompanying Recipes 219, 220, 334−5.

Chicken Information Council: Black and white photograph accompanying Recipe 178.

Citrus Fruits and South African Fruits: Black and white photographs accompanying Recipes 159, 294, 306, 423, 425, 436, 501.

Colman's Mustard: Colour pictures nos. 20, 26. Black and white photographs accompanying Recipes 226, 238, 552.

Colman's Semolina: Black and white photographs accompanying Recipes 243−4, 304, 385.

Cookeen: Black and white photographs accompanying Recipes 233, 460.

Creda: Colour picture no. 34.

Danish Agricultural Producers Information Service: Colour picture no. 23.

Elders and Fyffes Bananas: Colour picture no. 14. Black and white photographs accompanying Recipes 174, 372, 374, 467.

English Country Cheese Council: Colour picture no. 9. Black and white photographs accompanying Recipes 197, 213, 215, 217, 218.

Express Dairy Products: Black and white photographs accompanying Recipes 169, 173.

Farmer & Stock-Breeder: Black and white photographs accompanying Recipes 4, 246, 257, 308, 540, 556, 632.

Findus Frozen Foods: Black and white photographs accompanying Recipes 383, 402, 470.

Green Giant Corn and Mexicorn: Black and white photographs accompanying Recipes 47, 50, 83.

H. J. Heinz Co. Ltd: Colour pictures nos. 5, 31, 33. Black and white photograph accompanying Recipe 55.

Heerring Industry Board: Black and white photographs accompanying Recipes 103, 192.

Ideal Milk: Colour pictures nos. 13, 29.

The Italian State Tourist Office: Black and white photographs accompanying Recipes 594, 616, 646, 691.

Kraft Foods Ltd: Black and white photographs accompanying Recipes 144, 148, 158, 162, 166, 201, 225.

Maggi Bouillon Cubes: Black and white photograph accompanying Recipe 668.

Mushroom Growers Association: Black and white photograph accompanying Recipe 150.

National Federation of Women's Institutes: Black and white photographs accompanying Recipes 497, 683.

National Film Board of Canada: Black and white photograph accompanying Recipe 583.

National Milk Publicity Council: Black and white photographs accompanying Recipes 23, 284, 438, 674, 676, 677.

Nestles Condensed Milk: Colour picture no. 25.

Outspan Oranges: Colour picture no. 18.

The Pig Industry Development Authority Home Service: Colour picture no. 27. Black and white photographs accompanying Recipes 74, 291, 295.

Potato Desk: Colour pictures no. 3. Black and white photographs accompanying Recipes 75, 90, 105, 705.

Prestige Group Ltd: Black and white photographs accompanying Recipes 96, 155, 509, 510, 511.

Public Relations Associates Ltd: Colour pictures nos. 8, 16, 17, 19, 21, 24, 30. Black and white photographs accompanying Recipes 303, 362, 364−5, 366, 723.

Retailer Publicity Services Ltd: Colour picture no. 32.

Rice Council of U.S.A.: Colour picture no. 2. Black and white photographs accompanying Recipes 61, 253.

Swiss Gruyère Cheeses: Colour picture no. 10.

Swiss Knight Processed Cheese: Colour picture no. 13, 22.

Tomato and Cucumber Marketing Board: Black and white photograph accompanying Recipe 558.

United Fresh Fruit and Vegetables Association (U.S.A.): Black and white photograph accompanying Recipe 370.

T. Wall & Sons Ltd: Black and white photographs accompanying Recipes 112, 379, 418, 429, 472, 487, 674, 676, 677.

John West's Middle-cut Brand Tuna: Black and white photograph accompanying Recipe 248.

White Fish Authority: Colour pictures nos. 6, 15.

Zanzibar Cloves: Black and white photographs accompanying Recipes 484, 485, 486.

Crèmes Oranges à la Louise 425
Damson Amber, 390
Fruit and Ice Cream Melon, 418
Gingerbread Ring with Apple Compote, 364, 365
Gooseberry Fool, 394
Gooseberry Pudding, 395
Grape Baskets, 398
Greengage Pudding, 405
Greengage Sponge Pudding 406
Harvest Sundae, 379
Lemon Chiffon Mould, 408
Lemon and Grape Alaska, 399
Lemon Mousse, 409
Lime Sherbet, 411
Loganberry Sherbert, 413
Orange Curaçao Snowcups, 429
Orange Foam Pudding, 424
Orange and Redcurrant Ring, 428
Pan Baked Fruits, 366
Passion Fruit Jelly, 431
Peach Fruit Mould, 441
Peach Milk Jelly, 438
Pears Marguerite, 433
Pineapple Upside-Down Pudding, 446
Raspberry Galette, 455
Raspberry Ring, 456
Rhubarb Fool, 462
Rhubarb Snow, 463
Rosy Pears, 435
Strawberry Banana Meringue, 467
Strawberry Condé, 468
Strawberry Pineapple Cocktail, 470
Stuffed Peaches, Hot and Cold, 439, 440
Summer Glory, 469
Sunshine Sundae, 495
Tangerine Sundae, 472
Pumpkin:
  To Use, 4
  Pumpkin Jam, 602
Purée of Cauliflower, 41

Q

Quinces:
  To Store and Serve, 453
  Quince Jam, 603
  Quince Marmalade, 649

R

Radishes, 4
Raisins *see* **Dried Fruit**
Ratatouille, 111
Raspberries:
  To Store and Serve, 454
  Raspberry Galette, 455
  Raspberry Jam, 604, 605
  Raspberry Jelly, 627
  Raspberry Ring, 456
  Raspberry Wine, 692
Red Cabbage *see* **Cabbage**
Redcurrants:
  To Frost, 457
  To Store and Serve, 457
  Orange and Redcurrant Ring, 428
  Redcurrant Jelly, 628
  Redcurrant and Loganberry Jelly, 629
Red Peppers (Sweet) *see* **Peppers**
RELISHES *see* **CHUTNEYS**
Rhubarb:
  To Store and Serve, 458
  Rhubarb Amber Flan, 459
  Rhubarb and Angelica Jam, 609
  Rhubarb Cartwheel Flan, 460
  Rhubarb Conserve, 606
  Rhubarb Cream Pie, 461
  Rhubarb and Dried Fig Jam, 608
  Rhubarb Fool, 462
  Rhubarb Jam, 607
  Rhubarb Snow, 463

Rhubarb Wine, 696
Rice-Stuffed Peppers, 73
Rice-Stuffed Tomatoes, 122
Rice Whiskey, 719
Rich Chocolate Cup Custards, 285
Rose Hips:
  To Use, 464
  Rose Hip Jelly, 631
  Rose Hip Syrup, 504
  Rose Hip Wine, 697
Rosemary, 488
Rosy Pears, 435
Rowanberry Jelly, 630
Runner Beans *see* **Beans**
Russian Cabbage, 31
Russian Salad, 154
Rutabaga, 4

S

Sage, 488
Salad Burnet, 488
SALAD DRESSINGS *see* **MAYONNAISE**
SALADS:
  To Make, 137
  To Prepare with Cheese, 167
  To Prepare with Egg, 168
  To Prepare Ingredients, 138
  Apple Avocado Salad, 157
  Apple and Celery Cole Slaw, 142
  Apple Cole Slaw, 141
  Asparagus Salad, 139
  Banana Salad, 158
  Beetroot Salad, 145
  Butter Bean and Sardine Salad, 187
  Chicken Almond Salad, 176
  Chicken and Asparagus Salad, 177
  Chicken Platter, 178
  Chicory Salad, 144
  Cider Fruit Salad, 666
  Cole Slaw, 140
  Corn and Ham Cornets, 179
  Corn Salad, 146
  Cottage Cheese and Peach Platter, 173
  Cottage Cheese and Pineapple Platter, 169
  Creamed Tomato Rings, 181
  Cucumber Salad, 147
  Dried Fruit Salads, 493
  Dutch Supper Salad, 170
  Easy-to-Make Pear Salad, 166
  Egg Salad, 171
  Fruit Flowers, 159
  Fruit Salads, 476
  Fruits in Salads, 156
  German Herring Salad, 188
  Grape, Cheese and Banana Salad, 172
  Grapefruit Salad, 160
  Green Pea Salad, 182
  Green Pea and New Carrot Salad, 148
  Green Salad, 149
  Ham and Raisin Mousse, 183
  Lobster Relish, 184
  Macaroni and Sausage Mould, 185
  Meat Salads, 180
  Moulded Chicken Salad, 186
  Niçoise Salad, 189
  Nutty Banana and Cheese Salad, 174
  Orange Salad, 161
  Orange and Pineapple Salad, 163
  Orange and Tomato Salad, 164
  Peach Salad, 165
  Pineapple and Cheese Salad, 220
  Piquant Egg Salad, 175
  Potato Salad, 151
  Raw Mushrooms, 150
  Russian Salad, 154
  Salmon and Lettuce Shells, 190
  Shellfish Salads, 191
  Spiced Cole Slaw, 143
  Star Apple Salad, 357
  Summer Salad, 192
  Tomato Salad, 155
  White Fish Salads, 193

Salsify, 4
Salmon and Lettuce Shells, 190
SAUCES:
  With Eggs, 286
  Anchovy Sauce, 313
  Béarnaise Sauce, 332
  Béchamel Sauce, 324
  Brown Sauce, 330
  Caper Sauce, 315
  Cheese and Onion Sauce for Eggs, 254
  Cheese Sauce, 314
  Cheese Sauce with Chicory and Ham, 334
  Chicken and Ham Sauce for Omelette, 259
  Creamed Tomato Sauce, 320
  Cucumber Sauce, 321
  Egg Sauce, 317
  Fish Sauce, 316
  Ginger Sauce for Rhubarb Flan, 460
  Gooseberry Sauce, 396
  Hollandaise Sauce, 325, 331
  Horseradish Sauce, 322
  Maître d'Hôtel Sauce, 326
  Mayonnaise *see* Mayonnaise
  Mousseline Sauce, 332
  Mushroom Sauce, 323
  Onion Sauce, 318
  Orange Mayonnaise, 162
  Orange and Raisin Sauce, 495
  Oyster Sauce, 327
  Parsley Sauce, 319
  Prawn or Shrimp Sauce, 328
  Rich Cheese Sauce, 335
  Sauce for Artichokes, 6
  Tartare Sauce, 329, 352
  Tomato Sauce for Cabbage, 29
  White Sauce, 312
Sauerkraut *see* **Cabbage**
Sausage Ratatouille, 112
Sautéed Cauliflower, 42
SAVOURY, 488
Savoury Banana Toast, 376
Savoury Bean Bake, 17
Savoury Scrambled Eggs, 257
Savoury Soufflé Omelette, 263
Scalloped Potatoes, 99
Scotch Eggs, 247
Seakale, 4
Shallots:
  To Use, 4
  Shallots, Pickled, 529, 533
Shellfish Salads, 191
Short Crust Pastry, 227, 291
Sloe Gin, 720
Sloe Wine, 698
Sorrel, 4, 488
SOUFFLÉS:
  To Make, 265
  Blueberry Soufflé, 383
  Cheese Soufflé, 266
  Damson Soufflé Flan, 391
  Ham Soufflé, 267
  Plum Soufflé Flan, 448
  Soufflé Potatoes, 106
  Sweet Soufflé, 268
  Spanish Omelette, 264
SPICES:
  To Grow and Use, 488
  To Use with Coffee, 487
  To Use with Fruit, 484
  To Use with Tea, 487
  To Use in Milk Shakes, 484
  To Use with Vegetables, 483
  Spiced Dates, 538
  Spiced Dried Fruits, 539
  Spiced Fruits, 537
  Spiced Jellies, 636
  Spiced Vinegar, 521
Spiced Ham Balls, 305
Spinach:
  To Cook, 4
  Chopped Spinach, 116
  Creamed Spinach, 117
  Egg and Spinach Pie, 270
  Eggs Florentine, 234
  Poached Egg and Spinach, 254
  Spinach Soufflé, 118
Sponge for Fruit Gâteau, 445
Sponge for Fruit Pudding, 406
Spring Greens, 4
Squash, 4
St Martin's Boats, 100
Star Apple Salad, 357

Strawberries:
  To Store and Serve, 465
  Strawberry Babas, 466
  Strawberry Banana Meringue, 467
  Strawberry Condé, 468
  Strawberry Jam, 610, 611
  Strawberry Jelly, 632, 633
  Strawberry and Gooseberry Jelly, 634
  Strawberry Pineapple Cocktail, 470
  Summer Glory, 469
Stuffed Artichokes, 6
Stuffed Aubergines, 13
Stuffed Cabbage Leaves, 27
Stuffed Mushrooms, 62
Stuffed Onions, 67
Stuffed Vegetable Marrow, 127
Stuffed Whole Cabbage, 28, 29
Summer Casserole au Gratin, 229
Summer Salad, 192
Sunshine Sundae, 495
Swedes:
  To Use,
  Swede Wine, 706
Sweet Corn *see* **Corn on the Cob**
Sweet Corn Pie, 48
Sweet Pickles, 532
Swiss Eggs, 235

T

Tangerines:
  To Store and Serve, 471
  Tangerine Marmalade, 653
  Tangerine Sundae, 472
Tarragon:
  To Use, 488
  Tarragon Vinegar, 563
Tartare Sauce, 329, 352
TEA *see* **DRINKS**
Thyme, 488
Tomatoes:
  To Bake, 119
  To Cook, 4
  To Fry, 120
  To Grill, 121
  Bacon and Tomato Kebabs, 294
  Creamed Tomato Rings, 181
  Creamed Tomato Sauce, 320
  Fish Mayonnaise in Tomato Cases, 355
  Green Tomato Chutney, 559
  Orange and Tomato Salad, 164
  Red Tomato and Apple Chutney, 560
  Rice-Stuffed Tomatoes, 122
  Stuffed Tomato Cups, 210
  Tomato Chutney, 558
  Tomato and Horseradish Relish, 561
  Tomato Jam, 614
  Tomato Jelly, 635
  Tomato Juice Cocktail, 673
  Tomato Ketchup, 567
  Tomato Mayonnaise, 353
  Tomato and Onion Pie, 230
  Tomato Salad, 155
Tuna and Eggs Indienne, 248
Turnips:
  To Cook, 4
  To Glaze, 123
  To Mash, 124
  Turnip Tops, to Cook, 4
  Turnip Wine, 706

U

Ugli Fruit, 473
Ulster Eggs, 281

V

Vegetables:
  Charts and to Serve, 4

Bottling Vegetables *see* **Bottling**
To Can, 665
To Use Canned Vegetables, 133
To Cook Correctly, 3
To Cook in Pressure Cooker, 1
To Use De-Hydrated Vegetables, 135
To Dry, 513
To Add Eggs, 278
To Freeze, 723
To Use Frozen Vegetables, 132
To Use Spices, 483
Taste of Vegetable Wines, 708
Beans, to Salt, 514
Cheese and Vegetable Flan, 223
Cheese and Vegetable Platter, 224
Mixed Vegetable Grill, 134
Mutter Curry, 70
Ratatouille, 111
Sausage Ratatouille, 112
Vegetables in Casseroles and Stews, 136
Vegetable Pie, 231
Vegetable Scramble, 257
Vegetable Marrow:
  To Cook, 4
  To Fry, 125
  To Roast, 126
  To Stuff, 128
  Courgettes *see* Courgettes
  Marrow Chutney, 550
  Marrow Curd, 658
  Marrow Ginger Jam, 597
  Marrow Rum, 715
  Pickled Marrow, 524
  Stuffed Vegetable Marrow, 127
Vinaigrette Dressing, 354
Vinegar:
  To Flavour, 562
  Spiced Vinegar, 521
  Tarragon Vinegar, 563

W

Walnuts, Pickled, 534
Welsh Rabbit, 199
White Currants, 474
  White Fish Salads, 193
  White Sauce, 312
WINES:
  To Use Isinglass, 721
  To Make, 683
  Taste of Flower Wines, 708
  Taste of Fruit Wines, 699
  Taste of Vegetable Wines, 708
  Apple Wine, 684
  Beetroot Wine, 704
  Blackberry Wine, 685
  Blackcurrant Wine, 686
  Cherry Wine, 687
  Cowslip Wine, 700
  Damson Port, 688
  Dandelion Wine, 701
  Elderberry Wine, 689
  Elderflower Wine, 702
  Ginger Wine, 714
  Gooseberry Wine, 690
  Grape Wine, 691
  Loganberry or Raspberry Wine, 692
  Orange Wine, 693
  Parsley Honey, 722
  Parsley Wine, 703
  Plum Wine, 695
  Potato Wine, 705
  Raisin Wine, 694
  Rhubarb Wine, 696
  Rose Hip Wine, 697
  Sloe Wine, 698
  Turnip Wine, 706
  Wheat Wine, 707
Winter Casserole, 23

Y

Yams:
  To Cook, 4
  Baked Yams, 130
  Purée of Yams, 130

Lemon and Grape Alaska, 399
Lemon Marmalade, 641
Lemon and Melon Jam, 594
Lemon Mousse, 409
Lemonade, 669
Orange and Lemon Chutney, 553
Orange and Lemon Curd, 660
Orange and Lemon Marmalade, 646
Lentils, 4
Lettuce:
To Cook, 4, 56
Braised Lettuce, 57
Salmon and Lettuce Shells, 190
Lima Beans, 4
Limes:
To Store and Serve, 410
Lime Marmalade, 642
Lime Sherbert, 411
Limousine Potatoes, 89
Lobster Relish, 184
Loganberries:
To Store and Serve, 412
Loganberry Sherbert, 413
Loganberry Wine, 692
Redcurrant and Loganberry Jelly, 629
Lychees:
To Store and Serve, 414
Lychees in Syrup, 415
Lyonnaise Potatoes, 90

M

Macaroni Cheese, 228
Macaroni and Sausage Mould, 185
Maître d'Hôtel Sauce, 326
Mangoes:
To Store and Serve, 416
Mango Chutney, 549
Mango Cream Dip, 346
Marjoram, 488
MARMALADE:
To Make, 639
To Make in a Pressure Cooker, 664
To Make Without Sugar, 651
To Measure Yield, 656
Dried Apricot and Orange Marmalade, 640
Four-Fruit Marmalade, 655
Jelly Marmalade, 643
Lemon Marmalade, 641
Lime Marmalade, 642
Marmalade and Cheese, 218
Orange Marmalade, 647, 648
Orange Ginger Marmalade, 644
Orange and Grapefruit Marmalade, 645
Orange and Lemon Marmalade, 646
Orange Peel and Apple Marmalade, 643
Quince Marmalade, 649
Seville Orange Marmalade, 652, 654
Sweet Orange Marmalade, 650
Tangerine Marmalade, 653
Three-Fruit Marmalade, 654
Marrow, *see* **Vegetable Marrow**
Matchsticks, 92
MAYONNAISE AND SALAD DRESSINGS:
Atocha Mayonnaise, 338
Classic Mayonnaise, 337
Cocktail Dip or Salad Dressing, 339
Curried Mayonnaise, 340
Economical Salad Dressing, 341
Family Mayonnaise, 342
Fish Mayonnaise in Tomato Cases, 355
French Dressing, 343
Green Mayonnaise, 344
Magic Mayonnaise, 345
Mango Cream Dip, 346
Mayonnaise Without Eggs, 347
Orange Mayonnaise, 162
Salad Cream, 348
Slimming Salad Dressing, 349
Snappy Cheese Dressing, 350

Sweet French Dressing, 351
Tartare Sauce, 352
Tomato Mayonnaise, 353
Vinaigrette Dressing, 354
Mead, 716
Meat Salads, 180
Medlars:
To Store and Serve, 419
Medlar Jelly, 624
Melons:
To Store and Serve, 417
Fruit and Ice Cream Melons, 418
Lemon and Melon Jam, 594
Melon in Salad, 156
Meringues, 288
MILK DRINKS:
To Serve Children, 307
To Make Milk Coffee, 306
To Serve Milk Drinks, 306
To Make Milk Shakes, 306
To Spice Milk Shakes, 486
To Make Milk Tea, 306
Chocolate Milk Shake, 677
Coffee Milk Shake, 679
Egg and Brandy Milk Shake, 680
Orange Milk Shake, 681
Plantation Milk Shake, 682
Mincemeat, 661
Mint:
To Preserve in Sugar, 516
To Use, 488
Apple and Mint Chutney, 542
Mint Chutneys, 551
Mint Jelly, 624, 625
Mixed Vegetable Grill, 134
Moulded Chicken Salad, 186
Mousseline Sauce, 332
Mulberries:
To Store and Serve, 420
Mulberry Jam, 598
Mulberry Jelly, 626
Mushrooms:
To Cook, 4
To Fry, 60
To Grill, 60
Bacon, Mushroom and Egg Pie, 269
Creamed Mushrooms, 58
Curried Mushroom Eggs, 245
Ham, Egg and Mushroom Flan, 273
Mushroom with Cheese Filling, 59
Mushroom Ketchup, 566
Mushroom Rice, 61
Mushroom Sauce, 323
Pickled Mushrooms, 526
Raw Mushrooms, 150
Stuffed Mushrooms, 62
Mustard Pickles, 525
Mustard Relish, 552
Mutter Curry, 70

N

Nasturtium Seeds, Pickled, 527
Nectarines, 421
Nettles:
To Use, 4
Nettle Beer, 717
New Potato Bites, 93
Niçoise Salad, 189
Nursery Bird's Nest, 246
Nuts:
To Salt, 517
To Store, 517
Pickled Walnuts, 534

O

Oeufs Pochés Otéro, 255
Okra, 4
OMELETTES:
To Flavour, 258
To Make, 258
Bacon Omelette, 258
Chicken Omelette, 258
Fish Omelette, 258
Fruit Omelette, 262
Jam Omelette, 261
Meat Omelette, 258
Mixed Herb Omelette, 258
Omelette with Chicken and Ham Sauce, 259
Savoury Soufflé Omelette, 263
Soufflé Omelettes, 260

Spanish Omelette, 264
Onions:
To Cook, 4
To Bake, 64
To Fry, 65
To Roast, 66
Braised Onions, 63
Cheese and Onion Sauce for Eggs, 254
Onion Sauce, 318
Pickled Onions, 529
Stuffed Onion, 67
Tomato and Onion Pie, 230
Oranges:
To Store and Serve, 422
Banana and Orange Jam, 579
Crèmes Orange à la Louise, 425
Gooseberry and Orange Jam, 591
Ham and Orange Cookies, 304
Marmalade *see* Marmalade
Orange Curaçao Snowcups, 429
Orange Curd, 659
Orange Dessert Cake, 426
Orange Foam Pudding, 424
Orange and Lemon Chutney, 553
Orange and Lemon Curd, 660
Orange Mayonnaise, 162
Orange Milk Shake, 681
Orange and Pineapple Salad, 163
Orange and Raisin Sauce, 495
Orange Raisin Shortbread, 427
Orange and Redcurrant Ring, 428
Orange Salad, 161
Orange and Tomato Salad, 164
Orange Wedding, 423
Orange Wine, 693
Orangeade, 671
Oranges in Salad, 156
Sunshine Sundae, 495
Oyster Sauce, 327

P

Pancake Batters, 308
Pancakes, Fillings for, 308
Parsley:
To Use, 4, 488
Parsley Honey, 722
Parsley Sauce, 319
Parsley Wine, 703
Parsnips:
To Cook, 4
To Fry, 109
To Roast, 110
Parsnip Croquettes, 108
Passion Fruit:
To Store and Serve, 430
Passion Fruit Jelly, 431
PASTRY:
Almond Pastry for Apricot Tart, 368
Biscuit Crust Pastry for Fruit Pie, 461
Cheese Pastry, 202, 226
Cheese Rough Puff Pastry, 222
Flan Pastry, for Galette, 455
Pastry for Prune Pie, 452
Puff Pastry, 374
Short Crust Pastry, 227, 291
Suet Crust Pastry, 395
Peaches:
To Store and Serve, 437
Cottage Cheese and Peach Platter, 173
Dried Peach Jam, 664
Peach Fruit Mould, 441
Peach Milk Jelly, 438
Peach Salad, 165
Peaches in Salad, 156
Stuffed Peaches, Hot or Cold, 439, 440
Pears:
To Store and Serve, 432
Apricot and Pear Flan, 369
Compote of Pears, 485
Easy-to-Make Pear Salad, 166
Pan Baked Fruits, 366
Pear Cider, or Perry, 718
Pear and Mincemeat Pie, 434

Pear and Pineapple Conserve, 599
Pears Marguerite, 433
Pears in Salad, 156
Rosy Pears, 435
'Starry Gazie' Pie, 436
Peas:
To Cook, 4
Bacon Pease Pudding with Pork Sausages, 295
Green Pea and New Carrot Salad, 148
Green Pea Salad, 182
Hopping John, 68
Peas à la Française, 69
Pectin, Commercial, to Use in Jam, 573
Pennyroyal, 488
Pepperpot Shortbread, 244
Peppers:
To Cook, 4
Cheese Stuffed Peppers, 72
Peppers au Gratin, 71
Pork Stuffed Green Peppers, 74
Red Pepper Chutney, 556
Rice Stuffed Peppers, 73
Persimmon:
To Store and Serve, 442
Persimmon Cocktail, 443
Piccalilli, 528
PICKLING AND PRESERVING:
To Make, 518
To Make Brine for Vegetables, 519, 520
To Pickle for Show Purposes, 512
To Make in a Pressure Cooker, 664
To Make Spiced Vinegar, 521
Chutney *see* Chutney
Mincemeat, 661
Mustard Pickles, 525
Piccalilli, 528
Pickled Beetroot, 522
Pickled Cucumbers, 523
Pickled Fruits, 536
Pickled Hard-Boiled Eggs, 535
Pickled Marrow, 524
Pickled Mushrooms, 526
Pickled Nasturtium Seeds, 527
Pickled Onions, 529
Pickled Red Cabbage, 531
Pickled Walnuts, 534
Sweet Pickles, 532

PIES, FLANS AND TARTS:
To Add Eggs, 277
Apple Pie and Cheese, 213
Apricot and Pear Flan, 369
Apricot Tart, 368
Bacon Pie, 298
Bacon and Cream Cheese Flan, 227
Bacon and Egg Tart, 290
Bacon, Mushroom and Egg Pie, 269
Bacon and Sausage Pie, 292
Baked Apple and Flan, 214
Banana Horns, 374
Cheese Tartlets, 222
Cheese and Vegetable Flan, 223
Cornish Cheese Pie, 226
Country Prune Pie, 452
Creamy Plum Pie, 449
Creamy Quiche Lorraine, 274
Damson Soufflé Flan, 391
Egg and Cauliflower Pie, 272
Egg and Leek Pie, 271
Egg and Spinach Pie, 270
German Apple Tart, 360
Greengage Pie, 404
Ham, Egg and Mushroom Flan, 273
Harlequin Corn Pie, 49
Pear and Mincemeat Pie, 434
Plum Soufflé Flan, 448
Rhubarb Amber Flan, 459
Rhubarb Cartwheel Flan, 460
Rhubarb Galette, 455
Raspberry Galette, 455
'Starry Gazie' Pie, 436
Sweet Corn Pie, 48
Tomato and Onion Pie, 230
Vegetable Pie, 231
Wiltshire Bacon and Pig's Liver Pie, 291
Pineapple:
To Store and Serve, 444

Banana and Pineapple Jam, 580
Cottage Cheese and Pineapple Platter, 169
Orange and Pineapple Salad, 163
Pear and Pineapple Conserve, 599
Pineapple and Cheese Salad, 220
Pineapple and Cherry Gâteau, 445
Pineapple Upside-Down Pudding, 446
Quick Pineapple Relish, 554
Plums:
To Store and Serve, 447
Creamy Plum Pie, 449
Plum Chutney, 555
Plum Jam, 600, 601
Plum Soufflé Flan, 448
Plum Wine, 695
Victoria Plum Conserve, 615
Victoria Plum Jelly, 637
Pomegranates, 450
Pork Stuffed Green Peppers, 74
Potatoes:
To Bake in their Jackets, 76
To Cook, 4
To Roast, 97
To Shallow Fry, 101
To Store, 515
Bacon Barbecued Potatoes, 104
Baked Corn Potatoes, 83
Baked Stuffed Potatoes, 105
Cheese Stuffed Potatoes, 205
Chipped Potatoes, 77
Creamed Potatoes, 79
Curried Potatoes, 84
Dauphine Potatoes, 86
Duchesse Potatoes, 85
Game Chips, 87
Hashed Brown Potatoes, 88
Herring Stuffed Potatoes, 103
Limousine Potatoes, 89
Lyonnaise Potatoes, 90
Matchsticks, 92
New Potato Bites, 93
Potato and Cabbage Casserole, 82
Potato and Celery Salad, 152
Potato Cheese Cakes, 209
Potato Cream, 78
Potato Crisps, 80
Potato Croquettes, 81
Potato Pancakes, 95
Potato and Mushrooms, 94
Potato Salad, 151
Potato Wine, 705
Potatoes Anna, 75
Potatoes Macain, 91
Potatoes Parisienne, 96
Potatoes Savoyarde, 102
Potatoes Vichy, 107
Ribbon Potatoes, 98
Scalloped Potatoes, 99
Soufflé Potatoes, 106
St Martin's Boats, 100
Sweet Potatoes *see* Yams
Prawn or Shrimp Sauce, 328
PRESERVES
see **PICKLING**
PRESERVING FRUIT
see **BOTTLING**
PRESSURE COOKING:
To Make Chutneys, 569
To Bottle Fruit, Method and Timetable, 509
To Bottle Vegetables, Method and Timetable, 510
To Cook Fruit, 2
To Cook Dried Fruit, 493
To Make Preserves, 664
To Cook Vegetables, 1
Prunes *see* **Dried Fruit**
PUDDINGS AND SWEETS:
Apple and Banana Compote, 372
Apple Compote, 365
Apple Gingersnap Dessert, 362
Apple Meringue, 358
Banana Alaska, 373
Blueberry Soufflé, 383
Blushing Apple Dumplings, 359
California Rum Fudge, 496
Cherry Lemon Whip, 385
Compote of Pears, 485

Mango Chutney, 549
Marrow Chutney, 550
Mint Chutneys, 551
Mustard Relish, 552
Orange and Lemon Chutney, 553
Plum Chutney, 555
Quick Date Chutney, 547
Quick Pineapple Relish, 554
Red Pepper Chutney, 556
Red Tomato and Apple Chutney, 560
Rhubarb Chutney, 557
Spiced Dried Fruit as Relish, 539
Tomato Chutney, 558
Tomato and Horseradish Relish, 561
Cocktail Dip or Salad Dressing, 339
COFFEE *see* **DRINKS**
Cole Slaw, 140
CONSERVE *see* **JAMS**
Coriander, 488
Corn on the Cob:
To Cook, 4
Corn Bake, 47
Corn and Eggs Scramble, 257
Corn and Ham Cornets, 179
Corn Salad, 146
Corn Toasties, 50
Harlequin Corn Pie, 49
Sweet Corn Pie, 48
Cornish Cheese Pie, 226
Cottage Cheese Ring, 225
Courgettes:
To Cook, 4
To Stuff, 128
Courgettes Portugese, 129
Cowslip Wine, 700
Cranberries:
To Store and Serve, 387
Cranberry Sauce, 388
Creamed Carrots, 35
Creamed Curry, 241
Creamed Mushrooms, 58
Creamed Potatoes, 79
Creamed Spinach, 117
Creamed Tomato Rings, 181
Crème Caramel, 284
Cucumber:
To Cook, 4, 51
Cucumber Jelly, 619
Cucumber Salad, 147
Cucumber Sauce, 321
Cucumber Stuffed with Mushrooms and Beef, 53
Fried Cucumber, 52
Pickled Cucumbers, 523
Cumin, 488
CURDS:
Lemon Curd, 657
Marrow Curd, 658
Orange Curd, 659
Orange and Lemon Curd, 660
Curried Hard-Boiled Eggs, 240
Curried Mushroom Eggs, 245
Curried Potatoes, 84

D

Damsons:
To Store and Serve, 389
Damson Amber, 390
Damson Chutney, 546
Damson Jam, 586
Damson Port, 688
Damson Soufflé Flan, 391
Dandelion Leaves, 4
Dandelion Tea, 711
Dandelion Wine, 701
Dates *see* **Dried Fruit**
Dauphine Potatoes, 86
De-hydrated Vegetables, 135
Devilled Eggs with Creole Rice, 242
Devilled Sauce for Eggs, 242
Dill, 488
Dried Fuit:
To Cook in Pressure Cooker, 493
To Cook and Use, 492, 494
To Dry, 491
To Dry Apples, 490
To Store and Serve, 451
To Store and Serve Figs, 392
To Store and Serve Prunes, 451
To Spice Dried Fruit as Relish, 539

Apricot Jam, 575, 576
Country Prune Pie, 452
Dried Fruit Salads, 493
Dried Peach Jam, 664
Fig and Lemon Jam, 588
Ham and Raisin Mousse, 183
Orange and Raisin Sauce, 495
Orange Raisin Shortbread, 427
Quick Date Chutney, 547
Raisin and Cheese Pyramids, 221
Raisin Wine, 694
Rhubarb and Dried Fig Jam, 608
Spiced Dates, 538
DRINKS, HOT and COLD:
To Use Spices with Tea, 487
To Use Spices with Coffee, 487
Advocaat, 709
Appleade, 667
Banana Frappé, 676
Blackcurrant and Lemon Frappé, 677
Bouillon on the Rocks, 668
Cherry Brandy, 710
Cider, To Make, 712
Dandelion Tea, 711
Ginger Beer, 713
Grapefruit Soda, 670
Lemonade, 669
Lime Sherbet, 411
Loganberry Sherbet, 413
Marrow Rum, 715
Mead, 716
Milk Drinks *see* Milk Drinks
Mixed Fruit Cordial, 672
Nettle Beer, 717
Orangeade, 671
Perry or Pear Cider, 718
Rice Whisky, 719
Sloe Gin, 720
Summer Special, 675
Summertime Soda, 674
Tomato Juice Cocktail, 673
Duchesse Potatoes, 85
Dutch Supper Salad, 170

E

Eggplant *see* **Aubergines**
Eggs:
To Bake, 232
To Boil, 239
To Coat With, 276
To Use with Custard Powder, 282
To Flavour Custards, 283
To Make Custards, 283
To Prepare Egg Salads, 168
To Fry, 249
To Add to Pie, 277
To Poach, 252
To Preserve with a Coating, 237
To Preserve in Waterglass, 236
To Use in Sauces, 286
To Scramble, 256
To Add to Vegetables, 278
To Use Whites, 287
To Use Yolks, 287
Bacon and Egg Tart, 290
Bacon Mushroom and Egg Pies, 269
Cheddar Scotch Eggs, 204
Cheese Scrambled Eggs, 257
Corn and Eggs Scramble, 257
Creamed Curry, 241
Creamed Hard-Boiled Eggs, 240
Curried Mushroom Eggs, 245
Devilled Eggs with Creole Rice, 242
Easter Sunday Eggs, 233
Economical Egg Fingers, 250
Egg and Brandy Milk Shake, 680
Egg and Cauliflower Pie, 272
Egg and Ham Casserole, 302
Egg and Leek Pie, 271

Egg Salad, 171
Egg Sauce, 371
Egg and Spinach Pie, 270
Eggs Diable, 243
Eggs Florentine, 234
Eggs in a Nest, 253
Eggs Royale, 279
Fried Devilled Eggs, 251
Golden Ring, 280
Ham, Egg and Mushroom Flan, 273
Ham Scramble, 257
Individual Bread Baskets, 238
Nursery Bird's Nest, 246
Oeufs Pochés Otéro, 255
Omelettes *see* Omelettes
Pickled Hard-Boiled Eggs, 535
Piquant Egg Salad, 175
Poached Egg and Spinach, 254
Rich Chocolate Cup Custards, 285
Savoury Scrambled Eggs, 257
Scotch Eggs, 247
Soufflés *see* Soufflés
Swiss Eggs, 235
Tuna and Eggs Indienne, 248
Ulster Eggs, 281
Vegetable Scramble, 257
Wiltshire Bacon and Pig's Liver Pie, 291
Elderberries:
Elderberry Jam, 587
Elderberry Jelly, 620
Elderberry Wine, 689
Elderflower Wine, 702
Endive:
To Cook, 4

F

Fennel, 4, 488
Figs *see* **Dried Fruit**
Fish Mayonnaise in Tomato Cases, 355
Fish Sauce, 316
Flagelots, 4
Flower Wines *see* **Wines**
Flowers, to Crystallise, 479
Fondue, 207
Frankfurters with Cheese Sauce, 336
FREEZING FOOD:
To Package, 723
To Select Food, 723
French Beans *see* **Beans**
French Dressing, 343
Fried Aubergines, 11
Fried Cucumber, 52
Frozen Vegetables, 132
Fruit:
Bottling Fruit see Bottling
To Can, 665
To Cook in Pressure Cooker, 2
To Crystallise Fresh Fruit, 477
To Freeze, 723
To Poach, 482
To Use in Salad, 156
To Spice, 484
To Stew, 481
Cider Fruit Salad, 666
Compote of Fruit, 480
Dried Fruit *see* Dried Fruit
Four-Fruit Marmalade, 655
Fruit Butters, 662
Fruit and Cheese, 217
Fruit Cheeses, 663
Fruit Dips, 475
Fruit Flowers, 159
Fruit and Ice Cream Melons, 418
Fruit Omelette, 262
Fruit Salad Bowl, 375
Fruit Salads, 476
Fruit Syrups *see* Fruit Syrups
Fruit Wines *see* To Taste, 699
Harvest Sundae, 379
Mixed Fruit Cordial, 672
Pan Baked Fruits, 366
Peach Fruit Mould, 441
Pickled Fruits, 536
Spiced Fruits, 537
Summertime Soda, 674
Three-Fruit Marmalade, 654
FRUIT JUICES, TO BOTTLE, 507
FRUIT SYRUPS:
To Make and Bottle, 503

Elderberry Syrup, 505
Lemonade Syrup, 506
Rose Hip Syrup, 504

G

Game Chips, 87
Gammon *see* **Bacon**
Garlic, 4, 488
German Apple Tart, 360
German Herring Salad, 188
Ginger Beer, 713
Ginger Wine, 714
Globe Artichokes *see* **Artichokes**
Golden Ring, 280
Gooseberries:
To Store and Serve, 393
Gooseberry Fool, 394
Gooseberry Jam, 589, 590
Gooseberry Jelly, 621, 622
Gooseberry and Orange Jam, 591
Gooseberry Pudding, 395
Gooseberry Sauce, 396
Gooseberry Wine, 690
Green Gooseberry Jam, 664
Strawberry and Gooseberry Jelly, 634
Grapefruit:
To Serve Hot, 401
To Store and Serve, 400
California Prawn Cocktail, 402
Gammon and Grilled Grapefruit, 300
Grapefruit Salad, 160
Grapefruit in Salad, 156
Grapefruit Soda, 670
Orange and Grapefruit Marmalade, 645
Grapes:
To Store and Serve, 397
Grape, Cheese and Banana Salad, 399
Grape Ketchup, 565
Grape Wine, 691
Lemon and Grape Alaska, 399
Greengages:
To Store and Serve, 403
Greengage Jam, 592
Greengage Pie, 404
Greengage Pudding, 405
Greengage Sponge Pudding, 406
Green Pea Salad, 392
Green Peppers *see* **Peppers**
Green Salad, 149
Gumbo, 4

H

Ham *see* **Bacon**
Haricot Beans *see* **Beans**
Harlequin Corn Pie, 49
Harvest Sundae, 379
Hashed Brown Potatoes, 88
Hawaiian Baked Beans, 16
Hawaiian Fried Rice, 301
Hawaiian Sandwiches, 208
Herbs:
To Grow and Use, 48
To Preserve, 489
Herring Stuffed Potatoes, 103
Hollandaise Sauce, 325, 331
Hopping John, 68
Horseradish, 488
Horseradish Sauce, 322
Hot Beetroot, 21
Huckleberries:
Huckleberry Jam, 593

J

Jam Omelette, 261
JAMS AND CONSERVES:
To Use Commercial Pectin, 573
To Prepare for Competitions, 571
To Make Jams, 570
To Use the Right Pan, 572
To Make Without Sugar, 613
To Measure Yield, 656
Apple Ginger Jam, 577
Apricot Jam, 574–576
Banana and Lemon Jam, 578

Banana and Orange, 579
Banana and Pineapple Jam, 580
Blackberry and Apple Jam, 581
Blackcurrant Jam, 582, 664
Cherry Jam, 583–585
Damson Jam, 586
Dried Peach Jam, 664
Elderberry Jam, 587
Fig and Lemon Jam, 588
Greengage Jam, 592
Green Gooseberry Jam, 664
Gooseberry Jam, 589, 590
Gooseberry and Orange Jam, 591
Huckleberry Jam, 593
Japonica Jam, 596
Lemon and Melon Jam, 594
Loganberry Jam, 595
Marrow Ginger Jam, 597
Mulberry Jam, 598
Pear and Pineapple Conserve, 599
Plum Jam, 600, 601
Pumpkin Jam, 602
Quince Jam, 603
Raspberry Jam, 604, 605
Rhubarb Conserve, 606
Rhubarb Jam, 607
Rhubarb and Angelica Jam, 609
Rhubarb and Dried Fig Jam, 608
Strawberry Jam, 610, 611
Tomato Jam, 614
Victoria Plum Conserve, 615
JELLIES:
To Prepare for Competitions, 571
To Make, 570
To Measure Yield, 656
Apple Jelly, 616
Apple and Lemon Jelly, 617
Blackberry or Bramble Jelly, 618
Cucumber Jelly, 619
Elderberry Jelly, 620
Gooseberry Jelly, 621, 622
Jelly Marmalade, 638
Medlar Jelly, 623
Mint Jelly, 624, 625
Mulberry Jelly, 626
Raspberry Jelly, 627
Redcurrant Jelly, 628
Redcurrant and Loganberry Jelly, 629
Rose Hip Jelly, 631
Rowanberry Jelly, 630
Spiced Jellies, 636
Strawberry Jelly, 632, 633
Strawberry and Gooseberry Jelly, 634
Tomato Jelly, 635
Victoria Plum Jelly, 637

K

Kale, 4
KETCHUP:
Blackberry Ketchup, 564
18th Century Catchup, 568
Grape Ketchup, 565
Mushroom Ketchup, 566
Tomato Ketchup, 567
Kohl-rabi, 4
Jerusalem Artichokes *see* **Artichokes**

L

Leeks:
To Cook, 4
Braised Leeks, 54
Egg and Leek Pie, 271
Leek, Bean and Bacon Savoury, 55
Lemons:
To Store and Serve, 407
Apple and Lemon Jelly, 617
Banana and Lemon Jam, 578
Blackcurrant and Lemon Frappé, 677
Cherry Lemon Whip, 385
Fig and Lemon Jam, 588
Lemon Chiffon Mould, 408
Lemon Curd, 399, 657

Index

A

Advocaat, 709
Anchovy Sauce, 313
Angelica, 488
　To Crystallise, 478
　Rhubarb and Angelica Jam, 609
Anise, 488
Apples:
　To Store and Serve, 356
　Apple Avocado Salad, 157
　Apple and Banana Compote, 372
　Apple Chutney, 541
　Apple Compote, 365
　Apple Ginger Jam, 577
　Apple Gingersnap Dessert, 362
　Apple Jelly, 616
　Apple and Lemon Jelly, 617
　Apple Meringue, 358
　Apple and Mint Chutney, 542
　Apple Pie and Cheese, 213
　Apple Raisin Fingers, 363
　Apple in Salad, 156
　Apple Sauerkraut, 114
　Apple Welsh Rarebit, 212
　Apple Wine, 684
　Apple Yeast Ring, 361
　Appleade, 667
　Baked Apple and Flan, 214
　Blackberry and Apple Jam, 581
　Blushing Apple Dumplings, 359
　Cheese and Apple Toasties, 201
　Cider, to Make, 712
　German Apple Tart, 360
　Gingerbread Ring with Apple Compote, 364
　Harvest Sundae, 379
　Orange Peel and Apple Marmalade, 643
　Pan Baked Fruits, 366
　Red Tomato and Apple Chutney, 560
　Star Apple Salad, 357
Apricots:
　To Store and Serve, 367
　Apricot Chutney, 543
　Apricot Jam, 574—576
　Apricot and Pear Flan, 369
　Apricot Tart, 368
　Dried Apricot and Orange Marmalade, 640
Artichokes:
　Artichokes (Globe), To Cook, 4
　Artichokes (Jerusalem), To Cook, 4
　Artichoke Fritters, 5
　Stuffed Artichokes, 6
Asparagus:
　As an Accompaniment, 7
　To Cook, 4
　Asparagus Normande, 8
　Asparagus Parmesan, 9
　Asparagus Polonaise, 10
　Asparagus Salad, 139
Aubergines:
　To Cook, 4
　Aubergines Provençale, 14
　Fried Aubergine Slices, 12
　Fried Aubergines, 11
　Stuffed Aubergines, 13
Avocados:
　To Store and Serve, 370
　Apple Avocado Salad, 157

B

Babas with Strawberries, 466
Bacon, Ham and Gammon:
　To Bake, 293
　To Boil, 293
　Bacon Barbecued Potatoes, 104
　Bacon and Cream Cheese Flan, 227
　Bacon and Egg Tart, 290
Bacon Fingers, 297
Bacon, Mushroom and Egg Pie, 269
Bacon Pease Pudding with Pork Sausages, 295
Bacon Pie, 298
Bacon and Sausage Pie, 292
Bacon and Tomato Kebabs, 294
Bacon Twists, 296
Cheese Sauce with Chicory and Ham, 334
Egg and Ham Casserole, 302
Gammon and Butter Bean Platter, 299
Gammon and Grilled Grapefruit, 300
Ham and Apple Scallop, 303
Ham and Orange Cookies, 304
Ham Scramble, 257
Ham Soufflé, 267
Hawaiian Fried Rice, 301
Spiced Ham Balls, 305
Wiltshire Bacon and Pig's Liver Pie, 291
Baked Corn Potatoes, 83
Baked Stuffed Potatoes, 105
Balm, 488
Bananas:
　To Store and Serve, 371
　Apple and Banana Compote, 372
　Banana Alaska, 373
　Banana Frappé, 676
　Banana Horns, 374
　Banana and Lemon Jam, 578
　Banana and Orange Jam, 579
　Banana and Pineapple Jam, 580
　Banana Salad, 158
　Banana in Salad, 156
　Grape, Cheese and Banana Salad, 172
　Nutty Banana and Cheese Salad, 174
　Savoury Banana Toast, 376
Basil, 488
Bay, 488
Beans:
　To Salt, 514
Butter Beans:
　To Cook, 4
　Butter Bean Rarebit, 211
　Butter Bean and Sardine Salad, 187
　Gammon and Butter Bean Platter, 299
French or Runner Beans:
　To Cook, 4
　Beans and Macaroni, 132
　French Beans Lyonnaise, 18
　French Beans Paysanne, 19
Haricot Beans:
　To Cook, 4
　Hawaiian Baked Beans, 16
　Leek, Bean and Bacon Savoury, 55
　Savoury Bean Bake, 17
Béarnaise Sauce, 332
Béchamel Sauce, 324
Beetroot:
　To Cook, 4
　Beetroot Chutney, 544
　Beetroot Cups, 20
　Beetroot Salad, 145
　Beetroot Wine, 704
　Hot Beetroot, 21
　Pickled Beetroot, 522
Blackberries:
　To Store and Serve, 377
　Blackberry and Apple Jam, 581
　Blackberry Balls, 378
　Blackberry or Bramble Jelly, 618
　Blackberry Chutney, 545
　Blackberry Ketchup, 564
　Blackberry Wine, 685
　Harvest Sundae, 379
Blackcurrants:
　To Store and Serve, 380
Blackcurrant Fool, 381
Blackcurrant Jam, 582, 664
Blackcurrant and Lemon Frappé, 677
Blueberries:
　To Store and Serve, 382
　Blueberry Soufflé, 383
Blushing Apple Dumplings, 359
Borage, 488
BOTTLING AND PRESERVING:
　To Bottle Fruit in Brandy, 508
　To Bottle Fruit in Own Juice, 501
　To Bottle Fruit Juices, 507
　To Bottle Fruit in Oven, 498
　To Bottle Fruit Perfectly, 497
　To Bottle Fruit in Pressure Cooker, 509
　To Bottle Fruit for Show Purposes, 512
　To Bottle Fruit in a Steriliser, 500
　To Make Fruit Syrup, 499
　To Bottle Fruit Syrups, 503
　To Bottle Vegetables in Pressure Cooker, 510
　To Bottle Vegetables for Show Purposes, 512
　To Open Screw Topped Jars, 511
　To Pulp Fruit, 502
　Braised Cabbage, 25
　Braised Celery, 43
　Braised Onions, 63
　Bramble Jelly, 618
　Bread Baskets, 238
　Bread, Hot for Salads, 311
Brine, to Make, 519, 520
Broad Beans, 4
Broccoli:
　To Cook, 4
　To Use, 15
Brown Sauce, 330
Brussels Sprouts:
　To Cook, 4
　Brussels Sprouts au Gratin, 22
　Winter Casserole, 23
　'Bubble and Squeak', 24
Burnet, 488
Butter:
Butter Beans *see* Beans
　To Flavour, 309
　To Season, 310

C

Cabbage:
　To Cook, 4
　Apple and Celery Cole Slaw, 142
　Apple Cole Slaw, 141
　Braised Cabbage, 25
　'Bubble and Squeak', 24
　Cabbage with Mustard Dressing, 26
　Cole Slaw, 140
　Potato and Cabbage Casserole, 82
　Spiced Cole Slaw, 143
　Stuffed Cabbage Leaves, 27
　Stuffed Whole Cabbage, 28, 29
　To Cook, 4, 30
　Pickled Red Cabbage, 531
　Red Cabbage with Caraway Seeds, 32
　Russian Cabbage, 31
Sauerkraut:
　To Cook, 4
　Apple Sauerkraut, 114
　Choucroute Garnie, 115
　Sauerkraut, 113
CAKES:
　Apple Raisin Fingers, 362
　Apple Yeast Ring, 361
　Gingerbread Ring, 364
　Orange Dessert Cake, 426
　Orange Raisin Shortbread, 427
California Prawn Cocktail, 402
California Rum Fudge, 496
　Pineapple and Cherry Gâteau, 445
　Quick Cherry Cakes, 386
　Strawberry Babas, 466
Canned Vegetables, 133
CANNING, 665
Caper Sauce, 315
Capiscums *see* **Peppers**
Caraway, 488
Cardoons, 4
Carrots:
　To Cook, 4
　Carrot Soufflé, 33
　Carrots Vichy, 34
　Carrot Wine, 706
　Creamed Carrots, 35
　Green Pea and New Carrot Salad, 148
Cauliflower:
　To Cook, 4
　Cauliflower Cheese, 37
　Cauliflower au Gratin, 36
　Cauliflower and Mushrooms au Gratin, 38
　Cauliflower Noisette, 39
　Cauliflower Polonaise, 40
　Egg and Cauliflower Pie, 272
　Purée of Cauliflower, 41
　Sautéed Cauliflower, 42
Celeriac, 4
Celery:
　To Cook, 4
　Braised Celery, 43
　Celery and Leek Casserole, 44
　Celery Purée, 45
　Celery Seeds, 488
　Potato and Celery Salad, 152
Chard, 4
Cheddar Scotch Eggs, 204
Cheese:
　Chart, 197
　To Choose, 195
　To Fry, 206
　To Make, 198
　To Prepare in Salads, 167
　To Store, 196
　To Serve on Toast, 200
　Apple Pie and Cheese, 213
　Apple Welsh Rarebit, 212
　Bacon and Cream Cheese Flan, 227
　Baked Apple and Flan, 214
　Bel Paese, 197
　Bresse Bleu, 197
　Brie, 197
　Butter Bean Rarebit, 211
　Caerphilly, 197
　Cake and Cheese, 215
　Camembert, 197
　Cheddar, 197
　Cheddar Scotch Eggs, 204
　Cheese and Apple Toasties, 201
　Cheese Cake, 216
　Cheese and Ham Rolls, 219
　Cheese and Onion Sauce for Eggs, 254
　Cheese Pastry, 202, 226
　Cheese Rough Puff Pastry, 222
　Cheese Scrambled Eggs, 257
　Cheese Stuffed Peppers, 72
　Cheese Stuffed Potatoes, 205
　Cheese Rafts, 203
　Cheese Sauce, 314
　Cheese Soufflé, 266
　Cheese Tartlets, 222
　Cheese and Vegetable Flan, 223
　Cheese and Vegetable Platter, 224
　Cheshire, 197
　Cornish Cheese Pie, 226
　Cottage Cheese, 197
　Cottage Cheese and Peach Platter, 173
　Cottage Cheese and Pineapple Platter, 169
　Cottage Cheese Ring, 225
　Cheese Cream, 197
Creamy Quiche Lorraine, 274
Danish Blue, 197
Demi-Sel, 197
Derby, 197
Double Gloucester, 197
Dunlop, 197
Edam, 197
Emmenthal, 197
Fondue, 207
Frankfurters with Cheese Sauce, 336
Fruit and Cheese, 217
Fruit Cheeses, 663
Gjetöst, 197
Gorganzola, 197
Gouda, 197
Grape, Cheese and Banana Salad, 172
Gruyère, 197
Hawaiian Sandwiches, 208
Lancashire, 197
Leicester, 197
Macaroni Cheese, 228
Marmalade and Cheese, 218
Mozzarella, 197
Nutty Banana and Cheese Salad, 174
Parmesan, 197
Pineapple and Cheese Salad, 220
Port Salut, 197
Potato Cheese Cakes, 209
Processed Cheeses, 197
Raisin and Cheese Pyramids, 221
Rich Cheese Sauce, 335
Roquefort, 197
Sage Derby, 197
Samsöe, 197
Snappy Cheese Dressing, 350
St. Paulin, 197
Stilton, 197
Stuffed Tomato Cups, 210
Summer Casserole au Gratin, 229
Tomato and Onion Pie, 230
Tome au Raisin, 197
Vegetable Pie, 231
Welsh Rarebit, 199
Cherries:
　To Store and Serve, 384
　Cherry Brandy, 710
　Cherry Jam, 583—585
　Cherry Lemon Whip, 385
　Cherry Wine, 687
　Pineapple and Cherry Gâteau, 445
　Quick Cherry Cakes, 386
　Strawberry Pineapple Cocktail, 470
Chervil, 488
Chestnuts:
　To Cook, 4
　Chestnut Purée, 46
　Chicken Almond Salad, 176
　Chicken and Asparagus Salad, 177
　Chicken Platter, 178
Chicory:
　To Cook, 4
　Cheese Sauce with Chicory and Ham, 334
　Chicory Salad, 144
Chilli Peppers, 4
Chipped Potatoes, 77
Chives, 4, 488
Chopped Spinach, 116
Coucroute Garnie, 115
CHUTNEYS AND RELISHES:
　To Make, 540
　To Make in a Pressure Cooker, 569
　To Prepare for Show Purposes, 512
　Apple Chutney, 541
　Apple and Mint Chutney, 542
　Apricot Chutney, 543
　Beetroot Chutney, 544
　Blackberry Chutney, 545
　Damson Chutney, 546
　End of Season Relish, 548
　Green Tomato Chutney, 559

Freezing of Foods

Top quality foods only should be preserved by home-freezing. Fruits and vegetables should be frozen directly they are packed.

Meat and poultry should hang for the correct minimum length of time before freezing and do not freeze already frozen meat.

PACKAGING

Moisture-vapour proof packaging materials are essential. Unless well packed and sealed food will lose moisture, become dry, texture and colour deteriorate and flavours disappear. It can also spoil other produce stored in the same freezer. Choose packaging materials with care and expel as much air as possible inside the containers before sealing.

EQUIPMENT

Quality of frozen foods depends on speed in preparation and quick drop in temperature when in the freezer. For freezing set the home-freezer at — 20 °F. to — 30 °F.
  ,, storing ,, ,, ,,   ,, ,, 0 °F.

Meat is cut into the portions you will need later.

Probably the butcher will do this, then they are wrapped in moisture-vapour-proof covers. The edges are turned in and sealed with tape or by heat. Expel the air by squeezing gently. After sealing, over-wrap with mutton cloth or similar wrapping to protect from damage while in the home freezer. Poultry should be trussed ready for cooking. Wrap sharp ends to protect the container. Wrap giblets separately. Place the bird in a suitable container e. g. plastic bag. Place giblets by the side, expel the air, seal. Blanch vegetables by putting in frying basket and immersing in boiling water. Bring to boil again. Time boiling according to the size of vegetables e. g. boil peas for 1 minute. Cool quickly by lowering into cold water. Pack and seal. Blanched and cooled vegetables may be packed in various types of containers, polythene bags or boxes. Place in the bag, expel the air. Seal.

Fruits should be covered with sugar syrup (see Recipe 499), the air expelled and the bag sealed or packed with sprinkling of sugar.

The container should be firmly sealed to avoid possible loss of moisture by evaporation from the fruit owing to the low humidity in the home freezer.

Cheese and fruit for the end of a perfect meal

34　ROAST DUCK GARNISHED WITH ORANGE
(Recipe 422)

31   SUPPER SPAGHETTI WITH CHEESE AND SALAD (Recipe 137)

32   MEAT AND VEGETABLE CASSEROLE (Recipe 136)

717   NETTLE BEER
(or Nettle Pop)

Young nettles only should be used for this and 2 gallons of them must be washed well and put into a pan with 2 gallons of water, ½ oz. of bruised root ginger, 4 lbs. of malt, 2 oz. hops and 4 oz. sarsaparilla. Boil for 15 minutes and strain it over 1½ lb. castor sugar. Stir until the sugar dissolves then add 1 oz. of creamed yeast. When the beer starts to ferment, put it into bottles and cork these and tie down with string. This beer needs no keeping.

718   PERRY (PEAR CIDER)

For dry perry prepare in the same way as for dry cider (Recipe 712) using pears instead of apples.

For sweet perry chop the pears to a pulp, adding water then proceed as for sweet cider (Recipe 712). Allow 2½ lb. raisins and 3 lb. sugar and 1 oz. yeast to each gallon of juice.

719   RICE 'WHISKY'

3 lb. round rice	*3 lb. sugar*
1 oz. yeast	*8 pint warm water*
juice of a lemon	*1 lb. raisins*

Put the rice, the chopped raisins with the sugar, lemon juice and water into a large bowl. Add the yeast which should have been dissolved in a little warm water. Let mixture stand, covered with a cloth, for 12 days, but stir occasionally for first 3 days. See that it is kept in a warm place. A scum will rise to the top as it works but do not remove until the last day. Filter the wine into a clean cask or a stone jar. Store for 6 months in a cool place, then bottle.

This is similar in taste, colour and potency to whisky.

720   SLOE GIN

Prick the ripe sound sloes all over with needle and half-fill glass jars with them. Sprinkle on them granulated sugar at the rate of 6 oz. sugar to 1 lb. of the prepared fruit. If you use unsweetened gin, double the amount of sugar.

Keep tightly corked in a fairly warm place for 3 months, shaking the jars occasionally, then strain through flannel or filter into bottles and cork tightly. It greatly improves with keeping.

721   USING ISINGLASS IN WINES

Many people are disappointed because their wine is cloudy. If it is well strained it should be clear but certain fruits have more of a tendency to be cloudy than others. If, when the wine goes into the casks, it looks cloudy add ¼ oz. of isinglass to each gallon of liquid. You may, however, not notice the wine has become cloudy until the time comes to bottle it. Put the isinglass in at this stage and leave in the cask for 48 hours and then bottle.

722   PARSLEY HONEY

2 large handfuls of fresh	*1¼ pints water*
parsley (about 4 – 5 oz.)	*1 lb. sugar*
1 dessertspoon vinegar	

Wash and pick over the parsley and chop up with stalks, roughly. Put into a pan with the water and bring to the boil. Boil gently until the water is reduced to 1 pint. Rinse out the saucepan and pour in the strained parsley water, add the warmed sugar and when dissolved bring to the boil. Add the vinegar and boil slowly until a little, when tested on a plate, is of a clear honey consistency, which will probably take about 30 minutes. Pot and seal.

Other interesting drinks to make

Note: *Some are alcoholic.*

709   ADVOCAAT

6 large egg yolks   1 oz. castor sugar (little
¾—1 bottle brandy   less if wished)

Put the yolks and sugar into a bowl and stand this over a pan of hot water, beating until a smooth thick creamy consistency. Beat until cool, then gradually stir in the brandy. Bottle.

710   CHERRY BRANDY

cherries*   brandy

for each 1 lb. cherries:

1—2 cloves   2—3 oz. castor sugar
* Morello cherries are best for this

Prick the cherries with a wooden cocktail stick and put enough to half fill a bottle. Add cloves and sugar to each lb. cherries. Fill the bottle with brandy, cover tightly and leave for 3—4 months. Strain into another bottle.

711   DANDELION TEA

Pour boiling water over the chopped washed dandelion leaves — leave to infuse for a short time and strain off. To 2 pints of water I would use ½-1 teacup (about 1 gill) of dandelion leaves.

712   CIDER

The type of cider you make, i.e. sweet, dry or sparkling varies a great deal.

To make dry cider choose sour apples; a good cooking apple is ideal but make sure it is mature. Leave them in a warmish place for several weeks until they are just beginning to soften. Chop up and pound until they are a pulp. Strain through muslin, pressing very hard so that all the juice is extracted. Keep this juice in a warm place in the pan and allow to bubble. When bubbles rise to the surface of the liquid and the sediment drops to the bottom put into a cask and cover tightly. Leave for 6—7 months in a cool place and then strain and bottle.

For a sparkling cider follow exactly the same process but watch carefully the liquid in the cask and when fermenting well strain into bottles. The bottles should be corked and wired down.

A sweet cider is made rather differently. Choose the same type of apple but instead of leaving them dry to mature cut them up, put them in a pan and cover with water. Leave for 2 weeks, stirring every day. Strain carefully and warm the liquid. To each gallon of liquid add 2½ lb. sugar and 1 oz. yeast. Cover and leave in a warm place to ferment. When fermenting is beginning pour into casks. Seal the casks at the end of fermenting and at the end of 6 months bottle.

713   GINGER BEER

¼ oz. yeast   2 teaspoons ginger
1¼ cups warm   2 teaspoons sugar
    water

Stir well and feed daily. Feed with 1 teaspoon ground ginger and 1 teaspoon sugar. After 7 days strain plant through cloth. Dissolve 3 cups of sugar with 4 cups of water. Add the juice of 2 lemons and liquid from the plant. Add all this to 10 cups of water. MIX WELL. Bottle in screw top bottles and keep for 7 days. Return plant to bottle and add 3 cups of water — mix well and halve. To each half add 2 teaspoons of ground ginger and 2 teaspoons sugar.

714   GINGER WINE

4 oz. raisins   3 gallons cold water
4 oz. whole ginger   9 lb. loaf sugar
4 lemons   ¼ oz. yeast

Stone and halve the raisins, put into a large preserving pan with the water, sugar and ginger (bruised). Boil for 1 hour, skimming frequently. Add the rind of the lemons and turn into a large earthenware bowl or wooden tub. Allow the liquid to stand until lukewarm, then put in the yeast. On the following day put into a clean dry cask, add the fruit of the lemons and bung lightly. Stir the wine every day for a fortnight then tighten the bung. Let the wine remain undisturbed for 3—4 months, when it may be bottled for use.

715   MARROW RUM

3 lb. diced marrow   castor sugar
2 lemons   rum

Simmer with lemon juice and pared rind until pulp. Put through jelly bag and to each pint juice add 6 oz. sugar and 1½ pints rum. Stir until sugar has dissolved — then filter and bottle.

Another way to make marrow rum is to make a hole in the centre of the marrow and in this put brown sugar and rum. Suspend the marrow with a bowl underneath to catch the drips and the marrow-flavoured rum will drip through.

716   MEAD

Dissolve 4 lb. light-coloured honey in 1 gallon water and 1 oz. hops, ½ oz. root ginger and sliced peel and juice of 2 lemons. Boil for 45 minutes, pour into cask to brim and while still lukewarm add 1 oz. yeast and allow to ferment — this will take 5 weeks approximately.

When bubbling has ceased put in ¼ oz. isinglass and bung tightly. Keep for 6 months then strain into bottles.

Wines from Vegetables and Flowers

700   COWSLIP WINE

7 pints flowers

and rest ingredients as elderflower wine (Recipe 702).

701   DANDELION WINE

5 pints dandelion flowers

and rest ingredients as elderflower wine (Recipe 702).

702   ELDERFLOWER WINE

1 pint elderflowers	*1 oz. whole ginger OR*
8 pints boiling water	*grated rind of 1 lemon*

Sugar: 3 lb. to each gallon of juice and juice of 1 orange or
lemon to each gallon of juice
Yeast: ¼ oz. to each gallon of juice

Put the ginger or lemon rind with the elderflowers, then pour over the 8 pints boiling water. Allow to stand for 4 days, stirring from time to time. Strain through flannel or several thicknesses of fine muslin, then measure and stir in 3 lb. sugar and the juice of 1 orange or lemon and ½ oz. yeast TO EACH GALLON of juice. Keep in a warm room and allow to ferment, then when you are sure all bubbling has ceased stir the wine, allow 3 days to settle, strain again most carefully and put into a corked container (not bottles). After several months' maturing pour into bottles.

703   PARSLEY WINE

8 oz. parsley	*8 pints boiling water*
1 oz. ginger	

Simmer parsley and water for 10 minutes, then add ginger. Put in 3 lb. sugar and juice of 1 lemon while still warm and the ¼ oz. yeast. Continue after this as for potato wine (Recipe 705).

704   BEETROOT WINE

4 lb. beetroot	*6 pints water*

As potato wine (Recipe 705) but omit pearl barley and flavour with a few cloves instead of lemon and orange.

705   POTATO WINE

4 lb. potatoes	*6 pints water*

Wash and slice the potatoes, then pour the boiling water over them, adding 1½ oz. ginger. Leave for 4 days to infuse, then to each gallon of liquid add 2 lb. sugar*, 4 oz. raisins, 8 oz. pearl barley, ½ oz. yeast (spread on toast) and the juice of 1 lemon and 1 orange. Leave in a warm place to ferment. When bubbling has ceased the wine should be stirred, then left for a further 3 days to settle and strained through flannel or VERY THICK muslin into a cask — which should be corked and left for 6 months. Pour into bottles, cork and store in a cool dark place.

Parsnips can be used instead.

* *This gives a very dry wine. If sweeter wine is liked use up to 3 lb. sugar.*

706   TURNIP CARROT, SWEDE WINE

All make good wines and same method and quantities should be used as for potato wine.

707   WHEAT WINE

1 pint wheat	*8 pints water*
3¼ lb. sugar	*2 oz. yeast*
2 lb. raisins or	
sultanas	

Put the wheat, sugar and sultanas into a large container. Pour over the water — which should be boiling. Allow to become lukewarm, then stir in the yeast. Leave in the pan for 3 weeks, stirring from time to time. Strain into a cask, and when bubbling has ceased cork tightly.

Leave for at least 3 months and preferably 1 year before bottling.

This wine is similar to a white port in flavour and colour. Rye or barley can be used instead.

708   VEGETABLE AND FLOWER WINES TASTE RATHER LIKE THIS

While each vegetable and flower gives its own particular flavour to the wine the nearest comparison to a familiar wine is given below.

Cowslip	very light white wine
Dandelion	light, often sparkling wine
Elderflower	light dry white wine
Parsley	dry white wine
Beetroot	rather potent, like a port wine
Potato	dry, rather potent white wine
Turnip	dry, rather potent white wine
Wheat wine	very strong, like a light port

695   PLUM WINE

5 pints boiling water   4 lb. RIPE plums*
1 lb. sugar

* By using a different type of plum with each lot of wine you produce a good variety of flavours

Sprinkle sugar over halved plums then add boiling water. Proceed as for rhubarb wine (Recipe 696) but add 1½ lb. sugar only to each gallon juice, together with cracked plum stones and ¼ oz. yeast.

696   RHUBARB WINE

6 pints boiling water   4 lb. rhubarb

Cut the fruit into pieces, pour over the water and leave for 4 days to infuse. Strain off liquid and to each gallon allow 2½ lb. sugar and ¼ oz. brewers' yeast (which can be spread on a small piece of toast or mixed with a little of the liquid). Add the juice of ½ lemon and ½ orange to each gallon. Leave in a warm place, i.e. in temperature of 65°–75°F. to ferment (bubble). When bubbling ceases (this will be after 4–6 weeks, but for some wines a shorter period) the wine should be stirred, left for a further 3 days for the sediment to settle, then strained through flannel or VERY THICK muslin into a cask, which should be corked and left for 6 months. The cask MUST be completely filled, otherwise your wine will taste like vinegar. Pour into bottles, cork and store in a COOL DARK PLACE to mature for another few months at least.

697   ROSE HIP WINE

4 lb. rose hips   1 gallon boiling water
1 oz. citric acid or   3 lb. sugar
the juice of 3   ¼ oz. yeast
lemons

Gather the rose hips after the first frost, cut in half or mince. Put rose hips, sugar and citric acid (or lemon juice) into large bowl and pour over boiling water. Stir well. When mixture is lukewarm add yeast. Cover well and leave until fermentation ceases — this may be shorter than in some wines. Strain into cask then proceed as for rhubarb wine (Recipe 696).

698   SLOE WINE

5 pints boiling water   4 lb. sloes

Method as for rhubarb wine but to each gallon of juice add 3 lb. sugar and ¼ oz. yeast. A little brandy may be added.

699   FRUIT WINES TASTE RATHER LIKE THIS

While each fruit gives its own particular flavour to the wine the nearest comparison to a familiar wine is given below.

Apple	light white wine
Blackberry	rich red wine
Blackcurrant	port wine
Cherry wine	claret
Damson port	port
Elderberry	port
Gooseberry	sweet champagne
Grape	light dry white wine
Loganberry or	
Raspberry	vin rosé
Orange	light sherry
Plum	red wine
Raisin	light port
Rhubarb	very dry white wine
Rose hip	very dry white wine
Sloe	red wine

The grape harvest in Italy

688　DAMSON PORT

Pour a gallon of boiling water over 4 lb. damsons and leave until next day. Mash and stir daily for 5 days and strain through a jelly bag. Now add 4 lb, sugar and ½ pint boiling water and leave to ferment for 8 days. Skim, strain and bottle.

689　ELDERBERRY WINE

As for rhubarb wine (Recipe 696), but flavour with ¼ oz. root ginger and 8 oz. raisins.

690　GOOSEBERRY WINE

　9 pints boiling water　　　4 lb. fruit (use green
　　　　　　　　　　　　　　　　gooseberries)

As for rhubarb wine (Recipe 696) but to each gallon of juice add 3 lb. sugar, ¼ oz. yeast and 1 oz. ginger.

691　GRAPE WINE

　5 pints boiling water　　　4 lb. grapes

As for rhubarb wine (Recipe 696) but to each gallon of juice add 2 lb. sugar, ¼ oz. yeast and a little almond essence if wished.

692　LOGANBERRY OR RASPBERRY WINE

　Use 1 gallon boiling water to 1 gallon loganberries

Proceed as for rhubarb wine (Recipe 696) but add 5 lb. sugar to each gallon of juice.

693　ORANGE WINE

　6 lb. oranges　　　　　　8 pints boiling water

Method as for rhubarb wine (Recipe 696) but to each gallon of juice add the juice of 2 lemons, ¼ oz. yeast (spread on toast) and 3 lb. sugar.

694　RAISIN WINE

　7 pints boiling water　　　4 lb. dried raisins
　2 sliced oranges

Method as for rhubarb wine (Recipe 696) and to each gallon of juice add 2 lb. sugar and ¼ oz. yeast.

680 EGG AND BRANDY MILK SHAKE

Whisk together an egg or egg yolk, a little sugar and brandy. Add hot or cold milk and beat well. Serve at once in tall glasses.

681 ORANGE MILK SHAKE

The simplest yet most delicious drink imaginable, orange milk shake, needs only the strained chilled juice of 2 oranges, well shaken with ½ pint of cold, cold milk and topped with a sprig of mint and 1 slice of orange for decoration.

682 PLANTATION MILK SHAKE

1 tablespoon peanut butter
3 tablespoons sugar
nutmeg
¼ teaspoon vanilla essence
pinch salt
1 pint milk

Place peanut butter, sugar and salt in bowl, add 2 tablespoons milk, whip with rotary beater until smooth. Add remaining milk gradually, beat till smooth. Add vanilla. Chill in covered jar in refrigerator until ready to use. When serving top each glass with a pinch of grated nutmeg.

Wines with Fruit

683 HOW TO MAKE PERFECT WINES

Note. It is illegal to make home made wines for sale. A great deal of success in wine making depends on the storage conditions.

Fermentation should take place in a warm temperature i.e. from 65°—80°F. but when storing the wine, after fermentation has ceased, it should then be stored between 50°—60°F. no hotter.

The equipment for wine making is not difficult to obtain. The local branch of your womens's organisation will help you about this and the pictures shown are taken from Women's Institute wine making displays.

The cooking of the ingredients, where necessary, can be done in an ordinary pan. For extracting the juice use a large basin; or you can obtain a proper wine press. For fermenting large casks of wood or stone or earthenware containers are perfectly all right but on no account should you use metal, enamel or glazed containers. For straining, several thicknesses of well washed flannel or a very big pad of muslin or un-medicated cotton wool can be used or you can obtain filter paper from a chemist. These are put over hair or nylon sieves, NOT metal. Any wine can be made rather by the same process and recipe as rhubarb wine (Recipe 696) but where a slight variation of technique gives a better result this has been stressed.

684 APPLE WINE

8 pints boiling water
juice of 2 lemons
4 lb. apples

Method as for rhubarb wine (Recipe 696), but to each gallon of juice add ¼ oz. yeast and 3 lb. sugar. Do not core or peel apples — just cut into pieces.

685 BLACKBERRY WINE

As for rhubarb wine (Recipe 696). Add little cinnamon to taste.

686 BLACKCURRANT WINE

6 pints boiling water
4 lb. blackcurrants

Method as for rhubarb wine (Recipe 696) but to each gallon of juice ¼ oz. yeast and 3 lb. sugar.

687 CHERRY WINE

Stone cherries and follow instructions for blackcurrant wine (see above).

Women's Institute wine making displays

673 TOMATO JUICE COCKTAIL

To each 2 pints of cored and cut up tomatoes:

4 whole cloves
4 slices onion
2 teaspoons salt
1 tablespoon sugar
(if liked)

¼ teaspoon celery salt
2 tablespoons vinegar
or lemon juice

Simmer until soft and rub through a fine sieve. If it is to be stored, heat to boiling point, pour into bottles and sterilise as purée (Recipe 503).

674 SUMMERTIME SODA

Put the juice of fresh orange, lemon, grapefruit in the bottom of a long tumbler. Pour over soda water to come very near the top and finish off with a spoonful of ice cream. Serve at once.

675 SUMMER SPECIAL

Strictly for grownups, this is guaranteed to ease the cares of the day and put an edge on tired appetites. In the bottom of each glass put a good dash of angostura bitters, 2 teaspoons water and 2 lumps of sugar which have been rubbed hard on an orange to pick up the zest. Add a measure of gin and the juice of the orange. Chill thoroughly and top up with iced soda water. Decorate with a sprig of mint or, if you prefer, a cherry.

Milk Shakes

If you have an electric blender or liquidiser milk shakes can be made in that. These drinks have all the goodness of milk in a very exciting form.

676 BANANA FRAPPÉ

Mash 1 banana for each portion. Put it into a dish with a squeeze of lemon juice and a little sugar. Add a spoonful of ice cream and just about ¼ pint of very cold milk, whisk together until frothy. Pour into tall glasses, decorate with sliced banana and a few nuts. Serve with a spoon.

677 BLACKCURRANT AND LEMON FRAPPÉ

Put a good tablespoon of blackcurrant syrup, a squeeze of lemon and a spoonful of ice cream into a basin. Add a good ¼ pint milk. Whisk until frothy, pour into tall glasses and decorate with rings of lemon.

678 CHOCOLATE MILK SHAKE

Whisk chocolate powder or sieved cocoa and sugar with cold milk until frothy. Add sugar to taste. For a richer milk shake add a spoonful of ice cream.

679 COFFEE MILK SHAKE

Mix together soluble coffee powder and milk with a little sugar and ice or ice cream. Whisk until frothy.

Home Made Drinks and Wines

In this chapter you will find a selection of fruit drinks, milk shakes and home made wines.

667 APPLEADE

1 pint water
just about 1 lb. apples
1 lemon
sugar or glucose to taste

Wash the apples and cut them into pieces, retaining peel and core. Add the pieces of lemon rind. Pour over 1 pint boiling water, then leave until cold. Strain. Add glucose and lemon juice. (This is a cooling drink.)

668 BOUILLON ON THE ROCKS

Make up 1 packet beef bouillon with ½ pint boiling water. Stir in 1 pint cold water. Pour over cubes of ice in glasses. Decorate with cucumber or lemon slices.

669 LEMONADE

2 small lemons
1 pint boiling water
sugar to taste (instead of sugar you can use glucose)

Grate the rind from the lemons, being careful to use only the yellow 'zest'. Put this into a jug, pour over the freshly boiling water, then add the lemon juice and sugar. Leave until cold and strain.

670 GRAPEFRUIT SODA

2 grapefruit
soda water
a little sugar if liked
ice cream

Squeeze the juice from the grapefruit and sweeten to taste. Divide between four tall glasses or tumblers. When ready to serve, top up the fruit juice with soda water, leaving a little space for the ice cream. Add spoonfuls of ice cream and serve with a spoon and straws.

671 ORANGEADE

2 oranges
1 pint boiling water
sugar to taste

Grate the rind from the oranges, being careful to use only the orange 'zest'. Put this into a jug, pour over the freshly boiling water, then add the orange juice and sugar. Leave until cold and strain.

672 MIXED FRUIT CORDIAL

The thirst quenching sharpness of lemon and grapefruit juices makes a mixed fruit cordial one of the most refreshing of all summer drinks. First make a syrup by adding 8 oz. sugar to ½ pint water in a saucepan and bringing slowly to boiling point. Boil for 2 minutes and then cool. Blend the strained juice of 4 oranges, 2 lemons and 2 grapefruit and chill thoroughly. Sweeten to taste with the syrup and dilute with iced water or soda water. Decorate with lemon slices.

For an extra 'frosted' effect, dip the rims of the glasses in fruit juice and then in sugar.

29   CIDER FRUIT SALAD (Recipe 666);
RICH CHOCOLATE EGG CUSTARD (Recipe 285)

completed they should be immersed in a vessel (provided with a false bottom) of boiling water, and the water, which, in consequence, is slightly lowered in temperature, again brought to the boil. These are the times necessary for an A2½ can; if smaller cans are used the time of boiling may be reduced by 5 minutes.

PROCESSING TIMES FOR CANNED FRUIT

Fruit	Time taken for water to reboil	Additional time for cans to be kept in boiling water
Apples (in syrup), Apricots, Blackberries, Damsons, Gooseberries, Grapefruit, Greengages, Loganberries, Oranges, Plums (firm-ripe), Raspberries, Red Currants, Rhubarb, Strawberries	0 — 5	18 — 15
	6 — 10	15 — 13
	11 — 15	12 — 10
	16 — 20	10 — 8
Apples (solid-pack)*, Black Currants, Cherries, Peaches, Pears (ripe dessert), Pineapple, Plums (under-ripe), Whortleberries	0 — 5	22 — 20
	6 — 10	20 — 18
	11 — 15	17 — 15
	16 — 20	15 — 13
Tomatoes (in brine)	0 — 5	35 — 32
	6 — 10	32 — 30
	11 — 15	30 — 27
	16 — 20	27 — 25
Tomatoes (solid-pack)*	0 — 5	45 — 42
	6 — 10	42 — 40
	11 — 15	40 — 37
	16 — 20	37 — 25

* Solid-pack apples and tomatoes should be canned while still hot from scalding.

Cooling the cans. As soon as the cans have been processed, they should be taken out and placed in cold clean water (running water if possible), to prevent the fruit over-cooking. Cans should be removed when at blood heat. This can be ascertained by rolling them gently for ½ minute in the hand.

CANNING VEGETABLES

Vegetables suitable for canning. The same as recommended for bottling (Recipe 510).
The cans. Many vegetables contain sulphur, which during storage would act on the plain can to give black stains. Fruitlacquered cans should not be used as the lacquer may not withstand the high temperature used in vegetable processing. Cans coated inside with sulphur-resisting lacquer to prevent staining can be obtained for vegetables. It is better but not essential to use these sulphur-resisting lacquered cans. Cans should be rinsed well in clean water before use.
Preparing the vegetables. See bottling (Recipe 510).
Packing the cans. The cans should be well filled with vegetables, but these should not be pressed down.
Brine. The brine, made from salt and water as for bottling (Recipe 510), should be boiling when poured over the vegetables and the cans filled to within ⅜ inch of the top.

Exhausting the cans. Immediately the brine has been poured on the lid should be placed on the can, which is then put in water at simmering point with water coming up to 1 inch from the top of the can, and left there for 5 minutes before the lid is sealed on.
Sealing the cans. As soon as the can is removed from the hot water the lid should be sealed as in fruit.
Sterilising. As soon as a batch of cans is sealed, they should all be sterilised under pressure. The method is the same as that given for bottled vegetables (Recipe 510). In general, the times recommended for A2 ½ cans are 5 minutes less than for bottles of similar vegetables because cans are hotter when sealed. At the end of the sterilizing time the pressure in the cooker should be allowed to fall.

Cooling the cans. As soon as the cans are taken from the steriliser proceed as with fruit. See above.

666   **CIDER FRUIT SALAD**

(illustrated opposite)

canned fruit   sugar to taste
water   ¼ pint cider

Dissolve the sugar in the cider. Pour over the fruit with a little of syrup from tin. Top with whipped evaporated milk.

jams that are most suitable are the dried fruits and as an example here is a recipe for dried peach jam.

Dried peach jam

1 lb. dried peaches	*1½ teaspoons citric or tartaric*
1½ pints water	*acid or the juice of 1½*
3 lb. sugar	*lemons*

Soak the fruit in the water for 48—72 hours. Put into the cooker without the rack. Fix lid, bring to pressure. Lower the heat and cook for 10 minutes. Allow pressure to drop gradually. Very good jams to make in a pressure cooker are the following:

Blackcurrant jam

1¼ lb. sugar	*1½ gills water*
1 lb. blackcurrants	

Put fruit and water into pan. Fix lid, bring to pressure and lower heat. Cook for 3 minutes. Allow pressure to drop gradually. Stir in sugar and when dissolved boil jam rapidly until set.

Green gooseberry jam

1 lb. gooseberries	*¼ pint water*
1¼ lb. sugar	

Method as for blackcurrant jam, allowing 1 minute only pressure cooking time.

Seville or bitter orange marmalade
(Coarse cut and bitter)

1 lb. oranges or	*1 pint water*
3 medium sized oranges	*2 lb. sugar*

Wash the oranges well and put into the cooker with the water. Fix the lid, bring to pressure. Lower the heat and cook for 15 minutes. Reduce pressure gradually. Remove the oranges from the liquid, allow to cool, then cut up neatly. Put the pips into the liquid and boil steadily for 10 minutes to extract the pectin from them, then remove and replace the cut orange pulp. Bring to the boil, then stir in the warmed sugar. Continue stirring until all the sugar is dissolved, then bring the marmalade to the boil rapidly without stirring until setting point is reached.

Canning

665   CANNING

Cans are made in different sizes. There are two available for use with most machines, the A2½, with a capacity of 1½ pint and the 1 lb. size with 16 fl. oz. capacity. The diameter of the two sizes is the same, but different baseplates will be required. These baseplates must be fitted for each machine by the maker's agents. The cans have an open end with a flange at the top, and the lids are made with a groove which fits the flange. Two types of can are commonly used for fruit — plain and lacquered.

Plain Cans. These, made of tinned steel plate, may be used for green, yellow or colourless fruits, such as apples, gooseberries or green plums, but must not be used for red-coloured fruits.

Fruit Lacquered Cans. These special cans have a layer of golden-coloured lacquer over the inside surface, which prevents the fruit from coming into contact with the tin itself. They may be used for all fruits, and are ESSENTIAL for purple or red-coloured fruits, such as blackcurrants and raspberries, and for rhubarb. Before use, the lacquer should be examined to make sure there are no scratches on its surface. Store empty cans upside down in a dry place to prevent rusting and away from strong smells such as creosote, soap or onions, which may be picked up by the lacquer and subsequently taint the fruit.

Cans should be rinsed in *clean* water and if at all dirty, in boiling water before use, and any dents in the flange or rim of the can should be removed if good results are to be secured. After the cans have been rinsed, they should be inverted to drain but should not be dried with a cloth as this might scratch the lacquer.

FRUIT

Selection and preparation of the fruit suitable for canning is as bottling; the methods for preparing it are given in Recipe 498. It is necessary to emphasise that a really firstclass product can only be secured by carefully grading the fruit before it is placed in the cans. Uniformity of ripeness and evenness of size and colour should be aimed at. Inferior fruit should not be mixed with sound fruit. Low-grade fruit should not be canned.

Syrup to cover fruit. See Recipe 499. In home canning the syrup must always be used BOILING but if kept hot for long, a lid should be put on the pan to prevent evaporation which will alter the strength of the syrup. The boiling syrup should be poured over the fruit to within ⅜ inch of the top and the lid placed on at once. The steam rising from the syrup drives the air from the can and it is essential that the contents should not be allowed to cool before the lid is sealed on. If air is left in the can it may cause slight discoloration of the fruit at the top of the can and also 'pinholing' or corrosion of the tin plate. For this reason, therefore, the temperature of the syrup should not fall appreciably before the can is sealed, and it is advisable not to fill more than 6 cans at a time before sealing.

Sealing the cans. Several types of machines are on the market for fastening the lids on to the can — a process known as 'double seaming'. As the method of operating these machines varies, the instructions issued with the machine should be carefully followed. The machine should be screwed on to a firm table or bench.

Processing. Immediately the syrup has been added, the cans should be sealed. When a batch has been

Fruit Curd, Mincemeat, Butters and cheese

657   LEMON CURD

8 oz. sugar	rind of 3 lemons
4 oz. fresh butter	juice of 2 large lemons
2 eggs	

Grate the rind carefully, removing just the yellow 'zest' but none of the white pith. If using loaf sugar, rub this over the lemons until all the yellow has been removed. Squeeze the juice from the fruit. Put all ingredients — except eggs — into double saucepan or basin over hot water and cook, stirring from time to time, until the butter and sugar have melted. Add the well beaten eggs and continue cooking until the mixture coats the back of a wooden spoon. Pour into jars and seal down.

658   MARROW CURD

Peel the marrow and take away any skins. Put into a pan with just enough water to cover the bottom and cook until quite soft. Measure the pulp and to each lb. of pulp allow the grated rind and juice of 2 lemons or 1 very large lemon and 1 lb. sugar, 4 oz. butter and 2 eggs. Put altogether into a double saucepan and cook until very smooth.

659   ORANGE CURD

8 oz. sugar	rind of 3 oranges
4 oz. fresh butter	juice of 2 large oranges
2 eggs	

Grate the rind carefully, removing just the yellow 'zest' but none of the pith. If using loaf sugar, rub this over the oranges until all the yellow has been removed. Squeeze the juice from the fruit. Put all ingredients — except eggs — into double saucepan or basin over hot water and cook, stirring from time to time, until the margarine and sugar have melted. Add the well beaten eggs and continue cooking until the mixture coats the back of a wooden spoon. Pour into jars and seal down.

660   ORANGE AND LEMON CURD

8 oz. castor or loaf sugar	rind of 1 lemon
	rind of 2 oranges
4 oz. fresh butter or margarine	juice of 2 large oranges
	2 eggs

Method as for lemon curd (Recipe 657).

661   MINCEMEAT

4 oz. shredded suet or melted margarine	4 oz. grated apple
	1 lb. mixed dried fruit
4 oz. sugar — preferably demerara sugar	4 oz. mixed peel
	4 oz. blanched and well dried almonds
finely grated rind and juice of 1 large lemon	½ teaspoon cinnamon

1 level teaspoon mixed spice	¼ teaspoon grated nutmeg
4 level tablespoons brandy, whisky or rum	

Do not cut down on the quantities of sugar, fat or spirit if you wish this to keep well. Make quite certain the fruit is dry. If this has been washed, let it dry for at least 24 hours before making mincemeat. Mix all the ingredients together. Put into dry jam jars and cover thoroughly. Leave in a cool dry place.

662   FRUIT BUTTERS

Any of the recipes for jam can be used. The fruit is simmered to a pulp and then instead of adding the sugar straight away it should be rubbed through a sieve to give a very smooth pulp. Add 8 oz. — 1 lb. of sugar, bring to the boil and cook until a thick consistency.

This can be put into moulds and turned out to serve as a sweet. If you wish to keep the fruit butter for any length of time it should be put into hot bottling jars and sterilised like fruit pulp (Recipe 502).

663   FRUIT CHEESES

These are made in exactly the same way as fruit butters except 1 lb. sugar is used because of the higher sugar content. The fruit cheese will keep like jam.

664   MAKING PRESERVES IN A PRESSURE COOKER

A pressure cooker can be of invaluable assistance when making jam, jelly or marmalade — particularly with the latter because instead of simmering the peel for several hours it will be softened in 15 minutes.

In addition, since pressure cookers are made of particularly strong metal, jam made in them is very unlikely to burn. When softening fruit the cooker should be sealed and the fruit cooked under pressure. When the sugar is added the pan should be left open so that evaporation can take place, and the jam set. ON NO ACCOUNT SHOULD THE PAN BE SEALED WHEN ONCE THE SUGAR HAS BEEN ADDED. NEVER FILL THE COOKER MORE THAN HALF-FULL.

Although all fruit can be cooked in a pressure pan, only those recipes where a great saving of time can be effected are given. With other jams and jellies use an ordinary recipe — reduce the liquid to half the usual quantity and the time to about quarter the normal time. Never cook the jam under pressure when the sugar has been added.

Jam made from such quick-cooking fruits as raspberries or strawberries is better not pressure cooked. The

650 SWEET ORANGE MARMALADE

1 lb. sweet oranges | *2 lb. sugar*
2 pints water | *juice 1 lemon*

Method as for orange marmalade (2) (Recipe 648).

651 SUGARLESS MARMALADE

¼ oz. gelatine to every ½ pint pulp
8 grains saccharin
2 Seville oranges
2 lemons

Cut the rind from the oranges and lemons being careful to remove no white pith with the rind and chop it. Cut up the pulp and place it in a preserving pan with the rind and 1 pint water. Boil gently for about 30 minutes; cook until pulp and rind are tender. Add saccharin then stir in gelatine dissolved in a little of the hot syrup. Remove from the fire and bottle while still hot. Cover at once. DO NOT MAKE LARGE QUANTITIES AS THIS MARMALADE WILL NOT KEEP.

652 SEVILLE ORANGE MARMALADE

3 lb. citrus fruit (8 to 10 bitter oranges 2 lemons)
5 lb. sugar
2 pints water
1 bottle commercial pectin
1 level teaspoon bicarbonate of soda

Wash fruit and remove skins in quarters using sharp knife. Shave off and discard about half of white part. Shred skins very finely, and place in preserving pan with water and soda (this helps to soften the skins). Bring to the boil and simmer. Cover, but stir occasionally, for about 10 minutes, until the skins can be crushed easily between thumb and fore-finger. Next, cut up the peeled fruit, discarding the pips and tough skin. Add pulp and juice to cooked rind. Simmer, covered, 20 minutes longer.

Put sugar and 3 pints prepared fruit into large preserving pan, making up the quantity with water if necessary. Heat slowly, stirring occasionally, until the sugar has dissolved. Add a small piece of butter or margarine. Bring to a full rolling boil and boil for 5 minutes. Remove preserving pan from heat and stir in commercial pectin. Then stir and skim by turns for just 7 minutes to cool slightly to prevent fruit floating. Pour into clean hot jars and cover.

653 TANGERINE MARMALADE

1 lb. tangerines — approx. 5 medium sized tangerines
1 level teaspoon citric or tartaric acid or the juice of 1 lemon
1½ pints water
1½ lb. sugar

Cut the tangerines finely, removing the pips. Cook the peel and pulp overnight in the water, together with the pips, which should be tied up carefully in a piece of muslin. After soaking put the fruit, water and pips into a covered pan and simmer slowly until the peel is quite soft. This should take approximately 1½ hours. Take out the bag of pips and stir in the warmed sugar and lemon juice or acid. Bring the marmalade to the boil and boil rapidly in an uncovered pan until setting point is reached. This will take approximately 20 minutes.

654 THREE-FRUIT MARMALADE

*1 Seville orange or grapefruit**
*1 sweet orange**
*1 lemon**
2¼ pints water
2¼ lb. sugar

** all medium-sized fruit*

Prepare the fruit as for Recipe 648 and cook in the same way, adding the fruit juice with the warmed sugar. Continue as instructed in this recipe.

655 FOUR-FRUIT MARMALADE

*1 Seville orange**
*1 grapefruit**
*1 sweet orange**
*2 lemons**
3½ pint water
3½ lb. sugar

** all medium-sized fruit*

Prepare fruit as Recipe 654 and cook in the same way adding the fruit juice with the warmed sugar. Continue as instructed in this recipe.

656 YIELD OF JAM, JELLY, MARMALADE

Correctly made jam should contain 60 % sugar. That means:

1 lb. sugar should produce 1⅔ lb. jam
2 lb. sugar should produce 3⅓ lb. jam
3 lb. sugar should produce 5 lb. jam etc.

Jam made with commercial pectin often has a slightly different yield.

645 ORANGE AND GRAPEFRUIT MARMALADE

(with commercial pectin)

3 lb. citrus fruit (4 oranges,
2 grapefruit and 1 lemon)
5 lb. sugar

1½ pints water
1 bottle commercial pectin
1 level teaspoon
bicarbonate of soda

Wash fruit and remove skins in quarters using sharp knife. Shave off and discard about half of white part. Shred skins very finely, and place in preserving pan with water and soda (this helps to soften the skins). Bring to the boil and simmer. Cover, but stir occasionally, for about 10 minutes, until the skins can be crushed easily between thumb and forefinger. Next, cut up the peeled fruit, discarding the pips and tough skin. Add pulp and juice to cooked rind. Simmer, covered, 20 minutes longer. Put sugar and 3 pints prepared fruit into large preserving pan, making up the quantity with water if necessary. Heat slowly, stirring occasionally, until the sugar has dissolved. Add a small piece of butter or margarine. Bring to a full rolling boil and boil for 5 minutes. Remove preserving pan from heat and stir in commercial pectin. Then stir and skim by turns for just 7 minutes to cool slightly to prevent fruit floating. Pour into clean hot jars and cover.

646 ORANGE AND LEMON MARMALADE

1 lb. sweet oranges
2¼ lb. sugar

1 lb. lemons
2½ pint water

Method as orange marmalade (2) (Recipe 648).

647 ORANGE MARMALADE (1)

(coarse cut and bitter)

1 lb. Seville or bitter
oranges (3 medium-
sized oranges)

2 pints water
2 lb. sugar

Wash oranges thoroughly and put into a covered pan with the water. Simmer slowly for about 1½ hours or until a blunt wooden skewer will easily pierce the skin of the fruit. Remove oranges from liquid, allow to cool, then cut up neatly. Put pips into liquid and boil steadily for 10 minutes to extract the pectin from them, then remove and replace the cut orange pulp. Bring to the boil, then stir in the warmed sugar. Continue stirring until sugar is dissolved, then bring to the boil and boil rapidly without stirring until setting point is reached. It is advisable to start testing the marmalade after about 15 minutes.

648 ORANGE MARMALADE (2)

(a sweeter variety)

1 lb. Seville or bitter
oranges
3 pints water

3 lb. sugar
juice 1 lemon or 1 teaspoon
citric or tartaric acid

Cut or mince oranges finely, removing pips. Soak peel and pulp overnight in the water, together with the pips, which should be tied up in a piece of muslin. After soaking, put fruit, water and pips into a covered pan and simmer slowly until peel is quite soft. This should take about 1½ hours. Take out the bag of pips and stir in warmed sugar and lemon juice or acid. Bring marmalade to the boil, and boil rapidly in an uncovered pan until setting point is reached. This will take about 20 minutes.

649 QUINCE MARMALADE

1 lb. quinces
¼ pint water

1¼ lb. sugar
juice of 1 lemon

Peel, core and cut the quinces into fairly even slices. Put into the water and simmer gently until tender. If the quinces are very hard you may find you need a little more water. Add the sugar and lemon and boil until set.

Marmalade

639 PERFECT MARMALADE

Perfect marmalade consists of neat pieces of peel and a very clear syrup. It is important to soak the peel well or cook very gently so that it is really soft before turning into a preserve.

640 DRIED APRICOT AND ORANGE MARMALADE

(with commercial pectin)

4 oz. dried apricots	1½ pints water
2 Seville oranges or 3 sweet oranges	1 lemon
¼ teaspoon bicarbonate of soda	2½ lb. sugar
½ bottle commercial pectin	knob of butter

Soak the apricots overnight in ½ pint of the water. Peel the oranges and lemon, being careful not to include any pith. Remove the pith, shred the peel and simmer it in the remaining pint of water with the bicarbonate. Slice the oranges and lemon and discard the pips. Add the pulp, juice, apricots and 'soaking' water. Boil for 20 minutes then add the sugar and a knob of butter. Stir over a gentle heat until the sugar is dissolved, then boil for 5 minutes as fast as possible. Remove from heat, and stir in the commercial pectin. Skim and pot.

641 LEMON MARMALADE

1 lb. lemons (4 medium or 3 large lemons)	2½ pints water
	2½ lb. sugar

Method as for orange marmalade (2) (Recipe 648).

642 LIME MARMALADE

1 lb. limes	2½ pints water
2½ lb. sugar	

Cut or mince the limes finely, removing the pips. Soak the peel and pulp overnight in the water, together with the pips, which should be tied up carefully in a piece of muslin. After soaking put the fruit, water and pips in a covered pan and simmer slowly until the peel is quite soft. This should take approximately 1½ hours. Take out the bag of pips and stir in the warmed sugar. Bring the marmalade to the boil and boil rapidly in an uncovered pan until set. Approximately 20 minutes.

643 ORANGE PEEL AND APPLE MARMALADE

peel from 1 lb. oranges	1 lb. peeled cooking apples
3 lb. sugar	3 pints water

Soak the peel overnight in the water, then simmer until nearly soft. Add the apples and continue cooking until a smooth pulp. Stir in the sugar, then boil without stirring until setting point is reached.

644 ORANGE GINGER MARMALADE

3 lb. oranges	1½ pints water
2 lemons	1 level teaspoon bicarbonate of soda
4¾ lb. sugar	
4 oz. crystallized ginger	1 bottle commercial pectin

Wash fruit and remove skins in quarters using sharp knife. Shave off and discard about half of white part. Shred skins very finely and place in preserving pan with water and soda (helps to soften the skins). Bring to the boil and simmer. Cover, but stir occasionally, for about 10 minutes, until the skins can be crushed easily between thumb and fore-finger. Next, cut up the peeled fruit, discarding the pips and tough skin. Add pulp and juice to cooked rind. Simmer, covered, 20 minutes longer. Put sugar, chopped ginger and 3 pints prepared fruit into large preserving pan, making up the quantity with water if necessary. Heat slowly, stirring occasionally, until the sugar has dissolved. Add a small piece of butter or margarine. Bring to a full rolling boil and boil for 5 minutes. Remove preserving pan from heat and stir in commercial pectin. Then stir and skim by turns for just 7 minutes to cool slightly to prevent fruit floating. Pour into clean hot jars and cover.

631   ROSE HIP JELLY

1 lb. rose hips   *2 lb. apples*
water   *sugar*

Simmer the rose hips with ½ pint water and apples with ½ pint water then put both lots of fruit through separate jelly bags, mix together and allow 1 lb. sugar and the juice of 1 lemon to each pint.

632   STRAWBERRY JELLY

1 lb. strawberries   *8 oz. redcurrants*
2 tablespoons water

Simmer the strawberries, redcurrants and water together — put through a jelly bag — measure the juice and add 1 lb. of sugar to each pint of juice. If you haven't redcurrants, then simmer the strawberries by themselves and to each pint of strawberry juice allow the juice of 2 lemons and 1 lb. sugar — put the lemon juice in with the sugar.

633   STRAWBERRY JELLY

(with commercial pectin)

3 lb. strawberries   *3 tablespoons lemon juice*
¾ pint water   *1 bottle commercial pectin*
3¼ lb. sugar

Put the strawberries into a saucepan and crush thoroughly. Add the water, bring to the boil, cover and simmer for 15 minutes. Place in a cloth and allow the juice to drain. Measure the juice and if necessary add water to make up to two pints. Put the juice, sugar and lemon juice into a preserving pan. Heat gently, stirring occasionally until the sugar has dissolved. Bring quickly to a full rolling boil and boil hard for 2 minutes. Remove

from the heat and stir in the commercial pectin. Boil rapidly for a further minute. Remove from heat, skim if necessary, pot and cover in the usual way.

634   STRAWBERRY AND GOOSEBERRY JELLY

1 lb. strawberries   *1 lb. gooseberries*
sugar   *lemons*
¼ pint water

Simmer the gooseberries with the water until nearly soft, add the strawberries and continue cooking until very soft. Put through a jelly bag and to each pint add 1 lb. sugar and the juice of a lemon. Boil rapidly until set.

635   TOMATO JELLY

2 lb. tomatoes   *¼ pint water*
lemons   *sugar*

Simmer the red tomatoes with the water until soft. Strain through a jelly bag and to each pint add the juice of 1½ lemons and 1 lb. of sugar. Boil rapidly until set. Excellent with cold meat.

636   SPICED JELLIES

Apple, gooseberry, cucumber and rosehip jellies are all excellent if a small amount of spice is added to the juice. This makes them particulary suitable for serving with cold meats.

637   VICTORIA PLUM JELLY

2 lb. Victoria plums   *¼ pint water*
lemons   *sugar*

Simmer the plums in the water until soft. Put through a jelly bag and to each pint allow the juice of 1 lemon and 1 lb. sugar. Boil rapidly until set.

638   JELLY MARMALADE

Use either lemon marmalade (Recipe 641), lime (Recipe 642) or orange (Recipes 652 or 648).

While the ingredients are the same as these recipes the method is very different.

Shred half the peel from the oranges very finely indeed. The other half of the peel need not be shredded but tied in a bag of muslin. The pips, pith and pulp of the fruit should also be tied in another bag of muslin. Put the shredded peel and the 2 bags to soak overnight in the water. Simmer gently the next day for about 1 hour. Take out the 2 bags and discard, add sugar and lemon juice. Bring to the boil and boil until set.

If by chance you do not want any peel in the marmalade at all, as would be the case with someone suffering from an ulcer, then all the peel is tied in a bag.

620 ELDERBERRY JELLY

4 lb. elderberries
sugar
1 pint water
1 — 2 lemons

Simmer the berries with the water and when quite soft strain through a jelly bag. To each 1 pint juice add 12 oz. — 1 lb. sugar and the juice of 1 large or 2 small lemons. Stir well until sugar has dissolved then boil rapidly until setting point is reached.

621 GOOSEBERRY JELLY

1 lb. sharp green gooseberries
sugar
½ pint water

Wash fruit and put into pan. Simmer gently, put into a jelly bag to drain. Measure, allowing 1 lb. of sugar to each pint of juice, and boil rapidly until set.

622 GOOSEBERRY JELLY

(with commercial pectin)

3 lb. gooseberries
1½ pints water
3½ lb. sugar
½ bottle commercial pectin
green colouring

Wash the gooseberries (no need to top and tail them). Put them in a pan with the water and simmer, covered for 20 minutes, or until the fruit is soft enough to mash. Strain through a jelly bag. Measure the juice into a pan and if necessary add water to make 2 pints. Add the sugar and heat gently, stir occasionally until sugar is dissolved. Stir in the commercial pectin. Bring to a full rolling boil and continue boiling for 1 minute. Remove from geat, skim and stir in colouring if desired.

623 MEDLAR JELLY

1 lb. medlars
1 gill water
sugar
¼ teaspoon citric acid or tartaric acid or juice
¼ lemon

Simmer fruit and water until soft. Put through a jelly bag then measure juice and allow 1 lb. sugar to each pint. Stir in sugar and acid or lemon juice and continue stirring until dissolved. Boil rapidly until set.

624 MINT JELLY

Make a syrup of 8 oz. sugar and ½ pint water; add ¼ pint vinegar and 1½ dessertspoons of powdered gelatine. Stir in 2 — 3 tablespoons chopped mint, pour into jars, seal down most thoroughly and store in a cool place.

625 MINT JELLY

2 lb. apples — either a sharp cooking apple or crab apple or gooseberries
1 pint water
2 tablespoons vinegar

To each pint juice allow 1 lb. sugar and 2 tablespoons chopped mint. Wash the apples and if large cut into pieces but do NOT peel or core them. Cover with the water and simmer gently until a thick pulp. Put through a jelly bag or since these may not be available several thicknesses of muslin and leave dripping overnight. Measure the juice and to each pint allow 1 lb. sugar. Heat the juice and when boiling stir in the sugar, continue stirring until sugar has quite dissolved. Boil rapidly until setting point is reached — without stirring. Then add the vinegar and the mint. If you are not very fond of the flavour of vinegar it may be omitted. The jelly will be a better colour if a few drops of green colouring are added. Pour the jelly into jars and seal down as for jam.

626 MULBERRY JELLY

1 lb. mulberries
¼ pint water
1 apple

Cut up but do not peel or core the apple and simmer with the mulberries and water until soft. Put through a jelly bag and allow 1 lb. sugar to each pint water.

627 RASPBERRY JELLY

raspberries
sugar
¼ pint water to each lb. raspberries

Simmer fruit and water until soft. Place in a jelly bag and leave to drain. To each pint of juice add 1 lb. sugar; boil rapidly until set.

628 REDCURRANT JELLY

1 lb. redcurrants
1 gill water

Method as for apple jelly (Recipe 616).

629 REDCURRANT AND LOGANBERRY JELLY

8 oz. redcurrants
8 oz. loganberries
¼ pint water

Wash fruit and put into pan with water. Simmer gently, put into a jelly bag and leave to drain. Measure, allowing 1 lb. sugar to each pint of juice. Boil rapidly until set.

630 ROWANBERRY JELLY

4 lb. rowanberries
sugar
1 pint water
lemons

Simmer berries with the water and when soft strain through a jelly bag. To each pint of juice add 12 oz. (for sharp jelly) or 1 lb. sugar and the juice of 1 large or 2 small lemons. Stir well until sugar has dissolved then boil rapidly until setting point is reached.

Jellies

Apple time

616　　APPLE JELLY

cooking apples or   1 pint water
  crab apples   to each 2 lb. fruit
sugar

Simmer the fruit until a pulp; there is no need to either peel or core the fruit. Put the pulp through thick muslin or a jelly bag and leave hanging overnight. Measure the juice and allow to each pint of juice 1 lb. sugar. Stir in the sugar and boil rapidly until set.

617　　APPLE AND LEMON JELLY

1 lb. cooking apples   ½ pint water
2 lemons

Squeeze juice from lemons, pare off yellow part of rind. Chop up apples, but do not peel or core. Put apples, lemon rind and water into pan. Simmer until soft. Place the fruit in a jelly bag, leave to drain. Add lemon juice and measure. To each pint of liquid add 1 lb. sugar; boil rapidly until set.

618　　BLACKBERRY OR BRAMBLE JELLY

1 lb. blackberries   1 medium-sized cooking
¼ gill water   apple*
sugar

* *Instead of using an apple you can use juice of a lemon to each pound blackberries. Add this with sugar*

Put blackberries, water and apple into a pan and simmer until soft. Put the pulp through a jelly bag. Measure juice and allow 1 lb. sugar to each pint. Stir in sugar and continue stirring until dissolved, then boil rapidly until set.

619　　CUCUMBER JELLY

about 4 lb. cucumbers   ¼ gill water
  (including skin)   1 lemon
1 lb. sugar   ginger

Cut up the cucumbers, add the water and simmer until a soft pulp. Put through a jelly bag, then add the juice of 1 lemon, 1 lb. sugar and a pinch of ginger to each pint juice. Stir until the sugar has dissolved, then boil rapidly until jelly sets.
Note. This is an extravagant jelly in that the cucumber yields little juice.

609 RHUBARB AND ANGELICA JAM

1 lb. rhubarb, cut into   *juice of 1 lemon*
pieces   *1 lb. sugar*

Cover the cut up rhubarb with the sugar and lemon juice and leave to stand overnight. Chop up 2 oz. angelica to 3 lb. rhubarb and cook altogether until set. This is a delicious jam and a lovely colour.

610 STRAWBERRY JAM

1 lb. strawberries — good   *14 oz. sugar*
weight   *juice of 1 lemon or ¼ gill*
     redcurrant juice

Simmer the fruit until soft. Add the sugar and lemon juice and stir until dissolved. Boil rapidly until set.

611 STRAWBERRY JAM

(whole fruit jam)

Put sugar and fruit into pan. Heat very gently until sugar has dissolved, add lemon or redcurrant juice and boil steadily until set.

612 STRAWBERRY JAM

(with commercial pectin)

5 lbs. FRUIT.
6 ozs. lemon juice.

2¼ lb. small strawberries   *3 lb. sugar*
3 tablespoons lemon juice   *½ bottle commercial pectin*
knob butter or margarine

Hull fruit and put in pan with lemon juice and sugar. Stand for 1 hour, stirring occasionally. Place over low heat, stir occasionally. When sugar has dissolved, add small knob of butter or margarine to reduce foaming. Bring to full rolling boil, boil rapidly for 4 minutes, stirring occasionally. Remove from heat, add commercial pectin and stir well. Cool for at least 20 minutes to prevent fruit floating. Pot and cover in the usual way.

613 SUGARLESS JAM

1 lb. fruit   *1 tablespoon hot water*
little water   *½ oz. powdered gelatine*
8 — 10 (0.3 gram)   *½ gill water*
saccharine tablets

Simmer fruit with water until soft. Crush saccharine tablets dissolved in the tablespoon of hot water, add to hot but not boiling fruit. Add the gelatine dissolved in the ½ gill hot water. Stir briskly for several minutes, pour into small jars with firmly fitting tops and seal down. Stand in cool place. This will keep for some days.

To make jam that keeps, pour very hot jam into hot bottling jars. Seal down, giving screw band half turn back. Stand in pan of boiling water and boil briskly for 5 minutes. Lift out and tighten screw band. Test for seal next day by seeing if lid is tight.

614 TOMATO JAM

2 lb. tomatoes   *4 tablespoons lemon juice*
2 lb. sugar

Cut the tomatoes in quarters, put over the sugar and stand overnight. By the morning you will have a nice amount of liquid, so need add no water. Simmer gently, stirring well until sugar has dissolved, then continue simmering until tomatoes are soft. Add lemon juice and boil rapidly until set. You can alter the flavour by putting in a little ginger.

615 VICTORIA PLUM CONSERVE

1 lb. Victoria plums   *1 lb. sugar*
(weight when stoned)   *½ gill water*

Boil the sugar and water together stirring well until the sugar has dissolved. Put in the halved Victoria plums and cook steadily until the jam sets. Add some of the kernels from the stones.

600 PLUM JAM

1 lb. plums	*use no water if ripe,*
1 lb. sugar	*¼ gill water if under-ripe*

Method as for greengage jam (Recipe 592). If whole fruit jam is required cut the plums into halves, put into a bowl, sprinkle over the sugar and leave overnight. The next day proceed as usual.

601 PLUM JAM

(with commercial pectin)

5 lb. plums	*6¼ lb. sugar*
½ pint water	*½ bottle commercial pectin*

Wash the plums and cut into pieces, removing as many of the stones as desired. Put the fruit and water into a large pan. If the fruit is ripe or sweet add the juice of 1 lemon. Bring to the boil. Cover and simmer for 15 minutes, stirring occasionally. Add sugar, heat slowly until the sugar has dissolved, stir occasionally, then bring to a full rolling boil. Boil rapidly for 3 minutes, stirring occasionally, then remove from the heat and stir in commercial pectin. Skim if necessary. Allow to cool to prevent fruit floating. Pot and cover in the usual way. Makes 11 lb.

602 PUMPKIN JAM

3 lb. pumpkin, peeled	*3 lb. sugar*
and diced	*2 lemons*
4 oz. crystallised ginger	
or 2 oz. root ginger	

Boil the pumpkin until it is tender, drain well and mash. Add the grated lemon rind and juice and the ginger cut into neat pieces. If dried ginger is used, this should be bruised, put in a muslin bag, cooked with the jam and removed before putting into jars. Bring to boil, add sugar and boil for 20 minutes or until thick.

603 QUINCE JAM

1 lb. quinces	*½ gill water*
1 lb. sugar	*juice ½ lemon*

Peel, core and cut up the fruit. Simmer with the water until soft. Add the sugar and boil rapidly until set. If desired, the fruit could be grated instead of cut into pieces.

604 RASPBERRY JAM

1 lb. raspberries	*1 lb. sugar*

Heat the fruit until boiling. Stir in the hot sugar — heated for a few minutes in the oven. Boil rapidly until the jam has set. If the fruit is firm and fresh this should only take about 3 minutes' rapid boiling.

605 RASPBERRY JAM

(with commercial pectin)

4 lb. raspberries	*1 bottle commercial pectin*
5¼ lb. sugar	

Crush the berries. Add the sugar and heat slowly until dissolved, stir occasionally. Bring to a full rolling boil quickly. Boil rapidly for 2 minutes, stirring occasionally. Remove from heat and stir in commercial pectin. Skim if necessary.

606 RHUBARB CONSERVE

2 lb. rhubarb	*8 oz. raisins*
2 lb. sugar	*1 lemon*
	1 orange

Wash and cut up the rhubarb into 1½-inch pieces. Leave overnight. Boil rhubarb, raisins and sugar gently for 20 minutes. Add the juice of the lemon and orange and the grated rinds of the orange and lemon. Boil until the syrup is thick and jelly-like but do not boil until jam forms a thick wrinkled surface.

607 RHUBARB JAM

(with commercial pectin)

2 lb. rhubarb	*2 oz. crystallized ginger*
¼ pint water	*3 lb. sugar*
3 tablespoons lemon juice	*½ bottle commercial pectin*
½ oz. bruised root ginger	

Wash and chop rhubarb very finely. Place in preserving pan with the water. Add lemon juice and the bruised root ginger in a muslin bag. Bring to the boil and simmer gently for a few minutes until rhubarb is tender. Add chopped crystallized ginger and sugar. Heat slowly until sugar has dissolved. Bring to full rolling boil quickly. Boil rapidly for 3 minutes. Remove from heat and take out muslin bag. Stir in commercial pectin. Allow to cool slightly to prevent floating fruit. Pot and cover in the usual way.

608 RHUBARB AND DRIED FIG JAM

1 lb. dried figs	*1 pint water*
2 lb. rhubarb	*3 lb. sugar*
	juice 1 large lemon

Soak the figs in the water for 48 hours, or even 72 hours. Simmer until the fruit is nearly soft. Add the rhubarb and continue cooking until a thick pulp. Add the sugar, stir until dissolved, then boil rapidly until set.

Lemons

use: 1 lb. huckleberries, 1 lb. cooking apples, 2 lb. sugar. As huckleberries are lacking in pectin you MUST put something in to help the jam to set.

Blueberries can be used instead.

594   LEMON AND MELON JAM

1 lb. melon (weight when   1 lb. sugar
*   peeled)   2 lemons*

Dice the melon and allow to stand overnight with the sugar. Next day put into a pan, simmer gently, stirring well until the sugar has dissolved, then add the lemon juice and grated rind. Boil steadily until set.

595   LOGANBERRY JAM

1 lb. sugar   1 lb. loganberries

Simmer fruit until soft. Add sugar, stir until dissolved, then boil rapidly until set.

596   JAPONICA JAM

1 lb. japonica   1 — 1¼ pints water (depend-
2 lemons   ing on how ripe the fruit is)
*   ground ginger*

Do not peel or core the japonica — just cut into halves and simmer in the water until pulp, adding a pinch of ground ginger. Then sieve and to each pint or pound of pulp add the lemon juice and 1 lb. of sugar, stir in the sugar and boil until set.

597   MARROW GINGER JAM

1 lb. prepared marrow   1 teaspoon ground ginger
(weighed after peeling   or 1 — 2 oz. crystallised
and cutting into cubes)   ginger
1 lb. sugar   juice 1 large lemon

Method as for apple ginger jam (Recipe 577).

598   MULBERRY JAM

1 lb. mulberries   ½ gill water
1 lb. sugar

Simmer the fruit with the water until soft then add sugar.

A very pleasant jam is made by mixing 1 lb. mulberries, 8 oz. apples and 1 gill water. Simmer these together, rub through a sieve and add 1 lb. sugar to each pint pulp.

599 PEAR AND PINEAPPLE CONSERVE

3 lb. pears   1 orange
1 medium can small   ¼ pint bottle maraschino
*   pineapple cubes   cherries*
sugar

Cut pears into small ½-inch cubes. Add the pineapple and grated rind and juice of the orange. Weigh the fruits and to each lb. add 12 oz. sugar. Leave overnight in a bowl, then simmer till thick. Cut the cherries in half and add to the fruit with the liquid from the bottle. Stir well. Pour into wide necked bottles and seal at once.

590   GOOSEBERRY JAM

(with commercial pectin)

4 lb. gooseberries   6¼ lb. sugar
½ pint water   1 bottle commercial pectin

Top, tail and wash the gooseberries. Put them in a large saucepan or preserving pan with the water. Bring to the boil, and simmer, covered, for 15 minutes, or until the skins are soft, stir occasionally. Add sugar and heat slowly until dissolved, stirring occasionally. Bring to a full rolling boil quickly. Boil rapidly for 2 minutes, stir occasionally. Remove from the heat and stir in commercial pectin. Skim if necessary. Allow to cool slightly. Pot and cover in the usual way.

(When making half the quantity 1 minute's boiling of the fruit and sugar is enough.)

591   GOOSEBERRY
            AND ORANGE JAM

1½ lb. gooseberries   1½ lb. sugar
2 oranges   ¼ pint water

Prepare gooseberries. Simmer gently until tender with water, orange juice, grated rind. Add sugar, stir until dissolved then boil until setting point is reached.

592   GREENGAGE JAM

1 lb. greengages (weight   use no water if ripe
*   after stoning)   (¼ gill water if under-ripe)*
1 lb. sugar

The stones of the fruit can be cracked and the kernels included. Simmer fruit until soft, adding water if necessary. Stir in the sugar and continue stirring until dissolved. Boil rapidly until set.

593   HUCKLEBERRY JAM

1 lb. huckleberries   2 lemons
2 lb. sugar

Simmer the huckleberries with very little water. Add the sugar and lemon juice. Boil until set. If preferred

Cherry picking

583 CHERRY JAM

1 lb. stoned cherries or nearly 1¼ lb. before stoning*	*juice ½ lemon or ½ teaspoon citric or tartaric acid*
12 oz. sugar	

* *If using red morello cherries use only half the quantity of acid. Use black cherries for Swiss jam*

Put the fruit, and stones tied in muslin, into the pan, simmer until the fruit is soft. Stir in the sugar and continue stirring until dissolved. Boil rapidly until set.

584 CHERRY JAM

(with commercial pectin)

2½ lb. stoned morello cherries	*3 tablespoons lemon juice (1 lemon)*
¼ pint water	*1 bottle commercial pectin*
3 lb. sugar	

Simmer the cherries in the water and lemon juice in a covered pan for about 15 minutes. Add the sugar and heat slowly, stirring occasionally, until sugar has dissolved. Bring to a full rolling boil and boil rapidly for 3 minutes. Stir in the commercial pection and continue boiling for 1 minute. Remove from heat and skim if necessary. Cool slightly, pot and cover in the usual way. Makes 5 lb. For stronger cherry flavour add ¼ teaspoon almond extract before potting.

585 BLACK CHERRY JAM

(with commercial pectin)

2½ lb. black cherries (stoned)	*juice 2 lemons*
	3 lb. sugar
¼ pint water	*1 bottle commercial pectin*

Put prepared fruit in pan with water and lemon juice. Cook gently with lid on for 15 minutes, remove lid. Add sugar, stir over low heat until dissolved. Bring to rolling boil, boil rapidly for 3 minutes. Remove from heat, add pectin, stir well, cool for 15 minutes, stirring occasionally to prevent fruit rising. Pot and cover.

586 DAMSON JAM

½ gill water if fruit is ripe	*1 lb. damsons*
	1 lb. sugar

If fruit is very under-ripe use the following quantities:

1 lb. damsons	*1¼ lb. sugar*
½ pint water	

Put the fruit and water into a pan. Simmer until soft. Add sugar, stir until dissolved, then boil rapidly until set.

587 ELDERBERRY JAM

1 lb. elderberries	*1 lb. sugar*
1 lemon	

Crush the elderberries in preserving pan then simmer until soft. Add the sugar and stir well until dissolved, then put in the lemon juice and boil rapidly until setting point is reached.

588 FIG AND LEMON JAM

2 lb. dried figs	*2 lemons*
3 lb. granulated sugar	*1½ pints water*

Soak figs in water for 12 hours, rinse in fresh water, cut into small pieces, removing any hard pieces of stem. Put into a preserving pan with 1½ pints fresh hot water and simmer until tender. Stir in strained lemon juice and sugar and continue to cook until the preserve is thick. Pot while hot, cover when quite cold.

589 GOOSEBERRY JAM

½ gill water if fruit is ripe	*1 lb. gooseberries*
	1 lb. sugar

If fruit is very under-ripe use the following quantities:

1 lb. gooseberries	*1¼ lb. sugar*
½ pint water	

Put the fruit and water into a pan. Simmer until soft. Add the sugar and stir until dissolved, then boil rapidly until set.

575 APRICOT JAM

(dried fruit)

1 lb. dried apricots	*3 lb. sugar*
3 pints water	*juice 1½ lemons*

Soak the fruit in water for 48 or even 72 hours. Simmer gently until the fruit is soft. Add the sugar and lemon juice and boil rapidly until set. Dried peach jam is made in the same way.

576 DRIED APRICOT JAM

(with commercial pectin)

8 oz. dried apricots	*3 tablespooons lemon juice*
1½ pints water	*(1 lemon)*
3 lb. sugar	*1 bottle commercial pectin*

Wash fruit and leave to soak for at least 4 hours in the 1½ pints water. Simmer, covered, for about 30 minutes to break up the fruit. Measure 1½ pints prepared fruit pulp, making up the amount with water if necessary. Add lemon juice and sugar and heat slowly, stirring occasionally until the sugar has dissolved. Bring to a full rolling boil and boil rapidly for 1 minute, stirring occasionally. Remove from heat, stir in commercial pectin. Skim if necessary and pot and cover in the usual way.

577 APPLE GINGER JAM

1 lb. apples — weight after peeling and coring but both the peel and core should be saved, and it is advisable to use cooking apples	*1 lb. sugar* *1 teaspoon ground ginger*

Cut the apples into neat cubes, sprinkle over the sugar, leave to stand overnight with the cores and peel also in the bowl, but tied in a muslin bag. Put into a saucepan or preserving pan, simmer gently, stirring all the time until the sugar has quite dissolved, add ginger, then boil steadily until the cubes of apple look transparent and the syrup has set. Remove cores and peel.

578 BANANA AND LEMON JAM

6 bananas	*3 lemons*
1 lb. castor sugar	

Peel and cut up the bananas as small as possible. Grate the lemon rinds and squeeze and strain the juice. Put the bananas, grated rind and juice in a china or glass bowl. Cover with the sugar and allow to stand 1 hour for the sugar to dissolve. Place the contents of the bowl into a pan and bring to the boil in 1 hour. Boil until the jam sets. Pour into jars and cover.

579 BANANA AND ORANGE JAM

1 lb. bananas	*6 oranges*
12 oz. sugar	

Peel, slice bananas and put into preserving pan. Pour over them the strained juice, grated rind and pulp of the oranges. Add the sugar and leave for 30 minutes. Bring to the boil very slowly. Boil 25 minutes. Pot while hot.

580 BANANA AND PINEAPPLE JAM

(with commercial pectin)

5 ripe bananas	*3¼ lb. sugar*
1¼ lb. can crushed or chopped pineapple	*1 bottle commercial pectin*

Peel the bananas and mash thoroughly. Put into a preserving pan with the crushed or chopped pineapple and sugar. Heat gently, stirring occasionally until the sugar has dissolved. Bring quickly to the boil and boil hard for 1 minute. Remove from the heat and stir in the commercial pectin. Skim, pot and cover in the usual way.

581 BLACKBERRY AND APPLE JAM

1 lb. cooking apples (weight after peeling and coring)	*1 lb. blackberries* *2 lb. sugar* *¼ gill water*

Put the apples and water into the preserving pan, cook gently until the apples are becoming soft, add the blackberries, and continue cooking until all the fruit is soft. Stir in the sugar and continue stirring until dissolved. Boil rapidly until jam has set.

582 BLACKCURRANT JAM

1 lb. blackcurrants	*1¼ lb. sugar*
¾ pint water	

Put the fruit and water into the pan, simmer until the blackcurrants are quite soft. Stir in the sugar and boil rapidly until set.

12. Store in a cool, dry, DARK place.

13. If a jam shows signs of mould it is due to:
    a) damp fruit
    b) insufficient boiling — giving too low a proportion of sugar in the finished jam
    c) bad storage conditions (damp in particular)
    d) not filling jars sufficiently or covering well.

14. If a jam shows signs of fermenting and has a 'winey' flavour it is due to:
    a) over-ripe fruit
    b) not being sufficiently set
    c) too little sugar added or not boiled to give right proportion of sugar in finished jam
    d) bad storage conditions
    e) bad covering of jars.

15. If a jam crystallises it is due to:
    a) bad recipe — too much sugar in proportion to fruit, or if you have too little sugar it means too long cooking to stiffen jam
    b) not stirring to make sure sugar has dissolved before boiling
    c) too long cooking.

16. If jam or jelly is hard or dry it is due to:
    a) overboiling
    b) bad covering so that jam dries out in storage. With central heating it is always advisable to put jam or jelly either into bottling jars or use tightly-fitting caps over waxed circles — not just paper covers.

17. If jam or jelly is syrupy and not firm set it is because:
    a) the fruit juice was low in pectin (not enough natural setting quality)
    b) not boiled sufficiently, or over-boiling PAST setting point gives sticky, syrupy texture
    c) fruit juice in jelly left too long after straining — use as soon as ready.

18. If jam or jelly is a poor colour it is due to:
    a) too *quick* cooking to soften fruit
    b) over-boiling or too slow boiling
    c) poor quality fruit
    d) storing in bright light
    e) poor quality pan for cooking — aluminium or copper is best.

19. If jam or jelly has disappointing flavour it is because:
    a) too ripe, or under-ripe fruit used
    b) too much sugar, giving over-sweet taste
    c) too slow or long boiling takes away fresh fruit flavour.

20. If jelly is cloudy in appearance it is because:
    a) it was badly strained — use proper jelly bag (made of flannel generally) or several thicknesses of muslin over hair, not wire sieve
    b) the pulp was forced through bag or muslin — allow to drip itself without pressing or encouraging through with spoon.

571   JAMS AND JELLIES FOR COMPETITION

Marks are given for:

a) Appearance of the jar —

b) Contents are judged on colour — it should be bright.

c) *Condition of jam or jelly.*

d) Consistency — Firm but not over-stiff.

e) Flavour — The most important thing of all.
   Under the heading of flavour will come points like the taste of fruit peels or skins see point 5b). If tough you will lose marks.

f) Originality —
   In an open class you may win if you have used a less usual recipe, so look out for new ideas in jam-making.

Jams

572   YOUR PAN FOR JAM

Try to invest in a proper preserving pan — strong enough to prevent scorching and wide enough to encourage rapid boiling.

573   USING COMMERCIAL PECTIN

Many fruits are lacking in natural setting quality — pectin — and commercial pectin enables the jam to set quickly without prolonged boiling, which spoils flavour and colour.

574   APRICOT JAM

1 lb. apricots
¼ gill water, *unless the fruit is under-ripe, then ½ gill*
¼ teaspoon citric or tartaric acid or the juice of ½ lemon

Cut the fruit into pieces. If desired, crack the stones and take out the kernels. Put into a preserving pan with the water and simmer until the fruit is soft. Add the sugar and lemon juice or acid and boil rapidly until set.

Jams, Jellies and Marmalade

570 PERFECT JAMS AND JELLIES

1. Select firm, ripe but not over-ripe fruit.

2. Follow recipe carefully for amount of sugar to fruit. Many people think all fruits need 1 lb. sugar to 1 lb. fruit — this is quite wrong.
   Where a fruit has little natural pectin (setting quality) i.e. sweet cherries — you need MORE fruit than sugar, and in addition it helps to add acid in the form of commercial pectin, lemon juice or red-currant juice.
   Where a fruit has a lot of pectin i.e. blackcurrants, you get a better jam if you use MORE sugar than fruit.

3. Select a large pan so there is plenty of room for the jam to boil hard — without boiling over.

4. Preserving sugar is ideal but you can use loaf or granulated sugar. Warm sugar slightly; this speeds up dissolving.

5. Do soften fruit SLOWLY. This is very important for it
   a) extracts pectin (natural setting substance)
   b) softens skins — test most carefully for the skin MUST be soft before you add the sugar
   c) helps to keep jam a good colour.

6. Stir until sugar has dissolved — this is very important for it makes certain the jam or jelly does not burn or crystallise during cooking. You can tell if all the sugar has dissolved by tapping your wooden spoon on base of pan.

7. When the sugar has dissolved let JAM BOIL RAPIDLY without stirring. This is very important for the quicker the jam or jelly sets, the better the yield, the flavour and the colour. This is why it is essential to have plenty of room in the pan.

8. Test early for setting. Some jams are ready within 3 — 5 minutes, others take 10 — 15 minutes, or even more. Many fruits will *lose* their setting qualities if boiled TOO LONG and then the jam NEVER sets. There are several ways of testing:
   a) WEIGHT   Each 1 lb. of sugar should give 1⅔ lb. jam or jelly — i.e. 3 lb. sugar should produce 5 lb. jam; 4 lb. sugar 6⅔ lb. jam; 5 lb. sugar, 8⅓ lb. jam etc.
   If you have sufficiently large and strong scales you weigh preserving pan BEFORE cooking.
   If you feel jam or jelly is ready, weigh again. Deduct weight of pan from total weight and if it is more than the above the jam needs a little longer boiling.

   b) TEMPERATURE If you make a lot of jam or jellies it is worth investing in a sugar thermometer — stir round in hot jam. Jam has reached setting point at — 220 °F. — 222 °F., jelly at — 220 °F. — 221 °F.
   BE CAREFUL NOT TO PUT THERMOMETER ON COLD SURFACE.

   c) FORMING A SKIN   Put a little on an old saucer and allow to become quite cold then see if it forms a skin and wrinkles when pushed with a spoon or finger.
   TAKE PAN OFF HEAT WHILE WAITING FOR JAM TO COOL ON SAUCER.

   d) FORMING A FLAKE   Stir wooden spoon round in jam so that it becomes thoroughly coated, then allow to cool. Hold horizontally and inspect jam. If it drops off spoon readily it is not set. If it hangs in a firm drop or flake then it has reached setting point.
   TAKE PAN OFF HEAT WHILE WAITING FOR JAM TO COOL ON SPOON.

9. When you are satisfied that the jam is ready, remove from heat then get rid of scum. Most of this disappears if stirred steadily — for competitions though, remove with strainer, then stir; and for jelly, remove with strainer and a piece of *white* kitchen or blotting paper drawn quickly across the surface of preserve.
   A good knob of butter — if used to grease bottom of pan before cooking — helps to reduce scum.

10. For a jelly or jam that has no whole fruit in:
    a) Pour at once into HOT, DRY, CLEAN jars. Top jar as you fill to bring out air bubbles FILL to at least ¼ to ⅛ inch of top of jar. This not only gives a more attractive finish but, remembering jam or jelly will shrink a little as it cools, it also makes certain there is less air space in the jar and therefore less chance of it becoming mouldy.
    b) For a jam containing whole fruit allow jam to cool in pan until it stiffens slightly, then stir to distribute peel or whole fruit. Put into hot jars.

11. Put on waxed circles AT ONCE — put final cover on at once, or wait until jam is quite cold. Tie down firmly or use rubber band.

28   **STRAWBERRY JAM (Recipes 610–612)**

27 DISHES TO SERVE WITH PICKLES AND CHUTNEYS:
SCOTCH EGGS (Recipe 247);
BACON AND SAUSAGE PIE (Recipe 292);
QUICHE LORRAINE (Recipe 275);
GRILLED SAUSAGES AND CREAMED POTATOES

564 BLACKBERRY KETCHUP

Simmer the blackberries in the water until tender. Rub through a sieve very firmly, leaving only the pips behind. To each pint of purée add 2 oz. sugar and ½ pint spiced vinegar (Recipe 521). A little salt may also be added if you wish. Simmer steadily until fairly thick then put into heated bottles and sterilise as for fruit pulp (Recipe 502).

565 GRAPE KETCHUP

Ingredients as for blackberry ketchup, using grapes instead of blackberries. When adding sugar a better flavour is produced by using 4 oz. to each pint.

Both these fruit ketchups are excellent with cold meat.

566 MUSHROOM KETCHUP

3 lb. mushrooms	*½ pint spiced vinegar*
3 oz. salt	*1 level dessertspoon chopped onion (optional)*

Mince or break up mushrooms, sprinkle with salt and leave for 24–36 hours. Add spiced vinegar to the mushrooms and liquor (with chopped onion if liked) and simmer gently for 2½ hours. Strain carefully through muslin while boiling, bottle in sterilised jars and seal at once, coating corks with melted wax.

Note: TO ENSURE KETCHUP KEEPING bottles should be sterilised in water bath for 15 minutes at 180°F. (simmering) and then sealed AIRTIGHT.

567 TOMATO KETCHUP

4 lb. ripe tomatoes	*1 dessertspoon salt*
1 large onion	*1 dessertspoon pickling spices*
6 oz. sugar	*¼ teaspoon paprika or*
2 large apples	*cayenne pepper*
¾ pint vinegar	

Boil the vinegar and pickling spices together for 10 minutes, then strain vinegar. Cook the sliced tomatoes, onion and apples until you have a thick pulp, stirring well to prevent mixture burning. Rub through a sieve taking care to leave no pulp behind, otherwise ketchup will not thicken. Put pulp into pan with vinegar, sugar, salt and pepper and cook steadily until thick. Pour into sterilised bottles while boiling, seal down and if using corks paint at once with hot wax.

568 18TH CENTURY CATCHUP

'Take mushrooms and wipe them very clean, put them in a crock and strew salt between every 2 or 3 handfuls and let them stand 2 or 3 days, then strain them off and boil up ye licker with cloves mace nutmeg and pepper, a pretty while, when it is cold put it into a bottle and stop it very close.'

To make this today you might care to chop up the mushrooms coarsely and keep them in the liquor, after letting them stand. Adjust the spices, to taste, but, as mushrooms have a definite though delicate flavour, don't be too sparing.

569 USING A PRESSURE COOKER FOR CHUTNEYS

A pressure cooker softens the ingredients in chutney in a very short time. Use any of the recipes in this chapter but only two-thirds of the vinegar. Put all the ingredients, with the exception of the sugar, into the pressure cooker, *taking care it is never more than half-full.*

Put on the lid, bring to pressure and allow approximately 10–15 minutes. Allow pressure to drop in room temperature, take off the lid, stir in the sugar and proceed as if using an ordinary preserving pan.

558   TOMATO CHUTNEY

2 lb. tomatoes, green or red	8 oz. finely chopped onions
8 oz. sugar	8 oz. apples peeled and cored
¼ teaspoon ginger	
¼ pint malt vinegar	8 oz. sultanas
1 teaspoon pickling spice	½ teaspoon salt
1 rounded teaspoon mustard powder	¼ teaspoon pepper

First put the pickling spices into a piece of muslin. Put the onion into a saucepan with 2–3 tablespoons vinegar and simmer gently until nearly soft. Add the chopped apples, sliced tomatoes, spices, salt, pepper, mustard, ginger and sultanas. Simmer gently until all the mixture is quite soft, stirring from time to time. Add the remainder of the vinegar and the sugar. When the sugar has quite dissolved boil steadily until the chutney is the consistency of jam. Remove the little bag of spice. Pour the hot chutney into warm jars and seal down at once.

It is a mistake to put metal directly on top of the chutney — use paper, melted wax, THEN the paper or metal cover.

559   GREEN TOMATO CHUTNEY

2 lb. green tomatoes	8 oz. apples (weight when peeled and chopped)
8 oz. onions (grated or finely chopped)	
	½ teaspoon salt
8 oz. sugar	1 teaspoon pickling spices
¼ pint vinegar	

Put the onion into a saucepan with ½ gill vinegar and simmer until nearly soft. Add the chopped apples, chopped tomatoes, spices (tied in a muslin bag) and salt, and just enough vinegar to stop the mixture from burning. Cook gently until tomatoes and apples are soft, stirring from time to time. Add remainder of vinegar and stir in sugar. Boil steadily until the chutney is thick. Remove spices and pour into hot jars.

560   RED TOMATO AND APPLE CHUTNEY

1½ lb. red tomatoes	1 teaspoon ground ginger
1½ lb. apples — weight when peeled and chopped	12 oz. sugar
	1 teaspoon pickling spices
8 oz. onions, grated or finely chopped	½ pint vinegar (brown or white)
1 teaspoon salt	4 oz. dried fruit

Skin the tomatoes. Put onion into a saucepan with ½ gill vinegar and simmer until nearly soft. Add the apples, tomatoes, spice, tied up securely in a muslin bag, the salt, ground ginger and just enough vinegar to stop the mixture from burning. Cook gently until the fruit is soft, stirring from time to time. Add the remainder of the vinegar and thoroughly stir in the sugar; boil steadily until the chutney is thick. Remove the bag of pickling spices and pour the hot chutney into hot jars. Seal down at once.

Tomato chutney (Recipe 558) and tomato ketchup (Recipe 567)

561   TOMATO AND HORSERADISH RELISH

4 lb. ripe tomatoes	1 large onion
1 dessertspoon pickling spices	1 lb. sugar
2 large apples	½ teaspoon pepper — preferably cayenne or paprika
¾ pint vinegar	
horseradish	1 dessertspoon salt

Boil the vinegar and pickling spices together for 10 minutes. Cook the tomatoes, apples and onion until a thick pulp, stirring to begin with so this does not burn. Add the vinegar, salt and pepper and cook in an uncovered pan until becoming thick. This will take a fair time.

Add 2–3 tablespoons grated horseradish and the sugar and boil again for about 10 minutes.

Put into boiling bottling jars, seal down and sterilise by standing these (with screw tops loosened) in a pan of boiling water and boiling rapidly for about 10 minutes. Lift out jars carefully and tighten screw tops.

Note: The amount of horseradish added depends entirely on personal taste, so add it gradually, tasting as you do so.

562   FLAVOURED VINEGAR

Any herbs can be used to give flavour to vinegar. Below is recipe for tarragon vinegar but you can use sage, thyme, mint etc. Although you are advised to have herbs in vinegar for 6 weeks, from 3 weeks onwards they have imparted flavour. Flavoured vinegar is excellent for salad dressings.

Fruit vinegars are made by adding 1 pint vinegar to each 1 lb. of the soft fruit — raspberries and blackberries are particularly good. Leave for 3–5 days — stirring occasionally. Strain off liquid. Add 8 oz.–1 lb. sugar to each pint. Boil for 10 minutes and bottle.

563   TARRAGON VINEGAR

Bruise the tarragon leaves. Pack them into jars. Pour over cold vinegar (you can use malt vinegar which is more usual, or you can have white vinegar). Store for 6 weeks, shaking the bottles daily if possible, and then strain the vinegar through very fine muslin.

Salt and spices for chutneys

553 ORANGE AND LEMON CHUTNEY

3 large lemons	2 medium sized oranges
8 oz. onions	1 pint spiced vinegar (spiced
1 lb. castor sugar	white vinegar can be used
6 oz. white sultanas	to give a clearer colour)
salt to taste	1 teaspoon cinnamon
1 teaspoon powdered ginger	little pepper

Wash lemons and oranges and squeeze out the juice, mince or shred peel, pulp, etc. (as for marmalade) and soak for 24 hours in the cold spiced vinegar. Next day add the juice and thinly sliced onions and simmer very gently until peel and onions are tender. Add sultanas, seasoning, etc. to taste, together with sugar, and cook till thick.

554 QUICK PINEAPPLE RELISH

Gently fry until soft but not brown 1 tablespoon chopped onion in 1 oz. butter. Add 4 tablespoons shredded pineapple, 1 tablespoon chopped parsley, 2 tablespoons mild mustard. Use with any hot meat or poultry.

555 PLUM CHUTNEY

2 lb. plums	12 oz. sugar
1 teaspoon salt	1 teaspoon ground
½ pint vinegar	ginger
1 tablespoon pickling	2 — 4 oz. dried fruit
spices	(if desired)

Simmer stoned plums, dried fruit spices (tied securely in muslin bag), salt and ginger in a saucepan with just enough vinegar to stop the mixture from burning. Cook gently until the fruit is soft, stirring from time to time. Add remainder of vinegar and thoroughly stir in sugar. Boil steadily until the mixture is thick. Remove spices, and pour chutney into hot jars.

556 RED PEPPER CHUTNEY

4 red peppers (capsicums)	2 good-sized cooking apples
2 aubergines (eggplants)	8 oz. onions
2 cloves of garlic	¼ — 1 tablespoon curry
6 oz. raisins	powder
(can be omitted)	½ oz. root ginger
2 oz. brown sugar	6 chillis
1 teaspoon saffron powder	1 pint spiced vinegar
salt to taste	

Crush the cloves of garlic well, slice the peppers (removing the seeds) and the aubergines, apples and onions. Tie the root ginger and chillis in muslin, blend the curry powder and saffron with a little vinegar, add other seasoning. Proceed as apple chutney (Recipe 541.)

557 RHUBARB CHUTNEY

Using 3 lb. rhubarb instead of apples, follow Recipe 541 for apple chutney. If desired the quantity of dried ginger can be increased to 2 teaspoons.

547 QUICK DATE CHUTNEY

(No cooking required)

Chop dates finely, add little finely chopped onion, seasoning, and pour over enough hot spiced vinegar to moisten. Stir in good pinch ginger and/or mixed spice and stir well until the dates are softened. Use fresh, as this does not keep.

548 END OF SEASON RELISH

2 lb. green tomatoes	8 oz. ripe tomatoes
¼ head white cabbage	2 small green peppers
2 small red peppers	2 medium stalks celery
2 medium onions	½ medium cucumber, peeled
3 rounded tablespoons salt	5 oz. brown sugar
1½ pints mild vinegar	2 level tablespoons mild
1 level teaspoon paprika	mustard

Chop vegetables. Place in pan in layers, sprinkling each layer with salt. Stand overnight. Drain and press out all liquid. Add sugar, vinegar, mustard and paprika to vegetables. Cook for about 1½ hours, stirring often. Pour into clean hot jars and seal.

549 MANGO CHUTNEY

2 lb. mangoes	12 oz. onions
1 lb. cooking apples	1¼ lb. brown sugar
2 teaspoons ginger	2 teaspoons pickling spice

Tie the spices in a bag, chop the mangoes in very small pieces and put all ingredients with a little vinegar into the pan, except the sugar. Simmer gently until soft, adding the vinegar gradually. Remove the bag of spices, add the sugar and boil until thick.

It is advisable to keep the pieces of mango fairly large. Some people may like a little salt in this chutney but it is generally a sweet, rather hot, chutney.

550 MARROW CHUTNEY

Follow Recipe 541 for apple chutney but use marrow instead of apple — increase ginger to taste.

551 MINT CHUTNEYS

Recipe 542 gives a very good recipe for an apple and mint chutney but a little mint is very good added to a plum chutney, a rhubarb chutney or a green tomato chutney. Allow 1 dessertspoon to each lb. chutney.

552 MUSTARD RELISH

3 lb. apples*	8 oz. sultanas
(weight after peeling)	1 lb. sugar
1 lb. onions	3 teaspoons dry mustard
1 tablespoon salt	1½ pint vinegar
½ oz. mustard seed	

* or 1 lb. tomatoes, 2 lb. apples

Simmer the chopped onions and apples with half vinegar until tender, adding mustard seed tied up in muslin.

When soft put in the rest of the ingredients, blending the mustard with the vinegar. Stir well until the sugar

has dissolved then boil steadily until thick, stirring from time to time. Take out the bag of mustard seed. Pour into clean hot jars and seal.

and thoroughly stir in the sugar. Boil steadily until the chutney is thick. Remove pickling spices. Pour into hot jars.

542 APPLE AND MINT CHUTNEY

Recipe as apple chutney above but allow 1 dessertspoon or chopped mint to each lb. chutney. Stir this in just before putting into bottles.

543 APRICOT CHUTNEY

1 pint vinegar (white vinegar is good in this recipe but not essential)	4 oz. sultanas
	1 lb. brown sugar
8 oz. dried apricots	3 teaspoons pickling spice
1 lb. apples (after peeling)	1 good teaspoon salt
4 oz. raisins (stoned and cut in pieces)	2 cloves garlic
	juice and peel of 1 lemon

Cut dried apricots into small pieces and soak for 2—3 hours in cold water, drain and put into saucepan with a little of the vinegar and all the other ingredients *except apples and sugar*. The pickling spice to be tied in muslin. Boil steadily for 30 minutes, adding vinegar, then add grated or chopped apples and sugar. Stir until sugar dissolved. Boil for about another 20 minutes or until it thickens. Remove pickling spices. Put into hot jars and cover as directed.

544 BEETROOT CHUTNEY

3 lb. cooked beetroot	1 lb. apples
1 lb. onions	1 lb. white sugar
2 teaspoons salt	1 pint spiced white vinegar

Cook the chopped onions for a short time in a little of the vinegar. Add the rest of the ingredients and proceed as for apple chutney. The beetroot should be diced in very small pieces. 8 oz. light sultanas could be added to this recipe.

545 BLACKBERRY CHUTNEY

3 lb. blackberries	½ oz. mustard
1 lb. cooking apples	2 teaspoons powdered ginger
12 oz. onions	1 teaspoon powdered mace
1 lb. brown sugar	1 pint vinegar (white vinegar good here)
3 teaspoons salt	

Peel and chop the apples and onions put into a pan with the blackberries, spices and ¼ pint vinegar and cook for about 1 hour adding rest of vinegar gradually. Rub through a sieve to remove the pips, add sugar and cook until the desired consistency is obtained.

546 DAMSON CHUTNEY

3 lb. damsons	1 oz. pickling spices
2 pints vinegar	2 teaspoons ginger
1½ lb. apples	3 teaspoons salt
1 lb. onions	1 lb. sugar

Simmer damsons in 1 pint vinegar until tender enough to remove stones. Add chopped apples, onions, spices, pickling spice (tied in muslin) and salt, then continue cooking until fruit is completely soft. Add rest of vinegar and sugar and boil steadily until thick. Put into hot jars and seal down.

540 TO MAKE CHUTNEY

1. Don't put in all the vinegar at once as this rather 'takes away' the flavour of the ingredients — put in just about ¼ of the vinegar, then add rest gradually during the cooking period.
2. Cook chutney with lid OFF pan so it thickens — stir from time to time.
3. Never cut down on amounts of sugar or vinegar as this keeps the chutney.
4. Pour the chutney into jars while still hot — filling to neck of jar.
5. Cover very well — bottling jars are ideal as they have glass lids but never put metal tops directly next to the chutney otherwise the vinegar in the chutney will spoil both taste and colour and will also make the lid rust and be very difficult to remove. You can buy special pickling jars or instead put a round of waxed paper on chutney — then a thin layer of melted wax (paraffin wax) then the final cover OR put the waxed paper then several thicknesses of brown or parchment paper over this — tying it down tightly.
6. Always use pure malt vinegar — white vinegar can be used for light coloured chutneys if desired and where you desire to retain bright colour.
7. Store in cool dry place — preferably in dark — to keep warm.
8. Never use copper, brass or iron pans.

541 APPLE CHUTNEY

2 lb. apples (weight when peeled and chopped)	1 lb. onions (grated or finely chopped)
1 teaspoon salt	12 oz. sugar
½ pint vinegar	1 teaspoon ground ginger
1 teaspoon pickling spices	2—4 oz. dried fruit (if desired)

Put the onion into a saucepan with ½ gill vinegar and simmer until nearly soft. Add the chopped apples, dried fruit, spice (tied securely in a muslin bag), salt, ground ginger, and just enough vinegar to stop the mixture from burning. Cook gently until the fruit is soft, stirring from time to time. Add remainder of the vinegar

535 PICKLED HARD-BOILED EGGS

Hard-boil the eggs by placing them in cold water, bringing to the boil then turning out the heat, covering the pan and leaving for 15 minutes. Take out the eggs, immediately plunge them into cold running water so that they cool rapidly. Then shell. When quite cold, place the eggs in an ordinary glass jam jar and cover with cold vinegar. Leave for a day or so before using.

536 PICKLED FRUITS

These are delicious with cold meats etc.

Use pears, peaches, crab apples, damsons, plums or apricots.

To 2 lb. fruit allow 1 lb. sugar and ½ pint vinegar. To keep the colour of the fruit use a white vinegar. Spice this by adding 1 dessertspoon pickling spices to 1 pint vinegar. Tie spices in muslin and simmer in the vinegar for 10 minutes, then strain. Add the sugar to the vinegar, bring to the boil and simmer until the sugar has dissolved. Put the fruit — peeled and cut into quarters or halves into the vinegar syrup and simmer gently until just tender. Crab apples and damsons should be left whole. Take out the fruit and pack into bottling jars. Boil the vinegar (with the lid off the pan) for a few minutes to thicken liquid, then pour over the fruit and seal down at once.

Do not use metal tops next to the vinegar otherwise they will rust. Bottling jars are ideal. See instructions for covering pickles (Recipe 540, point 5).

537 SPICED FRUITS

These are particularly good when pickling apples and pears. Use recipe above but use ordinary malt vinegar and add little mixed spice, cinnamon bark and nutmeg to the vinegar and sugar. Cut apples into fairly thick slices and halve pears. Sliced lemons can be pickled in the same way and are very good with cold duck or pork. Do not remove peel but take out pips.

538 SPICED DATES

2 lb. stoned dates   1 pint spiced vinegar
2 teaspoons salt   (Recipe 521)

Dissolve the salt in the hot vinegar. Put the dates into bottling jars, pour over the spiced vinegar and seal down.

534 PICKLED WALNUTS

Be certain nuts are not over-ripe. Walnuts must be pricked deeply with a silver fork in 2 or 3 places. Then soak in standard brine (Recipe 519) for at least 3 days. Take them from brine and place on a tray or cloth in the sun, moving occasionally. Slowly they will turn black, this will take 2 or 3 days (if *very* hot 24 hours may suffice). When quite black, pack into jars and cover with spiced vinegar (Recipe 521). Tie down and mature for at least 1 month before use.

539 SPICED DRIED FRUITS

Prunes, dried apricots, peaches, figs are all excellent in a sweet spice. Prunes are particularly good since they blend so well with pork.

2 lb. dried fruit   2 pints spiced
8 oz. sugar   vinegar (Recipe 521)

Wash the dried fruit and soak overnight in the vinegar. Add the sugar and simmer until soft but unbroken. Pack into jars and seal down.

523   PICKLED CUCUMBERS

If the cucumbers are very small they can be left whole, but otherwise cut into convenient sized pieces.

Put into a brine made with 2 oz. salt to 1 pint cold water. Soak overnight or cover with salt. Boil vinegar and pickling spices together. Allow to each pint of vinegar 1 level tablespoon mixed pickling spices. Boil for 15 minutes, strain and cool. Remove the cucumber from the brine, rinse well under the cold tap, then drain thoroughly. Pack into jars, pour over the cold vinegar and seal carefully.

524   PICKLED MARROW

2 lb. marrow (after peeling)	¼ oz. curry powder
4 oz. sugar	6 peppercorns
¼ oz. ground ginger	¾ pint vinegar
4 oz. salt	¾ oz. mustard

Cut up the marrow, sprinkle with salt and allow to stand overnight. Add other ingredients to the vinegar, boil for 5 minutes, then add the drained and rinsed marrow and cook until tender. Pack pickle into jars and seal.

525   MUSTARD PICKLES ✓

2 lb. mixed vegetables i.e. cauliflower, marrow, onions, cucumber, small green tomatoes, beans	1 pint vinegar
	2 oz. sugar
	1 tablespoon flour or
	½ tablespoon cornflour
1 tablespoon mustard powder	1 dessertspoon ginger
½ tablespoon turmeric powder	1 tablespoon pickling spice

Cut the vegetables into neat pieces. Soak overnight in brine (Recipe 519). Wash well under the cold tap and drain thoroughly. Boil the vinegar and pickling spice together. Mix all the dry ingredients with a very little vinegar until a smooth paste, pour over the strained hot vinegar and stir well. Return to the pan and cook until just thickened. Put in the vegetables and cook for 5 minutes. Put into jars and seal well.

526   PICKLED MUSHROOMS

1 lb. small button mushrooms	¼ teaspoon ground mace
1 teaspoon black pepper	1 quart vinegar
1 oz. salt	

Peel or rub off the skin of the mushrooms with the help of a little salt, throw into boiling water with plenty of salt and boil for 5 minutes. Pack into jars and pour the vinegar over them while boiling, the pepper and spice having been boiled with the vinegar. White vinegar is the best for this purpose and the mushrooms will keep for a fairly long period.

527   PICKLED NASTURTIUM SEEDS

nasturtium seeds	to each pint of vinegar
vinegar to cover them	add ½ oz. salt and 6 peppercorns

When the blossoms are off the fruit (seed) is used as follows, instead of capers:

Boil the vinegar, salt and peppercorns together and when cold strain into a wide necked bottle. Gather the seeds on a dry day, put them into the vinegar and cork closely. These pickled seeds form an excellent substitute for capers. They are ready for use in about 3 months, but may be kept for a much longer time.

528   PICCALILLI

Use exactly the same ingredients as for mustard pickles (Recipe 525) but chop the pieces of vegetable rather smaller so that you get a greater blending of these in the mustard sauce.

529   PICKLED ONIONS OR SHALLOTS

Remove outer skins from the onions or shallots, using a stainless knife to prevent their discolouring. Soak in the brine for 36—48 hours. For quantities see Recipe 519. Then proceed as for pickled cucumbers (Recipe 523).

530   PICKLED COCKTAIL ONIONS

Choose very tiny onions indeed and pickle as onions (see previous recipe). Some people like to add a little colouring to the spiced vinegar to colour the onions but this is a matter of taste. To keep them very white use a white wine vinegar and you may like to add 1 or 2 teaspoons sugar for a sweet pickled onion.

531   PICKLED RED CABBAGE

Cut the cabbage into shreds. Put into a basin with a good sprinkling of salt between each layer. Leave for 24 hours. Drain thoroughly, pack into jars and pour over the cold spiced vinegar. For quantities of spiced vinegar see pickled cucumber (Recipe 523).

532   SWEET PICKLES ✓

2 lb. mixed vegetables, i.e. cauliflower, marrow, onions, cucumber, small green tomatoes, beans	6 oz. sugar
	1 pint vinegar
	2 tablespoons flour or
	1 tablespoon cornflour

Cut vegetables into small pieces. Soak overnight in wet brine. Wash well under the cold tap and drain thoroughly. Boil vinegar and pickling spice together. Mix all dry ingredients with a very little vinegar until a smooth paste, pour over the strained hot vinegar and stir well. Return to the pan and cook until just thickened. Put in the vegetables and cook for 5 minutes. Put into jars and seal well. If desired 4—6 oz. sultanas can be added with vegetables for cooking.

533   PICKLED SHALLOTS

These are pickled in exactly the same way as onions. Particular care should be taken, when peeling them; a stainless knife must be used so that they do not discolour.

Pickles Chutneys Relishes

518 TO MAKE PICKLES

1. Always use very good quality vegetables — firm and not discoloured.
2. Use pure malt vinegar — white vinegar if preferred.
3. Cover well — see Point 5 in chutneys (Recipe 540).
4. Never use copper, brass or iron pans.
5. You must see the vegetables are completely covered with vinegar.
6. It is essential to put vegetables in brine before covering with vinegar. See brine recipes (519 and 520).
7. You should boil vinegar before using even when allowing it to become cold afterwards — see spiced vinegar, Recipe 521.

519 WET BRINE FOR VEGETABLES

Dissolve 2 oz. kitchen salt (not refined table salt) in 1 pint cold water. Soak vegetables in this 24 hours (onions and shallots 36—48 hours) THEN RINSE WELL UNDER COLD TAP in colander or strainer. This wet brine is used for mixed vegetables, onions, shallots, cauliflower. Do not use for pickled cabbage.

520 DRY BRINE

You will have a 'crisper' texture for pickled cucumbers if you use dry brine, but many people prefer the softer texture given by soaking in wet brine. Sprinkle layers of kitchen salt between layers of shredded cabbage or sliced or whole small cucumbers — leave for 24 hours, then shake away surplus salt.

521 SPICED VINEGAR

Spiced vinegar is used for pickles and you can spice the vinegar for chutneys if you wish instead of tying the spices in a muslin bag.

Use a tablespoon of mixed pickling spices to 1 pint vinegar for pickles.

In the case of pickled fruits you may like to use a little less.

For chutneys use from 1 teaspoon upwards, according to personal taste.

522 PICKLED BEETROOT

Cut the cooked beetroot into slices or cubes as desired. Put into boiling salted water (1 tablespoon salt to 1 pint water). Simmer gently for about 10 minutes being careful not to break the slices. Drain and pack into jars. Cover with hot spiced vinegar, i.e. white malt or ordinary malt vinegar boiled with pickling spices and drained. I recommend 1 tablespoon pickling spices to each pint of vinegar. Seal down at once. Store in a cool dark place.

TOMATO CHUTNEY

TOMATO CHUTNEY

MUSTARD PICKLE

PICKLED RED CABBAGE

Left:
22   CHEESE RAFTS (Recipe 203)

Right:
24   APPLE YEAST RING (Recipe 361)

Below left:
23   BACON BARBECUED POTATOES

(Recipe 104)

Below right:
25   PLUM PIE (Recipe 449)

21 SPICED APPLES (Recipe 537);
APPLE JELLY (Recipe 616);
BLACKBERRY JELLY (Recipe 618);
APPLE AND MINT CHUTNEY (Recipe 542);
APPLE BUTTER (Recipe 662);
GREEN TOMATO CHUTNEY (Recipe 559)

Other methods of Preserving Vegetables

513   DRYING VEGETABLES

Runner Beans. All varieties of string beans can be dried. They should be young and perfectly fresh. The beans should be washed and strung carefully. The very young and tender beans can be dried whole, but older beans should be cut diagonally into strips, a sharp stainless steel knife being used or one of the numerous machines sold for the purpose. The prepared beans should be tied in a piece of muslin or cheese-cloth, or placed in a wire basket, and then the bag or basket put in a pan of boiling water from 2 – 5 minutes, according to the age of the beans. If desired, ½ oz. bicarbonate of soda can be added to each gallon of boiling water. This improves the colour of green vegetables. The beans should be removed from the boiling water, spread on trays and placed in the oven at a temperature of 120° F., increasing gradually to between 150° F. and 160° F. The beans should be dried until they are crisp, cooled for 12 hours and packed in tightly corked bottles which should be protected from the light. For use, the beans should be soaked in cold water for 12 hours then boiled in salted water until tender.

Peas. Generally speaking, with the exception of a few varieties, peas do not dry well. One variety that is quite satisfactory is Harrison's Glory. The method is the same as that for runner beans. Peas may be allowed to dry on the vines as for seed, then stored after shelling in a dry place. Marrow-fat varieties are the most suitable for this method.

Mushrooms. The mushrooms (or other edible fungi) should be very fresh. If the variety is normally peeled before use, this should be done, and the coarse stems removed. Spread on trays or thread on strings and dry at a temperature not exceeding 120° F. until quite crisp. Store in a dry place.

514   SALTING BEANS

Note. It is essential to use enough salt otherwise the beans become 'slimy' — 1 lb. KITCHEN salt to 3 lb. prepared beans. Slice and pack the beans into containers — use large jars or crocks. Put a layer of beans and a layer of salt, and press down firmly after each layer of salt.

You can fill the jars when convenient but always end with a layer of salt.

When the jars are completely filled then cover with glass lids or linen or several thicknesses of paper but *not metal*. It is a good idea to paste the paper round the edges to give a perfect seal.

If using glass jars tie brown paper round the outside to exclude the light and keep the beans a good colour.

To use the beans. Wash in about 6 lots of COLD water to get rid of the salt. Cover with really hot water, leave for 2 hours, then give a final cold rinse. Cook, without salt, in boiling water until tender.

NEVER SOAK OVERNIGHT: THIS TOUGHENS THE BEANS.

515   STORING POTATOES

While new potatoes can be stored by bottling some people bury them in sand in the garden, in a sheltered place, and use them for Christmas Day. They will not store for very much longer than this period.

516   PRESERVING MINT IN SUGAR

Chop the mint finely and put a layer into a jar with an equal depth of sugar. Continue to fill the jar in the same way until full and then seal down.

517   TO STORE NUTS

Gather the nuts when they are mature.

Almonds. Make certain that you are using the sweet almonds because bitter almonds should not be eaten although very small quantities can be added to cakes for flavouring. Spread the nuts out in one flat layer to dry. When dry put in containers, filling with a layer of nuts and a layer of salt and some kind of packing such as you use round grapes, if desired. If you cannot get this use a layer of salt and a layer of nuts.

Chestnuts. Store in boxes in a dry place.
Cob Nuts. Lay out in flat boxes in an airy space. Turn once or twice during storage.

Walnuts. Remove the green husk before storing. Clean away any pieces of the husk, dry the nuts and store as almonds.

TO SALT NUTS

Shell the nuts, heat in butter or olive oil until a faint golden colour and then toss in salt.
Store in airtight jars or tins.
Almonds should be blanched and dried before salting.

511 TO OPEN SCREW TOPPED JARS

Before putting screw topped jars away to store, oil the inside of the metal bands. If in spite of this they are difficult to remove there is a special screw cap opener (illustrated).

512 BOTTLING FRUIT AND VEGETABLES FOR SHOW PURPOSES

1. Check before leaving the jars that the seal is still airtight because carrying sometimes breaks this seal and your jars will be automatically disqualified.
2. Make certain that the jars are well polished on the outside. This helps to show the clarity of the fruit or vegetables inside.
3. When bottling fruit for show purposes use a fairly light syrup for this gives a better colour and prevents any possibility of the fruit rising in the jar.
4. See that the jars are labelled very carefully.
5. Pack very much more carefully and in a more original manner than you would for home bottling. Here are some suggested packs:

FRUIT

Apples. These look very good cut in rings rather than slices and the rings packed round the outside with a blackberry in the centre of each, where the core has been removed.

Whole Apples. Peeled and cored these look most interesting. If slicing apples make sure the slices are all turned the same way.

Apricots. Turn halved apricots with their cut side towards the jar and put a cracked kernel in the centre of each.

Blackberries. Fill jars with alternate layers of blackberries and sliced apples.

Cherries. These form a very attractive jar mixed with halved apricots.

Gooseberries. Take care to select gooseberries that are the same size and degree of ripeness.

Grapes. Pack alternate black and white grapes in a jar.

Grapefruit. Arrange the sections to form a very definite design round the sides of the jar.

Greengages. Be very careful to choose fruit that is not over-ripe.

Oranges. Whole oranges are most effective bottled and these can be bottled in water rather than syrup.

Pears. Take great care with the colour of pears (see Recipe 498) and it is quite a good idea, for show purposes, to put a little lemon juice into the syrup to make certain that the fruit keeps particularly white. Small pears look very effective if peeled, cored and packed whole. This means turning some one way and some the other.

Peaches. The yellow cling peaches are the best for bottling and look wonderful when halved.

Pineapple. This can be bottled as whole rings, or halved rings with cherries to give contrasting colour.

Raspberries. These are most effective if a white or red currant is put into the centre and this turned towards the outside of the jar.

Rhubarb. The right way to pack rhubarb for show purposes is to make sure every piece is exactly the same length.

Strawberries. The best way to keep the colour of strawberries is to let them stand in cold syrup overnight, take out of the syrup, pack in the jars, add the syrup and use the steriliser method.

Another most attractive pack of fruit for competition is a mixed fruit salad but do remember to sterilise this for the time required by the fruit wanting the longest period.

VEGETABLES

Choose vegetables of all the same size.

Potatoes should be put in a little salt water with lemon juice added to make certain they keep very white.

A few drops of green colouring can be added to the brine for peas and beans but some judges do not approve of this.

PICKLING AND CHUTNEY FOR SHOW PURPOSES

1. The flavour of the chutney is important so make certain this is the very best you can make.
2. Cover jars carefully and neatly.
3. With pickles, grade the vegetables, or whatever it may be, with the greatest care.
4. Strain the vinegar very carefully and use a white vinegar in order to show the colour of beetroot, fruit etc.

Bottling runner beans in a pressure cooker

510   VEGETABLE BOTTLING

Remember it is UNSAFE to bottle vegetables other than in a pressure cooker. Always follow the special instructions for your own make of pressure cooker. Below are the main points to remember.

1. Wash thoroughly to free vegetables from all traces of soil. Pre-cook or blanch by immersing in boiling water for the time stated in table below, then dropping into cold water. Drain well and pack into clean jars to within 1 inch of top. Do not pack too tightly.
2. Still leaving 1 inch at top, cover vegetables with a hot brine solution, made by dissolving 2—3 oz. salt to 1 gallon water, boiled before using. Work out air bubbles by quickly twisting the jar from side to side. Adjust rings and lids.
3. Process jars of hot food immediately. Pour 1 pint hot water into cooker, add 1 tablespoon vinegar. Stand jars on inverted trivet. Do not allow jars to touch each other or the sides of the cooker. Use paper between jars if necessary. Fix cover, place on LOW heat. Do not put on pressure control; allow air to be expelled through centre vent for 5 minutes. Put on 10 lb. pressure control valve, still at low heat, bring to pressure. Process for the time stated below. See that there is always a steady flow of steam from the pressure control as pressure must not drop below 10 lb.
4. As point 4 in fruit bottling (Recipe 509).
5. The loss of liquid does not interfere with the keeping quality of the food. Jars should never be opened, after processing, to replace liquid that has boiled out. When opening a jar of bottled vegetables do not taste the cold food. If the contents of the jar do not smell right and the food is soft and mushy, discard it at once. As a safeguard, heat bottled vegetables at boiling temperature for 10—15 minutes before tasting or using.

TIMETABLE FOR BOTTLING VEGETABLES
(Use 10 lb. Pressure Control)

Vegetables	Preparation	Minutes to blanch in boiling water	Minutes to process at 10 lb. pressure
Asparagus	Wash, trim off scales, cut in even lengths, tie in bundles, pack upright.	2—3 minutes	40 minutes
Beans, Broad	Pod. Choose very young beans.	5 minutes	55 minutes
Beans, Runner	Wash, string and slice.	5 minutes	40 minutes
Beetroot	Cut off top. Blanch before slicing or dicing.	15—20 minutes	40 minutes
Carrots	Wash, scrape, slice or dice. Young new, leave whole.	10 minutes	45 minutes
Celery	Wash, cut in even lengths.	6 minutes	40 minutes
Corn	Strip from cob.	2—3 minutes	50 minutes
Peas	Wash, shell and grade.	2—3 minutes	50 minutes
Potatoes, New	Wash, scrape carefully or peel thinly.	5 minutes	50 minutes

3

2. Pour 1 pint hot water into cooker, add 1 tablespoon vinegar to prevent cooker staining. Stand jars on inverted trivet. Do not allow jars to touch one another or side of cooker. Use paper between jars if they are likely to touch. If using ordinary jam jars, put cloth or layers of newspaper on trivet to prevent breakage. Add extra ¼ pint water to allow for absorption by cloth or paper. When using electricity, bring to pressure on low heat.

3. Fix cover, place on heat and bring to 5 lb. pressure in usual way. Process for time stated in table below.

4. Turn off heat and leave cooker on stove to reduce pressure at room temperature. When using an electric stove, move cooker gently away from heat. Do not reduce pressure with cold water as sudden cooling will crack jars. Open cooker, remove jars one at a time on to a cloth or wooden surface. Tighten screw band and allow to cool. Test seal after 24 hours by inverting jars. If seal is not perfect re-process.

TIMETABLE
FOR BOTTLING FRUIT
(Use 5 lb. Pressure Control)

Fruit	Minutes at 5 lb. pressure	Fruit	Minutes at 5 lb. pressure
Apples	3—4 minutes	Peaches	7 minutes
Apricots	3—4 minutes	Pears	3—4 minutes
Blackberries	3—4 minutes	Plums	3—4 minutes
Blackcurrants	7 minutes	Raspberries	3—4 minutes
Cherries	7 minutes	Redcurrants	7 minutes
Damsons	3—4 minutes	Rhubarb	3—4 minutes
Gooseberries	3—4 minutes	Tomatoes	7 minutes
Loganberries	3—4 minutes		

4

505 ELDERBERRY SYRUP

Recipe as for jelly (Recipe 620) but to each pint add just 8 oz. sugar. Simmer together until like a syrup. Pour into hot bottling jars or bottles. Seal while hot. With bottles dip the corks into melted paraffin wax to make a perfect seal.

506 LEMONADE SYRUP

Peel rind of lemons *thinly*, put into a pan and to each 4 lemons allow ¼ pint water. Simmer for 5 minutes then drain off liquid, add to the juice of the lemons and to every pint of liquid allow 8 — 12 oz. sugar. Boil together until like a syrup. Pour into hot jars and seal down. If in bottling jars this syrup should keep indefinitely.

507 FRUIT JUICES

Allow the same amount of water as for fruit syrups (Recipe 503) and proceed in the same way but allow just 2 — 4 oz. sugar to each pint juice. This gives a thinner liquid that needs less water for drinks and many people find it more refreshing than fruit syrup.

508 BOTTLING FRUIT IN BRANDY

For special occasions fruit can be bottled in brandy. Fruit is prepared in exactly the same way as in Recipe 498. The most suitable fruit to choose are pears, peaches, cherries, cherry plums and damsons.

Prepare the fruit, and in the case of damsons or any fruit with a fairly firm skin, prick this once or twice so the brandy syrup has a chance to penetrate.

Pack the fruit tightly in the jars, make a fairly heavy syrup (see Recipe 499), and to each pint of cold syrup add approximately ¼ pint brandy. Fill the jars in this way and use the steriliser method.

If preferred the oven method of bottling, (Recipe 498) could be chosen. The syrup is brought to the boil, the brandy added, heated but not boiled, otherwise it will evaporate. It is then poured over the fruit and sealed in the usual way.

509 FRUIT BOTTLING IN A PRESSURE COOKER

This is not a great saving of time, but the fruit remains an excellent colour and texture. Special instructions for your own make of cooker should be followed but below is a general guide to bottling by this method.

1. For preparation of fruit before bottling see Recipe 498. Only closures with clip tops may be used with ordinary jam jars. Special preserving jars are recommended. Scald jars and invert them on a clean folded cloth. Scald lids and rings by pouring boiling water over them. Do not boil but keep them in water until ready for use. Choose fruit of even size. Pack tightly without damaging the fruit, to within ½ inch of top of jar. Fill with boiling syrup (Recipe 499) or water. Tap jar on folded cloth. Adjust rings and lids. If using screw top jars, screw band tightly, unscrew ¼ turn.

1

Fruit bottling in a pressure cooker (Recipe 509)

2

this and the special string first of all into hot water for a few minutes, then tie on the skin as tightly as possible.

Put some sort of padding at the bottom of the steriliser. A wooden board, several thicknesses of paper or an old cloth will do. Stand the jars on this, being careful they do not touch the sides of the pan, or each other. It is always preferable to completely cover the jars in the steriliser with cold water, but if this is not possible, fill the steriliser with cold water up to the necks of the jars, then either put on the lid or cover with a board or tea cloth, so keeping in the steam.

Take 1½ hours to bring the water in the steriliser to simmering, i.e. 165 — 175 °F. for all fruits except pears and tomatoes, when the water should be brought to 180 — 190 °F. With all fruits, but for the following exceptions, maintain the temperature for 10 minutes. With pears, peaches and tomatoes maintain for 30 minutes. Before lifting out the jars bale out a little water so that it is easier and safer to lift them out. Stand the jars on to a wooden surface and in the case of jars with screw bands, tighten these.

Leave the jars for 24 hours, then test by removing the clip or band and seeing if the lid is tight. If it is, and the jar can be lifted by the lid, then the jars have sealed. (See notes at end of Recipe 498).

501 BOTTLING FRUIT IN ITS OWN JUICE

A less usual method of bottling fruit is to add no liquid at all, so that when the jars are opened they contain only the fruit. Obviously the flavour of fruit bottled by this method is much the best, for it is not diluted by water or syrup. This method is particularly suitable for tomatoes. Other fruits that can be done this way are raspberries, strawberries (although these bottle less successfully than any fruit), peaches and halved plums. Do not try to use other fruits containing less juice. To prepare the jars, wash them thoroughly and boil the rubber rings for 10 minutes. With tomatoes, skin these, then, if large, cut them into halves. Pack the tomatoes into the jars tightly, but being careful not to break them. Add ½ teaspoon salt and ½ teaspoon sugar to each lb. tomatoes. With other fruits simply pack the fruits into the jars with a sprinkling of sugar here and there in the jars. When the bottles are completely filled, put on the rubber rings, tops and clips or screw-bands.

NOTE CAREFULLY: These jars may not now be sterilised in the oven, but must be sterilised in a deep pan, so loosen the screw bands and proceed exactly as given in the directions for bottling in a steriliser (Recipe 500), giving exactly the same time and temperatures. When the jars are removed from the steriliser it will be found that the fruit has sunk a little down the jars; these cannot be filled up, so simply tighten the screw bands and test after 24 hours as usual.

502 PULPING FRUIT

Pulping is a very good way of preserving, for pulped fruit takes up comparatively little space in the jars. Stew the fruit, adding little or no water, and sugar to taste. In the case of tomatoes, add ½ teaspoon sugar and ½ teaspoon salt to each lb. (skinned if desired). If a smooth pulp is required, rub the cooked fruit through a sieve and re-boil. Put tops of jars and rubber bands to boil, and boil for 10 minutes. Also put the glass jars to get VERY HOT. Pour the boiling pulp into boiling hot jars, seal down as quickly as possible, and immediately stand the jars in the steriliser filled with boiling water. Boil fruit pulp for a good 5 minutes and tomato pulp for a good 10 minutes. Screw bands should be loosened the half turn before going into the boiling water and tightened when they come out.

503 FRUIT SYRUPS

All fruit syrups can be kept well — they tend to be a better flavour as well as a thicker texture if sugar is added — but they can be preserved without if it should be necessary for medical reasons.

> *Allow 8 — 12 oz. sugar to each pint juice.*
> *Allow NO WATER to soft juicy fruits — raspberries, loganberries, strawberries, etc.*
> *Allow ¼ pint water to each lb. blackcurrants, blackberries, redcurrants etc.*

1. Put the fruit into the top of a double saucepan or basin over hot water adding the water if required. Press down the fruit to squash it well and cook for about 1 hour until you are sure all the juice is extracted. Press down during cooking.
2. Strain through a jelly bag or through several thicknesses of muslin over a fine sieve.
3. Measure the juice and add sugar, heat together until the sugar is dissolved, stirring well during this time. DO NOT CONTINUE BOILING when sugar has dissolved.
4. Pour the hot syrup into hot bottling jars or use cordial bottles with well fitting screw topped lids, which should have been boiled before using.
5. Allow syrup to cool in the bottles, which should not be quite filled.
6. Stand them in a steriliser or deep pan with a rack at the bottom (see steriliser method of bottling, Recipe 500) or several thicknesses of cloth or paper.
7. Loosen screw bands ½ turn, then take 1 hour to bring water to simmering (170 °F.). Retain for 30 minutes for large jars or bottles or 20 minutes for smaller ones.
8. Lift out carefully, stand on a wooden surface and tighten screw bands.
9. Tie adhesive tape round the corks or caps of cordial bottles.
10. Dilute with water to serve.

504 ROSE HIP SYRUP

This is made in the same way as fruit syrup but you use 3 pints water to 1 lb. hips — grate the hips and simmer for about 5 minutes in 3 pints BOILING WATER. Allow to stand for 15 minutes then strain.

499   SYRUP FOR FRUIT

Heavy syrup can be used for most fruits if people have a very 'sweet tooth'. Use particularly with peaches, pears or fruit salad:

12 — 16 oz. sugar to 1 pint water.

Medium syrup is most usually chosen for all fruits except perhaps apples:

6 — 8 oz. sugar to 1 pint water.

Light syrup is ideal for apples or where a slightly sharp flavour is liked:

4 oz. sugar to 1 pint water.

Boil sugar and water together until sugar is dissolved. Strain if wished before using.

500   BOTTLING IN A STERILISER

Any deep container can be used as a steriliser, although a proper steriliser with a thermometer is obviously the most effcient to use.

Prepare the fruit and make the syrup. See instructions for doing this under the 'Oven Method' (Recipe 498). Pack the fruit into the jars, as tightly as possible. Fill to the very top of the jars with COLD water or COLD syrup. Put on the boiled rubber bands and the lids. If using the screw-band jars, turn these as tightly as possible, then unscrew for half a turn, so allowing for the expansion of the glass. If using the clip tops put the clip into position. When using the skin covering, put

Bottling

497   PERFECT BOTTLING

1. It is essential that fruit for bottling should be firm and ripe. Do not choose over-ripe fruit since it will break badly. Under-ripe fruit, on the other hand, has not a good flavour.
2. Fruit has a very much better flavour if it is bottled in syrup rather than water.
3. It is important to follow the timing for fruit preservation for if fruit is sterilised for too short a period it will not keep, and if for too long a period it will become over-softened.

The picture below shows fruit which has been sterilised at too high a temperature in the case of the left-hand bottle of apples and so has lost some of its liquid.

The jar on the right has been badly packed and so the fruit does not come right to the top.

The jar in the centre, however, does look quite excellent.

See also Recipe 512 for preservation for show purposes.

498   PREPARATION OF FRUIT
and
BOTTLING BY THE OVEN METHOD

Prepare the fruit. To do this, wash and dry the fruit, or wash and drain soft fruit. Be careful not to use fruit that is bruised or over-ripe.

Apples. Peel, core and slice, and immediately drop into a bowl of salted water, i. e. 1 level tablespoon kitchen salt to each quart of cold water. Let the apples stay there for 10 minutes, with a plate on top of them if desired, but this is not really necessary. This prevents their becoming brown in colour.

Peaches. Drop the peaches into boiling water and leave them there for ½-1 minute. Remove and put into cold water, then skin them. Leave them in water until ready to pack the jars. This prevents their discolouring.

Pears. Preparation of pears is similar to apples. If using hard cooking pears, simmer these until soft.

Tomatoes: Flavour is improved by adding to each 1 lb. tomatoes ½ teaspoon salt and ½ teaspoon sugar. Sprinkle this into the jar before pouring on the boiling water. Skin if wished.

Put the prepared fruits into clean jars, packing as tightly as possible. Since the fruit obviously shrinks during sterilising, it is suggested that the jars are filled just above the top. The jars are put into a cool oven (240 °F. — Gas Mark ½); where pressure is extra good use Gas Mark ¼.

Stand the jars either on an asbestos mat, several thicknesses of paper or cardboard, or on a wooden board. Cover the tops of the jars with an old, clean tin lid.

While the jars are in the oven, put the glass lids and rubber bands on to boil for 15 minutes. If using metal tops just drop these for 1 minute into boiling water so that the lacquer is not damaged.

Length of time to leave the fruit in the oven:

Raspberries, Loganberries - - - - - -	45 minutes
(Do not pack these fruits too tightly)	
Rhubarb, Redcurrants, Blackcurrants -	50 minutes
Plums, Apples, Blackberries, Damsons, Greengages and Cherries - - - - - -	1 hour
Whole Peaches, Whole Apricots - - -	1¼ hour
Halved Peaches, Halved Apricots, Pears, Tomatoes - - - - - - - - - - - - -	1½ hours

Fruit Salad — give time required by fruit needing maximum sterilising.

Have ready a kettle of boiling water or a pan of boiling syrup. Bring the jars one at a time out of the oven. Put on to a wooden surface, pour over the boiling liquid, tapping the jar as you do so, until it completely overflows. If using a screw top type of jar, put on the rubber ring first, put on the top, hold on to this tightly, then either screw down, clip down or put on weight. Do not handle the jars any more than necessary for 24 hours. After this time, remove the screw band or clip and test to see if the lid is firm. It should be possible to lift the jars by the lid. When the jars have sealed there is no need to replace either the clip or screw band.

If the screw band is put on the jar, do this only loosely, and it is advisable to lightly grease the inside of the band. The oven method is suitable for all fruits, but NOT FOR PULPING OR TOMATOES AND FRUIT BOTTLED IN THEIR OWN JUICE.

Dried Fruits

490   DRIED APPLE RINGS

Choose large good cooking apples. Peel, core and slice these, putting the rings into salted water (1 tablespoon kitchen salt to each 2 pints of water). Pat dry and thread on string or striks. Either put into an airing cupboard, if really warm, or put into the coolest possible oven — just under 200 °F. or Gas Mark 0 — and dry with the door slightly open, until leathery and creamy coloured. Make sure they are cold before putting into tins or jars.

491   DRYING OTHER FRUIT

Plums, grapes, peaches, apricots, figs can be dried at home. The fruit is washed, and then left to dry as suggested above for apple rings. However, due to the fact that the fruit one buys is often not the perfect variety for drying, and also that commercially dried fruit is processed under the finest conditions, you will probably be a little disappointed at the result. It is only worth while doing if you have a glut of fruits that cannot be dealt with in any other way.

492   TO COOK DRIED FRUITS

It is advisable to soak the fruit first, either overnight or for several hours in cold water. After this add sugar and flavourings and simmer very gently until tender.

Another way of cooking dried fruit is to bring it to the boil and then put it into a warmed vacuum flask and put on the lid. The fruit goes on cooking in this way.

493   DRIED FRUIT SALADS

Dried fruit is wonderfully tender if you use a pressure cooker. Soak fruit for 5—10 minutes in boiling water before cooking, then allow following times. Add sugar and flavouring to taste.

Fruit	Amount of water	Cooking time after 15 lb. pressure is reached
Apple Rings: 1 lb.	½ pint (little lemon juice)	10 minutes
Figs: 1 lb.	½ pint	10—15 minutes
Prunes: 1 lb.*	½ pint	10—15 minutes
Apricots: 1 lb.	½ pint	5—6 minutes
Peaches: 1 lb.	½ pint	5—6 minutes

* Excellent cooked in coffee

With dried fruit salad you can give all the fruit the same cooking time or reduce pressure half-way through cooking, then add the apricots and peaches.

494   TO USE DRIED FRUIT

Dried fruit, whether bought commercially or home dried, can be used in a variety of ways. You will find a number of recipes in this book where dried fruit is used to add flavour to savoury dishes. It can be added to fudge, toffee etc. and used in cakes and biscuits. If adding dried fruit to cakes care must be taken, if the fruit has been washed, that it is adequately dried again before going into the cake mixture, for damp fruit can cause a heavy cake.

495   SUNSHINE SUNDAE

mandarin oranges or fresh   vanilla ice cream
oranges or tangerines

Fill sundae glass with alternate layers of oranges and ice cream. Pour sufficient sauce over top to fill sides and cover top.

ORANGE AND RAISIN SAUCE

4 oz. orange marmalade   2 oz. seedless raisins
1 tablespoon cream

Heat marmalade gently until it comes to boiling point. Stir in cream and add plumped raisins. Serve hot.
To plump raisins, cover with cold water and bring to boil, cover and leave to stand for 5 minutes.

496   CALIFORNIA RUM FUDGE

1 lb. granulated sugar   ¼ pint water
2 oz. butter   1 teaspoon rum
¼ pint evaporated milk   4 oz. seedless raisins

Put the sugar, butter, milk and water into a large saucepan. Heat gently till the sugar has dissolved and the fat has melted, then bring to the boil. Boil rapidly, stirring until a temperature of 240 °F. is reached (to the 'soft ball' stage). Remove from heat, add the rum and seedless raisins, beat well until the mixture becomes thick and creamy. As the sugar begins to grain, pour into a greased tin about 6 × 8 inches. When nearly set, mark into squares with a sharp knife. Delicious served with plain ice cream or coffee ice cream.

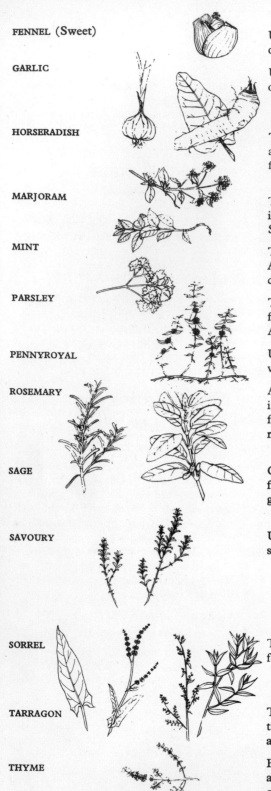

FENNEL (Sweet)	Use this thick stalk as raw vegetable or cooked like celery.	Sow annually.
GARLIC	Use very sparingly to give strong onion flavour in salads, stews etc.	Cloves should be planted annually in sunny enriched ground in February or March.
HORSERADISH	The grated root has a 'hot' flavour and is used for sauces for meat and fish.	Plant annually from pieces of root — if left spreads and becomes uncontrollable.
MARJORAM	These delicate-flavoured leaves are ideal for soups, stuffing and sauces. Sprinkle on lamb while roasting.	Perennial. Sow first in April.
MINT	The perfect accompaniment to lamb. A little sprig can be put into fruit drinks, and chopped and used in salads.	Perennial. Sow first in February or March.
PARSLEY	The most useful herb of all to give flavour and provide a gay garnish. Add to sauces.	Sow annually several times a year — very slow growing.
PENNYROYAL	Use sparingly in savoury dishes — very strong.	Perennial. Sow in spring.
ROSEMARY	A sprig put inside a roasting fowl instead of stuffing gives delicate flavour to the flesh; use also with rabbit, lamb and chopped in salads.	Propagated by soft cuttings in May or heeled cuttings in autumn, in sandy soil. Seed can be sown in April or May.
SAGE	Chopped fresh sage leaves are perfect for sage and onion stuffing or for giving flavour to savoury dishes.	Perennial. Buy plants rather than sow seed. Cuttings can be taken in April or May.
SAVOURY	Use when cooking broad beans, in stuffings and in soups.	Winter savoury is an almost evergreen perennial. New plants are raised from divisions or heeled cuttings or seeds in April. Summer savoury iss own in April.
SORREL	The acid-tasting leaves are cut up for use in omelettes, soups and salads.	Perennial. Raised from seed sown outdoors in April or by division of roots in early spring.
TARRAGON	The chief use of this herb is for making tarragon vinegar (Recipe 563), but a few leaves can be added to a salad.	Perennial. Propagate by division or cuttings in spring.
THYME	Both ordinary and lemon thyme give a delicious flavour if added to soups or stuffings.	Perennial. Renew every few years by division or cuttings or seeds sown in March or April.

489   TO PRESERVE HERBS BY DRYING

To dry herbs, wash them after picking in hot weather, dry well in a cloth, then lay them on baking trays, padded with plenty of paper and a piece of muslin over the top. Dry very slowly in the airing cupboard or very low oven, 200 °F. — Gas Mark 0 (with the door ajar), until brittle. Crumble and put into jars. In very hot weather they can be dried in the sun. Parsley is a better colour if dried for a few minutes in a hot oven.

Name	Use it like this	How to grow it

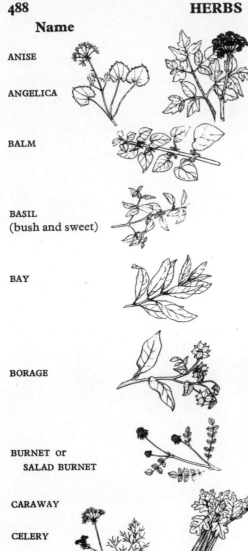

ANISE — Liquorice flavour. Dry seeds — crush, sieve, use in cake fillings etc. — Sow from seed in Spring.

ANGELICA — Stems and leaf stalks used in sweet dishes or for decoration. Crystallise — see Recipe 477. — Biennial, sown from seed in August.

BALM — Slight lemon flavour. Used in stuffings. Add to drinks. — An easily grown perennial herb, raised from root divisions in March or seeds or cuttings in April or May.

BASIL (bush and sweet) — Rather like bay leaf and used for same purpose (see below). A mild clove flavour. — Half-hardy annual. Sow from seed under glass in March or April and plant out in May.

BAY — The green shiny leaves from the bay tree should be well washed, then put into stews, soups or even custard. Use about 2 leaves for a stew and 1 for a custard. They can be bought dried and stored in air-tight jars. — Plant in April. Bay trees can be grown in tubs or pots and it is wise to move them to a sheltered position in autumn.

BORAGE — Both the flower and leaf can be used for flavouring fruit or other drinks. Borage has a slight cucumber taste and, if put into custard and removed before serving, gives a delicious flavour. — Hardy annual. Sow in April; can be propagated by root division or cuttings.

BURNET or SALAD BURNET — Slight taste of cucumber. Use leaves only when young. — Perennial. Propagate by seed or root division in spring or autumn.

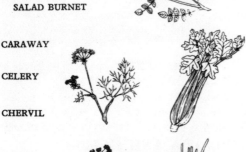

CARAWAY — Gather seeds, dry. Use for cakes etc. — Biennial. Sow in April.

CELERY — Dry seeds from celery flowers; use for pickles. — Sow annually.

CHERVIL — Fine parsley-like leaves useful for soups, salads, egg and fish dishes. As it withers quickly it is not so useful for garnishing as parsley. — A hardy annual which is best sown several times in the year.

CHIVES — These look like thick blades of grass, have a more delicate flavour than onion, and can be chopped finely and used in omelettes and savoury dishes. — Perennial. Grass-like tops which can be cut again and again from March to October.

CORIANDER — Hard seeds used in curries or cakes. — Sow annually, in spring or autumn.

CUMIN — Use ripe seeds in curry or with home made cheese. — Sow annually, first in pots then planted out: needs warmth and sun.

DILL — Chopped leaves can be used in white sauce like parsley, but chiefly grown for seeds which are dried when ripe and used in pickling vinegar. — Sow annually; tall plant — the seeds drop quickly.

FENNEL — Add little chopped leaf to sauce to serve with fish. Use seeds for flavouring pickles and soups. — Perennial. Sow in April from seed.

Using Spices and Herbs

483 SPICES IN VEGETABLE COOKERY

The judicious use of spices and herbs adds a great deal of interest to vegetable cooking. Bay leaves, for example, are very good if one is added when cooking a vegetable macedoine. Nutmeg is invaluable with mashed turnips. One or two cloves give a very good flavour when cooking carrots.

484 SPICES WITH FRUIT

Cloves are considered by many people an indispensable partner with apple and pears. Cinnamon, spice, nutmeg all go well with fruit.

485 COMPOTE OF PEARS

1 lb. pears	*a few cloves*
3 oz. sugar	*a little cinnamon*
¼ pint water	*a few drops of carmine*
¼ a lemon	*red wine (optional)*

Make a syrup of sugar and water. Add the juice of the lemon, cloves, cinnamon and carmine. Put all these ingredients into a thick saucepan and bring slowly to the boil and boil for 10 minutes. Peel the pears and cut them in half and core them without breaking the halves into pieces.

Stew the pears slowly in the syrup until they are tender and then lift them out carefully. Strain the syrup and add, if liked, a little red wine.

486 SPICED ICE CREAM MILK SHAKE

For more sophisticated tastes a milk shake made by whisking ice-cream, milk and sugar can be given interest by the addition of a little powdered clove or nutmeg.

487 ICED TEA AND COFFEE

One or two cloves are excellent in glasses of iced coffee or tea. This picture shows iced tea flavoured with cloves and iced blackcurrant flavoured with cloves, lemonade (Recipe 669) and iced cider garnished with orange and cucumber and once again flavoured with cloves and cinnamon.

To crystallise and Glacé Fruits

477   FRESH FRUIT

Sections of oranges, halved little pears, grapes are excellent when crystallised. Prepare the fruit, removing pips and white pith from oranges and dividing the fruit into neat segments. Proceed as follows:

1. Choose the fruits carefully — they should be firm.
2. Cook gently in water until just tender. Oranges and grapes need no cooking. They should just be put into the dish and the syrup poured over.
3. For each lb. of fruit allow ½ pint of syrup. Make this up by using ¼ pint of the water in which the fruits were cooked and 6 oz. sugar. Put the fruit into a fairly shallow dish and pour the syrup over while warm. See the fruit is well covered by putting a plate on top. Leave for 24 hours.
4. Next, pour off the syrup and reboil, adding another 2 oz. sugar. Pour over fruit again and leave for another 24 hours.
5. REPEAT THIS ANOTHER 3 TIMES — EACH TIME ADDING THE EXTRA 2 oz. SUGAR.
6. Drain off the fruit, return the syrup to the pan, this time adding 3 oz. sugar to the original ½ pint. When the syrup is boiling add the fruit and boil for 3 minutes. Return to the dish and leave for 24 hours.
7. Repeat step No. 6. The syrup should then take on the consistency of thick honey. If thin, repeat once again.
8. Drain off the syrup and place the fruit on to a wire cake sieve to dry — leave a plate underneath to catch the drips.
9. To give a crisp outside, as for crystallised fruits, put the fruit into the oven (200 °F. — Gas Mark ¼) with the door slightly ajar. Leave until crisp.

Note: The syrup can be coloured if desired.

WHEN USING CANNED FRUIT:

1. Drain the fruit from the syrup.
2. Measure the syrup and to each ½ pint add 2 oz. sugar. Boil together, pour over fruit and leave for 24 hours. Continue as for fresh fruit as from Note 4 to the end.

478   TO CRYSTALLISE ANGELICA

1. Choose stalks that are young, firm and tender.
2. Cut off the root ends and leaves, then place the stalks in a basin and pour over a boiling brine (¼ oz. kitchen salt to 4 pints of water).
3. Allow to soak for 10 minutes, rinse in cold water, place in a saucepan of fresh boiling water and boil for 5 minutes if very tender — a little longer if somewhat older.

4. Drain well, then scrape off outer skin.
5. Continue in exactly the same way as from note 3 in Recipe 477 on candying or crystallising fruits. When point 9 is reached the angelica can then be stored in dry jars. It will keep a better colour if stored in a dark place.

479   CRYSTALLISED FLOWERS

1 oz. gum arabic	*flowers*
rosewater (triple	*castor sugar*
strength)	

Cover the gum arabic with the rosewater and leave for 24 hours to melt. When properly melted paint each petal of the flowers all over on both sides, using a fine paint brush then hold each flower by the stem and sprinkle with castor sugar all over it.

The flowers must be fresh and never picked when wet. Care must be taken that the flowers are edible. Those suitable for crystallising are: roses, violets, primroses (and any other flower of the primula family such as polyanthus), also the blossoms of plum, cherry, apple, pear (the ornamental as well as the fruiting variety) and heather. The non-edible flowers are those which come from bulbs; in many cases these are poisonous.

480   COMPOTE OF FRUIT

This is a word used to describe cooked fruit but the fruit must be left in good sized pieces and not over-cooked. It can consist of a mixture of fresh and dried fruits cooked separately and mixed.

481   TO STEW FRUIT

The method used depends on the type of fruit. With hard fruit put into a pan with sugar and water, the amount of water depending on how much syrup is required and simmer gently. For very delicate fruit i.e. soft fruit, forced rhubarb, it is best to put the fruit in a basin over hot water, add sugar and little, if any, water and cook very gently.

482   TO POACH FRUIT

Where it is important to keep the shape of the fruit the best method of cooking is to prepare the syrup first and when this is really hot to put in the fruit. Soft fruits will not need any cooking; they just need to stand in the hot syrup as it cools. Other fruit should be cooked very gently in this.

469 SUMMER GLORY

1 lb. strawberries *1 6-oz. tin cream*
castor sugar

Place fruit, sugar, cream in layers. Serve.

470 STRAWBERRY PINEAPPLE COCKTAIL

8 oz. packet frozen *1½ gills undiluted orange*
strawberries *juice*
4 diced pineapple *2 tablespoons lemon juice*
rings *angelica*

Slice strawberries in half, leaving 6 whole strawberries for garnishing. Mix strawberries and pineapple together, combine orange and lemon juices together and keep chilled. Place strawberries and pineapple in individual dishes and pour the juice over. Decorate with whole strawberries and angelica. Serve chilled.

471 TANGERINES

TO STORE. Tangerines can be bottled (Recipe 498), canned (Recipe 665) or used for marmalade (Recipe 653).

TO SERVE. As a raw dessert or in any way that oranges are used.

472 TANGERINE SUNDAE

1 oz. seedless raisins *1 dessertspoon rum*
2 sugar lumps *6 tangerines*
1 level teaspoon arrowroot *½ oz. sugar*
1 brick dairy ice cream

Soak the raisins in the rum for about 30 minutes. Rub the sugar lumps over the tangerine skins until the oil is absorbed. Remove the peel and pith from two of the tangerines and cut the fruit into segments. Squeeze the juice from the remaining tangerines and make up to ¼ pint with water. Blend the arrowroot with a tablespoon of the juice, bring the rest to the boil in a small pan. Add the blended arrowroot, sugar lumps and sugar, cook for 2—3 minutes, stirring continuously, then stir in the orange segments and the raisins. Pile spoonfuls of ice cream into 4 sundae glasses and top with the sauce. Serve immediately.

This sundae sauce is equally good served cold.

473 UGLI

This is a cross between grapefruit and orange and can be used in any way that one uses these fruits.

474 WHITE CURRANTS

These currants are almost exactly the same in flavour as redcurrants and can be used like redcurrants. If you wish to make a jelly, however, you must tint this.

475 FRUIT DIPS

Try 'Fruit Dips' for a delightfully original 'tempter' for parties or buffet teas. Simply spear alternate strawberries and thick chunks of banana on cocktail sticks and arrange them round a shallow dish. Pile whipped cream, slightly flavoured with vanilla, in the centre and 'dip in'.

476 FRUIT SALADS

There are many ways of making a good fruit salad. The quickest and easiest is to open a can of some fruit that is not available, or in season, i.e. pineapple, peaches, apricots. Slice or dice the fruit and then add your fresh fruit to it. Grapes should be pipped and some people like them skinned. Apples should be added at the end of the preparations to keep them as crisp as possible. Slice thinly.

Bananas should be well covered in the syrup to keep them a good colour.

When using oranges, to avoid adding pips, pith, skins etc. to the salad, peel the orange with a knife but as you do this cut into the fruit very slightly so removing any of the outside pith. With the sharp knife cut slices of orange between the skin. If making a complete fresh fruit salad boil sugar and water to give the syrup, allowing 4—8 oz. to each pint of water. Add lemon or orange juice to flavour. Add this to the fruit. For special occasions a little sherry, kirsch, cherry or apricot brandy can be added. If no syrup is required the diced fruit should be mixed together and moistened with orange juice.

462　RHUBARB FOOL

12 oz. rhubarb
¼ pint thick custard
little whipped cream
few drops cochineal
sugar for cooking the rhubarb

Cook the rhubarb in a double saucepan, with the sugar — little, if any, water need be used. Rub through a sieve, add to the custard which should be very thick, and colour pale pink. Put into 4 glasses and serve very cold topped with lightly whipped cream.

463　RHUBARB SNOW

Cook the rhubarb with very little water and sugar until a very smooth purée — sieve if wished. When quite cold fold in stiffly whisked egg white (allowing 1 egg white to each ¼ pint purée). Pile into glasses and serve very cold. This is an excellent sweet for would-be slimmers since the rhubarb can be cooked with saccharin.

464　*ROSE HIPS*

It has been discovered during recent years that rose hips contain a great deal of Vitamin C and they are therefore worth storing for winter use in the form of rose hip syrup (Recipe 504), or as preserve (Recipe 664).

465　*STRAWBERRIES*

TO STORE. It is a pity that in bottling the flavour of this beautiful fruit is largely lost. If bottling use Recipe 498. Strawberries are excellent in jam (Recipes 610, 611, 612) though care must be taken to use a good recipe as they contain so little pectin, also in jelly (Recipes 632, 633).

TO SERVE. Raw or in various sweets; strawberries are quite delicious in a cream cheese salad, too.

466　STRAWBERRY BABAS

Babas:

4 oz. plain flour
½ oz. yeast
1 tablespoon water
1 egg
½ oz. castor sugar
¼ level teaspoon salt
2 oz. melted whipped-up cooking fat

Syrup:

¼ pint water
2 oz. sugar

To decorate:

8 oz. fresh strawberries
little cream

Babas: Sieve the flour into a warmed bowl and make a well in the centre. Add the yeast and the warm water and mix together with a wooden spoon or fingers, drawing in about a quarter of the flour. Dust a little of the flour over the yeast mixture and place in a warm place, covered with a damp cloth to prove (about 15 minutes). When yeast cracks through the flour add the beaten egg, sugar, salt, and melted fat. Beat thoroughly together. Again cover with a damp cloth and leave in a warm place until doubled in bulk (about 45 minutes). Divide dough into 8 portions and place in the dariole moulds which have been brushed with melted fat — the mould should be about half full. Leave again in a warm place covered with a damp cloth for a further 20 minutes. Bake near top of hot oven (425—450 °F. — Gas Mark 6—7) for 10—15 minutes. Turn out and leave to cool on a cake rack. Cut off tops and take out some of the centre of each baba.

Syrup: Bring the water and sugar to the boil, boil for 3—5 minutes then dip each baba in the syrup until thoroughly saturated with the syrup. Cut the strawberries in halves and fill the centre of the babas. Place a swirl of cream on top and place on the lids again.

467　STRAWBERRY BANANA MERINGUE

1 6-inch meringue flan case
6 bananas
8 oz. strawberries
a little fresh orange juice or canned pineapple juice

Reserve half a banana and half a dozen strawberries for decoration. Mash the remaining strawberries and bananas with the orange or pineapple juice. Fill the flan case with mixture and chill thoroughly. Just before serving, decorate with strawberries and banana slices (dipped in orange or pineapple juice to prevent them going brown).

468　STRAWBERRY CONDÉ

3 oz. rice
1 pint milk
1 oz. sugar
1 gill evaporated milk or cream
8—12 oz. strawberries
2—3 tablespoons redcurrant jelly
2 tablespoons water

Simmer rice in milk and sugar until very soft. Cool, then beat in evaporated milk. Pour into shallow dish. Arrange strawberries on top, halving these if large. Heat jelly and water together then pour over fruit.

457 REDCURRANTS

TO STORE. Redcurrants can be bottled (Recipe 498), frozen (Recipe 723), used in jelly and added to other fruit. They do not make a good jam by themselves because they are so full of pips but their juice is very rich in pectin and so helps to set jelly, strawberry and other jams.

TO SERVE. Mix with other fruit in fruit pies and tarts or eat raw.

FROSTED REDCURRANTS

When redcurrants are plentiful they look most attractive frosted for a centre-piece on a cake or sweet. Brush with egg white, shake over castor sugar and leave OR simply shake over icing sugar and leave in air to harden.

458 RHUBARB

TO STORE. Rhubarb can be bottled most successfully (Recipe 498), or canned (Recipe 665), but it is less good frozen. It makes a first class jam by itself or mixed with other fruits (see Recipes 606—609). It is, however, wise to use the second crop of rhubarb for jam making since its flavour is considered better. See also chutney (Recipe 557).

TO SERVE. Rhubarb, both forced and garden, is excellent in every type of pudding and pie and for cold sweets.

459 RHUBARB AMBER FLAN

6 oz. short crust pastry
(see Recipe 227)

Filling:

12 oz. rhubarb	*2 oz. sugar*
about 2 tablespoons water	*2 egg yolks*

Meringue:

2 egg whites	*2—4 oz. sugar*

Make and bake the flan case 'blind' until crisp and pale golden brown. Cook the rhubarb with just the 2 tablespoons water and sugar until very soft, mash or sieve and mix with the beaten egg yolks — do this while still hot so that the egg yolks get slightly cooked. Put into the flan case. Whisk the egg whites very stiff, fold in the sugar, pile over the filling. For a hot sweet you need only use the 2 oz. sugar and bake for approximately 20 minutes in the centre of a moderate oven (375°F. — Gas Mark 4) until the meringue is golden brown. If you wish to serve this sweet cold then use the larger amount of sugar and set for about 1—1¼ hours in the centre of a very slow oven (250—275°F. — Gas Mark ½—1).

460 RHUBARB CARTWHEEL FLAN

6 oz. short crust pastry (see Recipe 227)

Filling:

12 oz. rhubarb	*¼ pint water*
4 oz. granulated sugar	

Ginger sauce:

1 rounded dessertspoon cornflour	*¼ pint milk*
¼ heaped teaspoon ginger	*1 level tablespoon castor sugar*

Make the pastry, line 8-inch flan ring and bake 'blind' until crisp and golden brown. Wash the rhubarb well, trim the ends and cut into about 2½-inch pieces. Dissolve the sugar in water in a large saucepan, bring to the boil and add the rhubarb. Cook gently, just under boiling point, until tender, for about 10—20 minutes. When cooked, drain off the juice and allow to cool. Keep 6 of the strips, cut the others in half and place in the flan case. Fill with ginger sauce.

To make the ginger sauce:

Blend the cornflour and ginger with 1 tablespoon milk in a bowl. Put the remaining milk in a small saucepan and bring to the boil. Pour on to the blended cornflour; stir well; return to the saucepan and simmer for about 5 minutes, stirring all the time. Add the sugar and when cool, cover the rhubarb in the flan. Finally arrange the remaining strips of rhubarb on top to resemble the spokes of a cartwheel.

461 RHUBARB CREAM PIE

Biscuit crust pastry:

6 oz. wholemeal biscuits	*3 oz. butter*

Filling:

12 oz. rhubarb	*¼ lemon jelly*
1 gill cream or	*little sugar*
evaporated milk	*water*
glacé cherries	

To make the pastry, crush the biscuit crumbs, add the butter and form into the shape of a flan case in the serving dish. Allow to stand in a cool place until very firm.

Cook the rhubarb with about 1½ gills water and sugar to taste. When very soft but unbroken lift from the syrup. Dissolve the jelly in this and when cold, but not set, fold in most of the evaporated milk or cream (this need not be whipped). Put into the biscuit crumb case when just beginning to set. Smooth flat and arrange the cooked drained rhubarb on top in a neat pattern. Decorate with the whipped evaporated milk and glacé cherries.

450 POMEGRANATES

This fruit is not suitable for storing in any form but is used simply as a dessert.

451 PRUNES AND OTHER DRIED FRUIT

TO STORE. Details are given in Recipe 491 for drying fruit, but with the exception of apples it is really better to buy the commercially dried product for the quality is very high. Store in jars or in tins. Prunes make an excellent pickle (Recipe 536). Dried apricots are first class in jam (Recipe 575).

TO SERVE. Dried fruits are suitable for a great variety of sweets and puddings.

452 COUNTRY PRUNE PIE

Filling:

4 oz. prunes, soaked and
   stoned in 1 gill cold
   water
2 oz. soft brown sugar
pinch salt
nut of butter

squeeze of lemon juice
juice of ½ orange
1 level tablespoon cornflour
2 tablespoons cold water

Pastry:

4 fluid oz. (6 tablespoons)
   corn oil
3 tablespoons iced water

10 oz. plain flour
¼ level teaspoon salt
grated rind of ½ orange

To make the filling; soak and stone the prunes then cut in small pieces. Put the chopped prunes, the water in which they have been soaked, the brown sugar, salt, butter, lemon and orange juices in a saucepan and simmer gently for 5 minutes. Mix the cornflour smoothly with 2 tablespoons cold water, add to the ingredients in the saucepan and bring to the boil. Leave to cool while the pastry is being made. To make the pastry, blend the corn oil and water together well with a fork in the mixing bowl. Sift together the plain flour and salt and add gradually, mixing with a fork or palette knife to form a rollable dough. (Slightly more or less flour may be required.) Mix in the grated orange peel with the last of the flour. Roll out half the dough between 2 sheets of greaseproof paper and use to line an 8-inch flat plate. Spread the filling on the pastry, dampen the edge and cover with the remaining pastry. Brush with milk and decorate as liked. Bake 30—35 minutes in a moderately hot oven (400 °F. — Gas Mark 6). *Illustrated in colour picture no. 19.*

453 QUINCES

TO STORE. Quinces can be bottled by themselves or a little quince can be added to apples (Recipe 498). They make an excellent jam (Recipe 603) or marmalade (Recipe 649) and a small amount of quinces could flavour apples in apple jelly.

TO SERVE. They cannot be eaten raw but should be cooked either by themselves or with other fruit.

454 RASPBERRIES

TO STORE. Raspberries can be bottled (Recipe 498) or frozen (Recipe 723), and used to make jam (Recipe 604) and jelly (Recipe 627).

TO SERVE. Raspberries are considered by many people the most delicious of all fruits. As such they feel they require no cooking. If they are cooked they need a very short time.

455 RASPBERRY GALETTE

Flan pastry:

8 oz. plain flour (or self-
   raising flour)
pinch salt
4 oz. whipped-up
   cooking fat

1 rounded teaspoon castor
   sugar
1 tablespoon water
1 egg yolk

Filling:

8 oz. raspberries
2 rounded tablespoons
   redcurrant jelly

1 dessertspoon water
cream to decorate

To make pastry, sieve the flour and salt into a basin and rub in fat until the mixture resembles fine breadcrumbs. Mix the sugar into the water and egg yolk, beat lightly together. Stir into the dry ingredients and mix well to form a firm dough. Roll out on a lightly floured board to an 8-inch circle, flute the edges and prick all over with a fork. Place on a baking tray and bake in a moderately hot oven (400 °F. — Gas Mark 5) near the top of the oven for 20—25 minutes. Cool on a cake rack.

When the galette is cold place the raspberries all over the surface. Bring the redcurrant jelly and water to the boil and boil for 2 minutes. Pour over the raspberries immediately and leave to set. Decorate with whipped cream.

456 RASPBERRY RING

For the outer ring:

8 oz. raspberries
little sugar
little water

1 raspberry-flavoured
   jelly

Filling:

¼ pint cream (or whipped
   evaporated milk)
2 — 3 meringue cases

8 oz. raspberries
little sugar

Prepare outer ring first. Mash raspberries, add sugar and enough water to give 1 pint. Heat and dissolve jelly in this. Pour into ring mould previously rinsed out in cold water. When set, turn out. To make the filling, whip cream lightly until it just holds its shape. Crumble meringues, fold into cream together with whole raspberries and a little sugar, pile into centre of jelly ring.

Gas Mark 4) for 30—35 minutes. Cool on a wire tray. To make the meringues, whisk the egg white until stiff. Add a little of the castor sugar and whisk again until stiff. Finally fold in the remaining castor sugar. Pipe small meringues on to a greased baking tray or one previously lined with greaseproof paper. Bake in a very slow oven (225°F. — Gas Mark 0—½) until dry and crisp. Cool on a wire tray. To finish and decorate the gâteau, whisk the cream until stiff. Cut the Genoese through the centre. Fill with some of the cream and sandwich the two halves together. Spread remaining cream around the sides and on top of the Genoese. Mark the top with a fork to give a 'swirling' effect and mark with a knife into 8 portions. Press the meringues all around the sides. Peel the fresh pineapple and cut into 6 slices or open the can of pineapple rings and drain off the juice. Place on top of the gâteau and decorate with cherries. Leave in a cold place until ready to serve.

446 PINEAPPLE UPSIDE-DOWN PUDDING

4 oz. self-raising flour		4 oz. plain flour
1¼ level teaspoons baking powder	or	2½ level teaspoons baking powder
4 oz. castor sugar		3 rounded tablespoons brown sugar
4 oz. whipped-up cooking fat		3 rings pineapple
1 dessertspoon water		2 eggs

Pineapple sauce:

| 1 level dessertspoon cornflour | 1 gill pineapple juice |

Sieve flour, baking powder and sugar into a bowl. Add 3 oz. fat, eggs and water and, mixing all ingredients, beat for 1 minute. Brush a 6-inch round cake tin with fat. Melt brown sugar and 1 oz. fat together over a low heat. Place the pineapple rings at the bottom of the tin, spread over the sugar mixture, then place the cake mixture on top. Bake near the bottom of a slow oven (300°F. — Gas Mark 2) for approximately 2 hours. Turn out and leave upside down. Serve hot, as a sweet, with a pineapple sauce. To make the sauce, blend the cornflour with a little of the juice, place remainder in a saucepan and bring to the boil. Pour over blended mixture, return to the saucepan, bring to the boil, then cook for 3 minutes, stirring all the time.

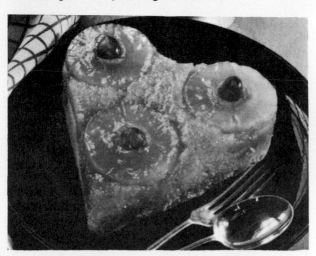

447 PLUMS

TO STORE. Probably one of the most successful of all fruits for bottling (Recipe 498) or using in jam (Recipes 600, 601).

TO SERVE. Really ripe plums are delicious as a dessert but all types of plums are excellent in cooking. Some people dislike the slight almond flavour given by the stones. In this case take these out before cooking.

448 PLUM SOUFFLÉ FLAN

Sponge flan:

| 2 eggs | 3 oz. castor sugar |
| 2 oz. self-raising flour | |

Filling:

| 8—12 oz. plums | 2 egg whites |
| 2 tablespoons sugar plus extra sugar for plums | |

Halve the plums and cook in a basin over hot water or a double saucepan with a little sugar but no water. When cooked either mash most of them or rub through a sieve. Save a few halves for decoration.

To make the sponge flan, whisk the eggs and sugar until very thick and creamy, fold in the sieved flour and bake in a well greased and floured sponge flan tin for about 12—15 minutes in a moderately hot oven (400°F. — Gas Mark 5). Turn out and put on to ovenproof dish. Whisk the egg whites until very stiff indeed, fold these into the thick plum purée, add the sugar, put into the flan case and set for about 15 minutes in a very moderate oven (350°F. — Gas Mark 3). Decorate with the plum halves and cream just before serving.

449 CREAMY PLUM PIE

| 6—8 oz. short crust pastry | 1½ lb. plums |
| 3 tablespoons condensed milk | 1 tablespoon boiling water canned or fresh cream |

Mix condensed milk and water and pour over the washed plums in a 1½ or 2-pint dish. Cover with the pastry. Brush with a little condensed milk and water. Bake in centre of a moderately hot oven (425°F. — Gas Mark 6) for approximately 30 minutes. *Colour picture no. 25.*

437 PEACHES

TO STORE. Peaches are one of the very best fruits for bottling (Recipe 498) or canning (Recipe 665). They can be frozen (Recipe 723). They are not so successful in jams but very good for pickling, although rather extravagant.

TO SERVE. Most people prefer ripe peaches as an uncooked dessert but the canned peaches lend themselves to innumerable sweets.

438 PEACH MILK JELLY

*1 can peaches or
4 fresh peaches
few strawberries or
cherries for decoration*

*1 lemon jelly
½ pint milk
little whipped cream*

If using fresh peaches skin, slice and poach in syrup of sugar and water for a few minutes. Lift out of the syrup, dissolve the lemon jelly in ½ pint fruit syrup, add half the chopped peaches and when cold put in the milk. Turn this out and decorate with the rest of the peaches, cream and strawberries.

439 STUFFED PEACHES (Hot)

Fill the halved peaches, canned or preferably raw, with a filling made by mixing equal quantities of butter, brown sugar and coconut. Bake for approximately 30 minutes in the oven.

440 STUFFED PEACHES (Cold)

Halve fresh peaches (or use canned) and stuff with a mixture of whipped cream, chopped nuts, glacé cherries and a little sugar. Frost lightly in the freezing compartment of the refrigerator.

441 PEACH FRUIT MOULD

1st Mixture

*1 envelope gelatine
(enough for 1 pint)
½ pint fruit syrup
cochineal*

*4 or 5 stewed peaches,
nectarines, several
cherries, or other fruit
1 dessertspoon lemon juice
2 tablespoons sugar*

Dissolve gelatine in 3 tablespoons hot water. Add to fruit syrup, lemon juice and sugar and make up ¾ pint with cold water. Colour a faint pink. Arrange the fruit in whole or halves or cut in small pieces in a plain mould or cake tin. When the syrup is thickening, pour carefully over the fruit. Leave to set.

2nd Mixture

*3 teaspoons gelatine
½ pint milk
green colouring*

*3 tablespoons hot water
1 tablespoon sugar
almond essence*

Dissolve gelatine in hot water, add gradually to milk, add sugar and a few drops of almond essence. Colour a delicate green and pour carefully on the fruit layer.

442 PERSIMMON

This rather rare fruit does not preserve well. Halve and serve with a spoon as an hors-d'oeuvre.

443 PERSIMMON COCKTAIL

Halve the persimmon, take out the pulp and mix with pieces of grapefruit, fresh or canned. Sweeten slightly, pile in cocktail glasses and serve as an hors-d'oeuvre.

444 PINEAPPLE

TO STORE. Pineapple can be canned (Recipe 665) or bottled (Recipe 498). It can be used in preserves (Recipe 664) and also in Pineapple Relish (Recipe 554).

TO SERVE. Pineapple is equally good as part of a savoury dish with chicken or ham or as a sweet. One very important point to remember is never to add *fresh* pineapple to a jelly because it destroys the setting quality completely.

445 PINEAPPLE AND CHERRY GÂTEAU

Genoese sponge:

*3 oz. castor sugar
3 eggs*

*3 oz. plain flour
1 oz. margarine*

Meringues:

1 egg white

2 oz. castor sugar

Filling and topping:

*½ pint thick cream
fresh or canned cherries*

*1 small fresh pineapple or
1 small can pineapple rings*

To make the Genoese, put the castor sugar and eggs into a mixing bowl, place over a saucepan of hot water and whisk until the mixture is light and creamy and thick enough to hold the impression of the whisk. Remove and whisk until cool. Lightly fold in the sieved flour and melted margarine. Pour into an 8-inch sandwich cake tin previously brushed with melted margarine. Bake in the middle of a moderate oven (375 °F. —

PEARS

TO STORE. Pears are excellent when bottled (Recipe 498) or canned (Recipe 665). They can be used in jam, like apples, (Recipes 577, 599), but are not particularly successful since they have so little flavour.

TO SERVE. Ripe pears can be served uncooked as dessert, and when canned or bottled in innumerable sweets. They are excellent in a cheese salad.

433 PEARS MARGUERITE

4 oz. seedless raisins
3 tablespoons brandy
3 large pears or 1 large can pear halves
¼ pint double cream or ice cream
1 oz. glacé cherries
1 oz. angelica

To decorate:
angelica

Chop cherries and angelica. Place seedless raisins in small pan and bring slowly to boil. Leave to get cold. Peel, core and halve the pears. (If using canned pears drain off syrup.) Whisk cream until beginning to thicken, stir in raisins and brandy, cherries and angelica. Pile cream mixture on pear halves, decorate with angelica leaves and chill for approximately 30 minutes.

434 PEAR AND MINCEMEAT PIE

6 oz. puff pastry*
2 heaped tablespoons mincemeat
1 large can pears
currants

* If using frozen puff pastry buy a small packet

Defrost the pastry then roll out to approximately 9 inches square. Using a plate, flan ring or cake tin as a guide, cut an 8-inch circle with a sharp knife and place gently on a baking sheet. Score the pastry all round ½ inch from the edge taking care not to cut right through. Spread with mincemeat up to this cut. Roll the pastry trimmings thinner and cut 8 holly leaf shapes, 1½ inches long and place in a small tin. Drain the pears and brush the edge of the pie and the holly leaves with pear juice. Bake the pie in a very hot oven (475 °F. — Gas Mark 8) for approximately 15 minutes and the holly leaves for approximately 5 minutes. Arrange the pear halves, cut side down and radiating from the centre, on top of the mincemeat. Serve warm and arrange the holly leaves in pairs around the edge of the dish. Place two currants for berries between each pair of leaves.

435 ROSY PEARS

This is a very good way of softening hard cooking pears. Simmer them in a syrup made with very little sugar, with redcurrant jelly, port wine and a little lemon juice.

436 'STARRY GAZIE' PIE

Filling:

6 large pears
preserved stem ginger
1 — 2 oz. coconut*
1 oz. sugar

Crust:

8 oz. flour
little syrup from the ginger
2 oz. butter
milk
* If using sweetened coconut omit sugar

Core, but do not peel the pears. Stuff centres with sweetened coconut mixed with finely chopped ginger. Arrange pears in pie dish, stem ends upwards.

Prepare some mixture: rub the butter into the flour and moisten with enough milk and ginger syrup to make a soft dough. Roll out dough lightly, and pat into shape to fit pie dish. Cut circles in dough to fit round tops of pears and place in position. Brush with milk and bake in centre of moderately hot oven (400 °F. — Gas Mark 5) till crust is crisp and golden. Before serving top each pear with an extra lump of ginger and decorate with pieces of angelica to simulate the pear stems.

427 ORANGE RAISIN SHORTBREAD

4 tablespoons orange juice   6 oz. plain flour
   or orange squash   2 oz. castor sugar
4 oz. seedless raisins   4 oz. butter

Put orange juice and seedless raisins into small sauce-pan, bring slowly to the boil. Turn into basin and leave to cool, preferably overnight. Sieve flour into basin, add sugar and rub in butter until mixture resembles fine breadcrumbs. Knead into dough, divide into 2. Form into 2 equal-sized rounds. Place 1 round on greased baking sheet, spread raisins over surface, top with second round pressing down firmly. Pinch edges with floured fingers. Prick well. Bake in a very moderate oven (325 °F. — 350 °F. — Gas Mark 3) for 45 minutes. Mark into segments and when cool remove from tin.

428 ORANGE AND REDCURRANT RING

Press vanilla ice cream into very cold ring mould and leave in the freezing compartment of the refrigerator. Meanwhile peel and slice oranges and frost redcurrants by dusting with icing sugar. Mix some of the sliced oranges with canned pineapple and raspberries. Turn out the ice cream ring and fill centre with the orange, pineapple and raspberry mixture. Top the ring with the frosted currants and arrange halved slices of orange and raspberries round. *Illustrated in colour picture no. 18.*

429 ORANGE CURAÇAO SNOWCUPS

2 large oranges   1 brick vanilla ice cream
1 miniature bottle curaçao   raisins and angelica

Cut the oranges in half and carefully remove the fruit, divide into segments and remove the pips. Soak the fruit in the liqueur for 2—3 hours. Just before serving

put the prepared segments into the orange 'cups'. Spoon ice cream on top of the fruit and decorate with raisins and angelica. Serve at once.

430 PASSION FRUIT

This is generally obtainable canned and can be served with cream or ice cream, or serve fruit raw.

431 PASSION FRUIT JELLY

Measure passion fruit purée (fresh or canned) and add enough water to give just over 1 pint. Dissolve a lemon jelly in this. Turn out and decorate with nuts and cream.

422   *ORANGES*

TO STORE. Whole oranges can be bottled (Recipe 498) which means that several oranges could be preserved ready for a convenient time for marmalade of all kinds (Recipes 639—655). The fruit sections can be bottled but on the whole the results tend to be disappointing.

TO SERVE. Use in salads, flavouring cakes, biscuits etc., sauces and sweets of every kind. Oranges can also be sliced and baked in the oven. Sliced orange makes a delicious garnish for roast duck (illustrated in colour picture no. 34).

Cut the oranges in half and remove pulp, being careful not to cut through the skin. Squeeze pulp in a strainer with the back of a spoon and strain off juice. Measure ½ pint of lemon and orange juice; if necessary add a little water. Blend cornflour with a little of the orange juice and put in a saucepan with the rest of the fruit juices, sugar and rind. Bring slowly to the boil, stirring constantly. When cold, fold in whipped cream. Heap the mixture in four orange halves, pipe a little whipped cream round the edges and replace the tops. Decorate with piece of angelica cut in leaf and stalk shapes.

423   ORANGE WEDDING

The scent of orange blossom fills the air. This amusing little table decoration can be made with 4 large Jaffa oranges. Apart from these, you only need a few bits of coloured crêpe paper, 12 ball-headed pins, a piece of white net, and dexterous fingers. Even when the bloom has worn off this ecstatic couple, you can eat their sweet, juicy interiors!

424   ORANGE FOAM PUDDING

3 oz. whipped-up cooking fat	1 level teaspoon baking powder
4 oz. castor sugar	grated rind and juice of 2 oranges
4 oz. breadcrumbs	
2 egg yolks	

Apple meringue:

1 egg white	1 grated apple
2 oz. castor sugar	

Cream the fat and sugar together. Add the egg yolks, breadcrumbs, orange juice and rind and baking powder. Put into a 1-pint mould brushed with fat. Cover with greaseproof paper, also brushed with melted fat, and steam for 45 minutes.

To make meringue, whisk egg white stiffly. Whisk in 1 heaped dessertspoon of sugar, fold in remaining sugar and lastly the grated apple. Turn out the pudding and serve hot with apple meringue piled on top.

425 CRÈMES ORANGES À LA LOUISE

4 large Jaffa oranges	2 oz. sugar
2 level tablespoons cornflour	1 teaspoon orange rind
juice of 1 lemon	¼ pint whipped cream
	angelica

426   ORANGE DESSERT CAKE

3 eggs	4 — 5 medium sized oranges
4 oz. castor sugar	2 heaped tablespoons boiled sieved apricot jam
3 level dessertspoons cornflour	1 tablespoon rum or orange liqueur
2 oz. whipped-up cooking fat	2½ oz. plain flour

Break the eggs into a basin and stir in the sugar. Place the basin over a pan of hot water and whisk eggs and sugar for 5 minutes. Remove basin to the table and continue to whisk for 5 minutes without heat. Sieve the flour and cornflour and very lightly fold into the whisked mixture. Lastly fold in very slowly the melted whipped-up cooking fat. Place in a 7-inch greased and floured tin. Bake in the middle of a moderate oven (375 °F. — Gas Mark 4) for 35—40 minutes. Cool on a cake rack. When cold split open and put a layer of thinly sliced orange rings. Sprinkle over with rum or liqueur and sandwich together. Brush over the top with boiled sieved jam, cover with overlapping slices of orange and remaining jam. Decorate with whipped cream.

416   *MANGOES*

TO STORE. Mangoes make a perfect chutney (Recipe 549).

TO SERVE. This fruit is delicious eaten fresh and to be at its best must look almost bad. It can also be stewed.

417   *MELON*

TO STORE. This is not a very good fruit to preserve since its delicate flavour is lost. It can be used in jam (Recipe 597) in place of marrow.

TO SERVE. A perfect hors-d'oeuvre with sugar and ginger or with slices of Parma ham or ripe figs.

418   FRUIT AND ICE CREAM MELON

1 cantaloup melon	*1 lb. mixed fresh fruits*
2 — 3 oz. castor sugar	*1 brick vanilla ice cream*

Cut off the top of the melon, scoop out the seeds and discard them. Remove the pulp from inside the melon and cut it into cubes. Mix the melon with the fresh fruits and dredge with sugar. When ready to serve place the fruit into the melon and top with spoonfuls of ice cream. If desired decorate with fresh fruit. Serve immediately.

419   *MEDLARS*

TO STORE. Medlars can be bottled (Recipe 498) or canned (Recipe 665) but are best in jam or jelly.

TO SERVE. Because of their rather strong flavour and the fact that they are now becoming very rare medlars are generally found in a preserve. They can, however, be eaten raw or stewed.

420   *MULBERRIES*

TO STORE. Mulberries can be bottled (Recipe 498) although their soft appearance makes them look very unappetising. They can be used in jam (Recipe 598) or jelly (Recipe 626).

TO SERVE. Another fruit that has become extremely rare. It looks like a very over-ripe loganberry and is delicious in a preserve, or can be eaten raw.

421   *NECTARINES*

Store and serve like peaches (Recipe 437).

Orange foam pudding (Recipe 424, see opposite)

407 *LEMONS*

TO STORE. Lemons can be bottled but tend to become very soft and not very satisfactory. The juice is often obtained canned or in concentrated form. Lemons can be used in marmalade (Recipes 641, 646) and chutney (Recipe 553).

TO SERVE. A lemon is an invaluable fruit for the juice adds flavour to sauces and savoury dishes as well as providing wonderful sweets. Many people prefer lemon juice to vinegar on salads. A lemon will keep rather fresher if it is put into a jar of cold water and kept in a cold place.

408 LEMON CHIFFON MOULD

3 oz. seedless raisins
1 orange or lemon jelly
¼ pint hot water
1 small can evaporated milk
1 lemon

Plump seedless raisins by covering with cold water, bring to boil and leave to stand for 5 minutes. Drain. Dissolve jelly in hot water, allow to cool and place in refrigerator until it begins to set. Whip evaporated milk until it is thick enough to leave a trail behind. Stir into lemon or orange jelly, add grated lemon rind, juice and raisins. Pour into 1 pint mould and chill until set.

409 LEMON MOUSSE

6 medium or small eggs
¼ pint double cream
juice of 1½ lemons
½ oz. powdered gelatine
1 oz. icing sugar
1 tablespoon water

Separate the eggs. Beat yolks and sugar together until thick and light coloured, then beat in the lemon juice. Beat the cream until just thick, but not too stiff, and the egg whites until very stiff. Soak gelatine in the water,

then melt over a very low heat. Stir in the yolks and when starting to stiffen, remove from heat and fold in the whites. Add half the cream, mixing well so that the mixture becomes light and fluffy. Turn into a serving dish rinsed with cold water. When set, decorate with the remainder of the cream.

410 *LIMES*

TO STORE. As lemons (Recipe 407), excellent in marmalade (Recipe 642) or in place of lemons in syrup (Recipe 506).

TO SERVE. As lemons (Recipe 407). If using in any sweet recipes in place of lemons you will find more sugar is required.

411 LIME SHERBERT

Remove peel from 1 lb. limes and squeeze out all the juice. Simmer the peel with 4 oz. sugar and ¼ pint water for 10 minutes. Strain, add liquid to juice. Freeze for 30 minutes in freezing tray then add 2 stifflybeaten egg whites and freeze until firm.

412 *LOGANBERRIES*

TO STORE. Loganberries can be bottled (Recipe 498), canned (Recipe 665) or frozen (Recipe 723) and used for jam (Recipe 595) or jelly (Recipe 629).

TO SERVE. Loganberries can be eaten like raspberries (Recipe 454) but most people prefer loganberries cooked rather than raw since they are so much sharper than raspberries.

413 LOGANBERRY SHERBERT

2 – 3 oz. sugar
¼ pint water
1 lb. loganberries
grated rind and juice of lemon
2 egg whites

Heat sugar, water, loganberries and lemon rind until soft. Rub through sieve, add lemon juice, taste and add more sugar if desired. Put into freezing tray, leave for 20 – 30 minutes until lightly frozen, then stir into the 2 egg whites which should be stiffly beaten. Re-freeze until firm. Serve by itself or with wafer biscuits.

414 *LYCHEES*

TO STORE. Lychees can be bottled (Recipe 498) or canned (Recipe 665).

TO SERVE. This Chinese fruit is delicious fresh as well as canned. It is fairly expensive and therefore most people will serve it with cream, ice cream etc. to make it go further.

415 LYCHEES IN SYRUP

Shell the lychees and remove the fruit; make a syrup of sugar and water and poach them gently in this.

400 GRAPEFRUIT

TO STORE Grapefruit can be bottled (Recipe 498), canned (Recipe 665) or made into marmalade (Recipe 645).

TO SERVE. Although grapefruit is most popular as a cold hors-d'oeuvre it is also extremely good when heated. Segments of grapefruit can be added to fruit and savoury salads.

401 HOT GRAPEFRUIT

Prepare the grapefruit as usual but spread the top with a little butter, sprinkle on brown sugar and a little spice or sherry and heat under the grill or in the oven.

402 CALIFORNIAN PRAWN COCKTAIL

2 Servings

1 grapefruit   *lettuce, shredded*
1 packet frozen prawns   *mayonnaise*
tomato purée

Serve ½ grapefruit per person. Scrape out the flesh and mix with chopped prawns and shredded lettuce. Combine with mayonnaise which has been tinted with a little tomato purée. Put the mixture back into the grapefruit halves and garnish with prawns.

403 GREENGAGES

TO STORE. Greengages can be bottled (Recipe 498) or canned (Recipe 665) or made into jam (Recipe 592). Very often large handsome greengage plums are called greengages but in fact a true greengage is a small neat fruit. Bottled greengages are often cloudy but this is no detriment at all.

TO SERVE. Excellent stewed hot or cold and really ripe greengages are delicious served raw.

404 GREENGAGE PIE

Put the fruit into a pie dish with sugar to taste and a little water. Cover with short crust pastry (see Recipe 227) and bake in the centre of a hot oven for 20 minutes then lower the heat to moderately hot for a further 15—20 minutes.

405 GREENGAGE PUDDING

As gooseberry pudding (Recipe 395).

406 GREENGAGE SPONGE PUDDING

12 oz. — 1 lb. greengages   *little water*
sugar to taste

For the sponge:

3 oz. margarine   *4 oz. flour (with plain flour*
2 eggs   *1 teaspoon baking*
3 oz. sugar   *powder)*

Put fruit, water and sugar at the bottom of a pie dish. Cream margarine and sugar until soft and light. Beat in eggs gradually then stir in flour. Spread over fruit and bake for approximately 1 hour in centre of moderate oven (375°F. — Gas Mark 4), reducing heat after 35—40 minutes if the pudding is becoming too brown.

392   FIGS

TO STORE. Figs can be bottled (Recipe 498), dried (Recipe 491), canned (Recipe 665) or used for jam (Recipe 588).

TO SERVE. When ripe serve as a dessert fruit or they can be cooked in syrup. As a dried fruit figs are excellent stewed or in fruit salads.

393   GOOSEBERRIES

TO STORE. Gooseberries can be bottled (Recipe 498), canned (Recipe 665), frozen (Recipe 723) and used for jelly (Recipe 621) and wine (Recipe 690).

TO SERVE. Dessert gooseberries are delicious when raw. Most people prefer gooseberries cooked and served in pies, puddings, etc.

394   GOOSEBERRY FOOL

Top and tail gooseberries and cook with no water, or if very under-ripe with 2 or 3 tablespoons only, and sugar to taste. Rub through a sieve and add an equal quantity of thick custard or whipped cream. A few drops of green colouring can be added if wished.

395   GOOSEBERRY PUDDING

Top and tail gooseberries. Line a basin with wafer-thin suet crust pastry (see below) and fill with fruit and sugar. Cover with pastry and greased paper, steam for approximately 2—2½ **hours.** Serve with custard or cream.

SUET CRUST PASTRY

8 oz. flour (with plain flour use 2 level teaspoons baking powder) water to mix	2—4 oz. finely shredded suet pinch salt

Sieve flour, salt and baking powder. Add suet. Mix to rolling consistency with cold water. Roll out thinly as this pastry rises.

396   GOOSEBERRY SAUCE

8 oz. gooseberries	1 or 2 tablespoons sugar
1 gill water	½ oz. margarine

Top and tail fruit. Put into a saucepan with the water, sugar and margarine. Simmer slowly until a very smooth mixture, then either rub through a sieve or beat with a wooden spoon until smooth. This fruit sauce is delicious with mackerel.

397   GRAPES

TO STORE. Grapes can be bottled (Recipe 498) but tend to be flavourless. They can be used for jam or jelly (substitute grapes for strawberries in Recipe 610) and wines (Recipe 691); but are best served fresh.

TO SERVE. Add to fruit salads, removing pips and skinning if wished. Use for cake decoration, trifles etc.

398   GRAPE BASKETS

4 oz. margarine	4 oz. self-raising flour
4 oz. castor sugar	(or plain flour with
2 eggs	1 teaspoon baking powder)

Filling and decoration:

2 tablespoons apricot jam	1 small bunch each green
2 oz. chopped nuts or coconut	and black grapes angelica
1 gill double cream	

Cream margarine and sugar together until light and fluffy. Beat in the eggs one at a time, adding a little of the sieved flour with the second egg. Fold in the remaining flour with a metal spoon. Place in a Swiss roll tin, 11 inches × 8 inches, previously brushed with melted margarine and lined with greaseproof paper. Bake in the middle of a moderate oven (375 °F. — Gas Mark 4) for 15—20 minutes. Cool on a wire tray.

Cut out 9 rounds with a 3-inch plain cutter and with a 2-inch plain cutter mark half-way through the centre of each. Remove this centre cake (and if liked use for trifle together with the other remaining sponge). Brush the sides with boiled, sieved apricot jam and roll in nuts or coconut. Whisk the double cream until stiff. Fill the centre of each 'basket' with cream. Cut the green and black grapes in half, remove the pips and decorate with these. Cut 9 thin strips from the angelica about 5—6 inches long and stick in to form a 'handle'.

399   LEMON AND GRAPE ALASKA

1 8-inch baked flan case (see Recipe 227)	8 oz. grapes, halved and seeded

Lemon curd

1 oz. butter or margarine	2 oz. castor sugar
2 egg yolks	rind and juice of 1 lemon

Meringue

2 egg whites	3 oz. castor sugar
1 brick vanilla ice cream	

Preheat the oven (475° F. — Gas Mark 9) for 20 minutes. Meanwhile, melt the butter in a small basin over a pan of hot water, add the 2 oz. sugar, egg yolks, the lemon rind and juice and stir until thick. Stand the flan case on an ovenproof plate, spread the lemon curd over the bottom and cover with the grapes. Whisk the egg whites until very stiff and dry, add half the sugar and continue whisking until again stiff, then gently fold in the remainder of the sugar with a metal spoon. Place the ice cream on top of the grapes then, working with a palette knife, quickly spread the meringue over the ice cream so that it is covered completely. 'Flash' cook, i. e. leave in hot oven 2—3 minutes until the meringue is tinged golden brown. Serve immediately.

384 CHERRIES

TO STORE. Cherries can be bottled (Recipe 498), are particularly good canned (Recipe 665), produce a wonderful jam if correctly made (Recipes 583, 584, 585), but are not very satisfactory frozen.

TO SERVE. Cherries can be eaten raw or cooked in pies, but when cooked they do need a little extra flavour added since, with the exception of morello cherries, they are inclined to lack flavour.

385 CHERRY LEMON WHIP

8 oz. fresh sweet cherries	2 egg yolks
1 pint water	1 gill cream (may be
juice of 2 lemons	omitted)
rind of 1 lemon	2 egg whites
4 oz. sugar or to taste	extra 2 tablespoons sugar
3 oz. fine semolina	1 tablespoon chopped walnuts

Pip the fresh cherries, leaving 4 with stems on for decoration, and chop roughly. Warm water, lemon juice, grated rind and sugar. Sprinkle in the semolina and cook, stirring, until thick and then cook very slowly for 2 minutes. Cool a little and beat in the egg yolks. Whisk in whipped cream. Beat egg whites to a stiff froth, gradually add the 2 tablespoons sugar and then fold into the cream mixture. Fold in the cherries and spoon the mixture into 4 individual dishes. Serve cold, each garnished with nuts and a cherry.

386 QUICK CHERRY CAKES

4 oz. luxury margarine	4 oz. self-raising flour
4 oz. castor sugar	1 level teaspoon baking
2 eggs	powder

Decoration:

¼ pint double cream	4 oz. fresh cherries

Place all the cake ingredients in a mixing bowl. Quickly mix together, then beat thoroughly with a wooden spoon. Place the mixture in 12—16 paper cases previously placed on a baking tray. Bake near the top of a moderately hot oven (400° F. — Gas Mark 5) for 15—20 minutes. Cool on a wire tray.
To decorate: Whisk the cream until thick. Pipe or spoon a 'swirl' of cream on to the top of each cake and decorate with fresh cherries.

387 CRANBERRIES

TO STORE. Cranberries can be bottled (Recipe 498), canned (Recipe 665) or frozen (Recipe 723).

TO SERVE. They can be stewed but they are at their best made into cranberry sauce to serve with poultry or this can be used with ice cream. See below.

388 CRANBERRY SAUCE

12 oz. cranberries	2 tablespoons water
3 oz. sugar	1 tablespoon port or sherry

Heat water and sugar together, add the fruit and cook until tender. Add port or sherry if wished.

389 DAMSONS

TO STORE. Damsons can be bottled (Recipe 498) or canned (Recipe 665) and used for jam (Recipe 586), damson 'port' (Recipe 688), pickles (Recipe 536) and chutney (Recipe 546).

TO SERVE. Damsons have a very rich flavour in cooking and can be served either by themselves or with apples. They tend to be rather full of stones so in cold sweets it is a good idea to sieve the fruit.

390 DAMSON AMBER

5—6 oz. short crust pastry	2 eggs
(see Recipe 227)	sugar to sweeten when
1 lb. damsons	cooking
2 oz. castor sugar	knob of butter
for meringue	

Cook the damsons with plenty of sugar, but very little water, until soft. Take a few for decoration, but sieve the rest of the fruit. Meanwhile, line a flan ring or sandwich tin with the pastry and bake 'blind' in a hot oven (425—450° F. — Gas Mark 6—7) until crisp and golden but not too brown. Whisk the egg yolks into the damson pulp, taste and add sugar if wished. Put into the flan case and bake for a further 15 minutes in just a moderate heat (375° F. — Gask Mark 4). Whisk the egg whites until very stiff, fold in the castor sugar, pile over the damson mixture and brown for a few minutes in a moderate oven. Decorate with whole damsons.

391 DAMSON SOUFFLÉ FLAN

Use the same recipe as for plum soufflé flan (Recipe 448) but with a thick damson purée.

savoury butter on the fingers, also some chutney. Spread the remainder on the bananas and grill for a few minutes. Place grilled bananas on fingers of toast and serve very hot garnished with a tiny sprig of parsley.

377 BLACKBERRIES

TO STORE. Blackberries are highly perishable so do not keep too long a period when fresh. They can be bottled (Recipe 498), frozen (Recipe 723) or canned (Recipe 665) and used for jam (Recipe 581), jelly (Recipe 618) and chutney (Recipe 545).

TO SERVE. Cook by themselves or with apples, to which they give a richness of flavour.

378 BLACKBERRY BALLS

4 oz. blackberries   1 tablespoon sugar
2 good tablespoons cake crumbs   icing sugar

Crush the blackberries, mix with the crumbs and sugar, form in balls and roll in icing sugar. Serve with ice cream.

379 HARVEST SUNDAE

8 oz. cooking apples   4 oz. blackberries
2 oz. sugar   vanilla ice cream

Peel, core and slice the apples and place in a pan with blackberries, sugar and 1 tablespoon water. Stew until tender. Arrange spoonfuls of vanilla ice cream in individual dishes and top with the hot stewed fruit.

380 BLACKCURRANTS

TO STORE. Blackcurrants can be bottled (Recipe 498), canned (Recipe 665) or frozen (Recipe 723), and used for syrup (Recipe 503), jam (Recipe 582), and wine (Recipe 686).

TO SERVE. There are innumerable ways to serve blackcurrants — in pies, in tarts, stewed and added to jellies, rubbed through a sieve and made into a fool. Care must be taken when simmering that the skins really are soft.

381 BLACKCURRANT FOOL

Cook blackcurrants with very little water and sugar to taste so that you have a thick purée. Rub through a sieve and add an equal quantity of thick custard or whipped cream.

382 BLUEBERRIES

TO STORE. Blueberries can be bottled (Recipe 498), canned (Recipe 665) or frozen (Recipe 723).

TO SERVE. Blueberries are one of the names given to a delicious fruit that generally grows wild. They are also called whortleberries or blaeberries. American huckleberries are a very similar fruit. Blueberries are extremely good cooked in pies, tarts etc., and can be obtained ready frozen.

383 BLUEBERRY SOUFFLÉ

1 packet frozen blueberries   2 eggs
   or about 8 oz. fresh   1 oz. castor sugar
   blueberries   1 gill cream (whipped)
chopped nuts and cream   ¼ oz. gelatine

Separate yolks from whites of eggs, whip the cream. Prepare soufflé case by tying a piece of stiff paper around the outside of the mould and standing well above the top of the mould. Defrost and sieve the blueberries and whisk together with egg yolks and sugar in a bowl standing over a saucepan of hot water until thick and creamy. Remove bowl from heat and water and continue whisking until cool. Dissolve gelatine in a little hot water and stir into mixture with half whipped cream. Finally fold in stiffly beaten egg whites, pour into soufflé case and chill. When set, remove paper. Decorate edge with chopped almonds dipped in green colouring and pipe with remaining cream.

BANANAS

TO STORE. Unless purchased green, bananas should be eaten fairly quickly. When rather black on the outside they are in perfect condition for small children. They can be bottled but it is not particularly satisfactory. They can be used in jam (Recipes 578, 579, 580).

TO SERVE. Bananas are at their best raw but are excellent cooked. They can be served as fritters, dipped in egg and breadcrumbs or batter and fried and these can be served either as a savoury dish with fried chicken Maryland or as a sweet. Baked with a little sugar, rum and butter they are delicious. In salads they blend well with cheese and vegetables

372 APPLE AND BANANA COMPOTE

Peel and slice apples and poach gently in a lemon flavoured syrup. Put into shallow dish and decorate with sliced bananas, glacé cherries and angelica. Serve hot or cold. Add banana just before serving to keep a good colour or put these with the cooked apples in the lemon flavoured syrup.

373 BANANA ALASKA

large block ice cream	3 egg whites
4 bananas	3 oz. castor sugar
8 oz. strawberries	whipped cream

Slice half the bananas on to a shallow, ovenproof dish and pile the ice cream in a pyramid shape on top. Stud the sides of the ice cream with alternate rows of strawberries and banana slices and spread the whipped cream on top. Cover the whole pyramid with a meringe made of the stiffly beaten egg whites into which the castor sugar has been carefully folded, 'flash' bake (2—3 minutes only) in a very hot oven (475°—500° F. — Gas Mark 8—9) and serve immediately.

374 BANANA HORNS

| 8 oz. puff pastry (see below) | little warmed jam |
| 3 or 4 not quite ripe bananas | fat for deep frying |

Roll out pastry about ¼ inch thick and cut in 4-inch squares. Peel bananas and cut in halves crosswise. Place ½ banana diagonally in centre of each square. Brush with jam or redcurrant jelly and roll up squares of pastry from corner. Brush edges of pastry with a little cold water to help rolled edges to stick together and press firmly. Heat fat (frying oil or a hydrogenated vegetable fat is best as it gets really hot without smoking) to 375° F. or until a 1-inch cube of bread browns in 40 seconds, and drop banana horns in, one at a time, giving the fat time to heat up again after

each horn has gone in before adding the next. Cook each for about 2 minutes until golden brown and crisp. Drain on absorbent kitchen paper and serve hot with a sprinkle of granulated sugar. The banana will be like cream inside the pastry.

PUFF PASTRY

8 oz. plain flour	cold water to mix
7—8 oz. fat	good pinch salt
few drops lemon juice	

Sieve flour and salt together. Mix to rolling consistency with cold water and lemon juice. Roll to oblong shape, make fat into neat block and place in centre of pastry and fold over it first the bottom section of pastry, and then the top section, so that fat is quite covered. Turn the dough at right angles, seal edges, 'rib' (depress with the rolling-pin at intervals) and roll out. Fold dough into envelope, turn it, seal edges, 'rib' and roll again. Repeat five times, so making seven rollings and seven folding in all. Put pastry to rest in a cold place once or twice between rollings to prevent it becoming sticky and soft. Always put it to rest before rolling for the last time.

375 FRUIT SALAD BOWL

¼ rings dessert apple	lettuce
¼ pieces banana	watercress
lemon juice	thick mayonnaise
crispbread	cheese spread or cream cheese

Prepare the fruit and brush lightly with lemon juice to preserve colour. Arrange a few lettuce leaves attractively in an individual bowl and the fruit neatly on top. Put a large spoonful of thick mayonnaise over the fruit, garnish with a sprig of watercress and serve with crispbread and cheese spread as a light meal.

376 SAVOURY BANANA TOAST

2 bananas	pinch curry powder
2—4 slices bread	few drops lemon juice
1 oz. butter	seasoning
chutney	

Toast the bread, peel the bananas, slice each in 2 lengthwise and then crosswise to make 4 pieces. Cut toast into fingers to fit the bananas. Cream butter and beat in the curry powder, lemon juice and seasoning. Spread a little

367   *APRICOTS*

TO STORE. Apricots will not store for any length of time when raw but are excellent bottled (Recipe 498), canned (Recipe 665), in jams (Recipes 574, 575, 576) or dried (Recipe 491). They are not so successful when frozen.

TO SERVE. Apricots have a very pronounced flavour in all dishes after being cooked and make delicious sweets, hot or cold.

368   APRICOT TART
Almond pastry

3½ fluid oz. (5 tablespoons) corn oil	7 oz. plain flour
2½ tablespoons iced or cold water	¼ level teaspoon salt
	1 oz. chopped blanched almonds

Filling

1 lb. fresh apricots	2 level teaspoons cornflour
1 gill water	few blanched almonds and
4 oz. sugar	cherries for decorating

To make the pastry:

Blend the corn oil and the water together well with a fork in a mixing bowl. Gradually add the salt sifted together with flour and work in the chopped almonds with the last of the flour. Mix with a fork or palette knife to form a rollable dough (slightly more or less flour may be required). Roll out between 2 sheets of greaseproof paper and use to line a 10-inch flat plate. Prick well and decorate the edge as liked. Bake 'blind' (empty) about 20 minutes in a hot oven (425 °F. — 450 °F. — Gas Mark 6—7).

To make the filling:

Make a syrup of the water and sugar. Wash, halve and stone the apricots then poach till tender in the syrup. Drain off the syrup and use to make a glaze. Arrange the apricots in the baked pastry case and decorate with glacé cherries and blanched almonds. Cover with the glaze.

To make the glaze:

Put the syrup from the apricots on to heat. Mix the cornflour smoothly with a little cold water, add to the syrup and boil for 3 minutes, stirring constantly. Allow to cool slightly before using.

This apricot tart is illustrated in colour picture no. 17.

369   APRICOT AND PEAR FLAN

¼ pint water	approx. 6 dessert pears
2 heaped tablespoons apricot jam	1 cooked pastry flan case (see Recipe 227)
few blanched almonds	1 teaspoon arrowroot

Peel and core the pears, keeping them in a weak brine until ready to coat them with the sauce. For the brine use 1 dessertspoon — quite flat — salt to 1 pint water. Drain and dry the pears well and arrange in the flan case. Blend the arrowroot with water and put into a saucepan together with the apricot jam. Brind slowly to the boil, stirring all the time; and cook gently until thickened and clear. Cool slightly; then pour over the pears and decorate with the almonds.

370   *AVOCADO PEARS*

TO STORE. These are very unsatisfactory if bottled or cooked. They must be purchased and eaten fresh.

TO SERVE. Unlike other fruit avocado pears are best served as a savoury. Take out stone, sprinkle avocado with French dressing (Recipe 343) and fill centre with shrimps, prawns etc.

361 APPLE YEAST RING

1 teaspoon sugar	1 fluid oz. corn oil
½ oz. yeast	1 egg
½ pint milk (approx.)	1 teaspoon salt
1 lb. flour	glacé icing
1 lb. red dessert apples	angelica

Cream the sugar and yeast together, and add a little warm milk. Sieve the flour and salt into a warm basin, and make a well in the centre. Pour in yeast mixture, corn oil and egg, and sufficient warm milk to make a pliable dough. Knead thoroughly. Put aside to prove for about 1 hour, in a warm place, until dough has doubled its size. Knead again lightly, and form into a ring. This quantity will make 2 small rings or 1 large one.

Prove again for about 20 minutes in a warm place. Mark the dough round the sides with a knife, and insert slices of apple, leaving the red skin on. Brush the ring with beaten egg and bake in a hot oven (425° F. — Gas Mark 6) for about 15 minutes, then reduce the heat to moderate and bake for about 15 minutes more, until ring sounds hollow when tapped on the bottom. When cold, coat with glacé icing, and decorate with chopped angelica. *Illustrated in colour picture no. 24.*

362 APPLE GINGERSNAP DESSERT

12 large gingersnaps or ginger biscuits	juice of 1 lemon
12 oz. cream or cottage cheese	2 tablespoons chopped walnuts
2 oz. castor sugar	4 rosy Worcester Pearmain eating apples
grated rind of 1 lemon	angelica

Sieve cheese. Arrange gingersnaps around the edge of a round shallow pie dish, fitting them closely together. Sweeten sieved cream cheese, or cottage cheese to taste with sugar, and flavour with 2 tablespoons lemon juice and the rind of 1 lemon. Stir in 2 tablespoons chopped walnuts and the diced flesh of 1 eating apple. Fill centre of the dish with the cheese mixture. Core remaining apples, but do not peel, and slice thickly. Dip apple slices in lemon juice to keep colour bright and arrange in a cartwheel round the dish on top of the cream cheese. Decorate centre with angelica 'leaves'.

363 APPLE RAISIN FINGERS

8 oz. short crust pastry (see Recipe 227)	3 oz. raisins
1 oz. fine cake crumbs or chopped nuts	3 large cooking apples
	1 — 2 oz. sugar
	pinch spice

Line square tin or round flan ring with half the pastry. Grate apples rather coarsely and mix with other ingredients. Spread over pastry. Cover with rest of the dough. Bake for 20 minutes in hot oven (425 – 450° F. — Gas Mark 6 – 7) then a further 20 minutes in moderate oven (375° F — Gas Mark 4). Serve whole or cut into fingers. The crumbs or nuts absorb apple juice.

364 GINGERBREAD RING WITH APPLE COMPOTE

5 oz. butter or margarine	2 level teaspoons baking powder
4 oz. brown sugar	1 oz. ground almonds
5 oz. black treacle or golden syrup	1 teaspoon grated lemon rind
1 tablespoon water	2 teaspoons powdered ginger
7 oz. plain flour	2 eggs

Put the butter, sugar, treacle and water into a thick pan and heat gently until the butter is melted. Sieve the dry ingredients and pour the treacle mixture into a well in the centre, beating hard until thoroughly mixed. Beat in the eggs gradually. Pour the mixture into a greased ring mould and bake in the centre of a very moderate oven (350° F. — Gas Mark 3) for about 1 hour until well risen and set. Allow to shrink slightly and unmould. Serve hot or cold, filling the centre with apple compote. Garnish with whipped cream and walnuts.

365 APPLE COMPOTE

2 lb. cooking apples	½ teaspoon cinnamon or ground ginger
2 dessertspoons water	
4-6 oz. castor sugar	lemon juice to taste

Peel, core and slice the apples and put in a thick saucepan with the water, sugar and cinnamon or ginger. Cover and cook till tender. Flavour to taste with lemon juice and add more sugar if desired. Lift into centre of gingerbread with a perforated spoon.

366 PAN BAKED FRUITS

4 pears, peeled but not cored	½ oz. cornflour
4 apples, peeled halfway down and cored	1 oz. butter
	¼ pint orange juice
3 oz. brown sugar	1 gill water
2 — 3 oz. stoned raisins	

Stuff the centre of each apple with chopped raisins and 1 oz. brown sugar and top with a nut of butter. Put the fruit into the frying pan. Add the orange juice, water and the rest of the sugar, cover and cook gently till tender, basting occasionally with the syrup. When cooked, remove from the pan and put into a serving dish. Mix the cornflour smoothly with a little cold water, add to the syrup and boil until it thickens. Add a little colouring as required and pour over the fruit.

Fruit

Fresh fruit is one of the easiest as well as the most delicious of desserts — so serve it often. In this book you will find not only new ideas for using fruit but ways to preserve each fruit where possible.

356 APPLES

TO STORE. First class dessert or cooking apples may be stored in a cold place. Keep the apples well spread out and discard any that are imperfect for long storage. Apples may also be stored by bottling (Recipe 498), canning (Recipe 665), drying (Recipe 490) and deep freezing, and used in jam (Recipe 577), jelly (Recipe 616) and chutney (Recipes 541, 542).

TO SERVE. Apples can be served in a variety of ways: raw, in salads, in sauces, pies and hot and cold puddings. They have a tendency to discolour if left in the air so either squeeze over a little lemon juice or keep in brine (Recipe 520) until ready to serve.

357 STAR APPLE SALAD

3 oz. black grapes, peeled   2 stalks celery, chopped
3 oz. black grapes, unpeeled   2 oz. chopped walnuts
2 eating apples, pared,   parsley to garnish
   cored and diced   mayonnaise
1 eating apple, cored and
   sliced

Mix ingredients together and toss in mayonnaise. Arrange cored unpeeled apple slices in the centre in a star shape. *Illustrated opposite.*

358 APPLE MERINGUE

6 eating apples   1 tablespoon redcurrant
¼ pint lemon juice   jelly
4 oz. castor sugar   2 egg whites
1½ oz. granulated sugar

Peel and core the apples. Cut them in half and simmer in water in which there is a little lemon juice. Reserve rest of juice. Do not allow the apples to break. Place in a buttered ovenproof dish. Combine remainder of lemon juice, the granulated sugar and the redcurrant jelly in a pan. Bring to the boil and pour over apples. Whip the egg whites very stiffly. Fold in the castor sugar. Pipe in circles on the apples and brown slowly in the oven. The centres should be filled with chocolate sauce after cooking.

359 BLUSHING APPLE DUMPLINGS

4 medium-sized baking   red colouring
   apples   pinch salt
½ pint water   3 oz. whipped-up cooking fat
4 oz. sugar   3 dessertspoons cold water
6 oz. plain flour   pinch nutmeg

Peel and core the apples. Put parings with the ½ pint water, cook for 5 minutes and strain. Add 2 oz. sugar, cover and cook for a further 5 minutes to make a syrup. Add red colouring. Sieve flour and salt and rub in the cooking fat until the mixture looks like fine breadcrumbs. Add the water and mix to a smooth dough. Roll out fairly thinly and cut into 9-inch × 3-inch strips with a pastry wheel. Wrap one strip of pastry round each apple, sealing at the bottom only. Mix the remaining 2 oz. sugar with the nutmeg and put into the centre of each apple. Top each with a small pat of fat. Place in a fireproof dish, pour the syrup over and bake in centre of a moderately hot oven (400° F. — Gas Mark 5) for 50 minutes. Baste with the syrup after baking for 40 minutes. Serve hot, with or without cream.

360 GERMAN APPLE TART

6 oz. short crust pastry   2 oz. sugar
   (see Recipe 227)   1 large or 2 small eggs
1 lb. cooking apples   ½ gill cream from the top of
2 oz. margarine   milk or evaporated milk or
2 oz. blanched almonds   fresh milk
1 dessertspoon grated lemon
   rind

Line a deep pie plate with the short crust pastry and bake 'blind' in the middle of a hot oven (450° F. — Gas Mark 7) for 10 minutes. Melt the margarine, then mix with all the other ingredients. The apples should be cut into thin fingers and the almonds halved. Pour into the pastry case, after it has been partially cooked, and put back into the oven, reducing the heat to 375° F. — Gas Mark 4. Leave for another 25 minutes. Serve hot or cold, dredged with sugar.

15 FISH MAYONNAISE IN TOMATO CASES (Recipe 355)

13   FRANKFURTERS AND CHEESE SAUCE (Recipe 336)

14   ASPARAGUS WITH MEAT BALLS AND BANANA FRITTERS (Recipe 7)

12   MIXED VEGETABLES

345   MAGIC MAYONNAISE

1 small can full cream condensed milk	½ teaspoon salt
1 gill salad oil or melted butter	1 teaspoon mustard
	dash cayenne pepper
2 egg yolks	1 gill vinegar or lemon juice

Place all the ingredients in a bowl and beat well with a whisk until the mixture thickens. The mayonnaise can be stored in a refrigerator for a very long time.

346   MANGO CREAM DIP

1 gill double cream	1 level dessertspoon mango chutney, chopped if necessary
1 dessertspoon Worcestershire sauce	
¼ level teaspoon made mustard	salt and pepper
	paprika

Half whip the cream, add remaining ingredients and mix together, being careful not to overwhip the cream. Serve with chicken salad.

347 MAYONNAISE WITHOUT EGGS

1 level teaspoon mustard	pinch pepper
¼ teaspoon salt	1 small can evaporated milk
1 teaspoon sugar	¼ pint olive oil
	2 — 3 tablespoons wine vinegar

Put the mustard into a bowl with sugar, salt and a large pinch of pepper. Add the evaporated milk. Mix and beat in by degrees the olive oil. Add the vinegar, when the mixture will thicken. Season to taste.

This is a specially quick and easy way of making mayonnaise because there is no danger of curdling.

348   SALAD CREAM

1 oz. butter or 1 tablespoon oil	¼ gill vinegar
1 oz. flour	1 teaspoon sugar
1 egg	¼ teaspoon salt
¼ pint milk	good pinch pepper and dry mustard

Mix the flour and seasonings together with a little of the cold milk. Bring the remainder of the milk to the boil and pour over, stirring thoroughly. Put the mixture into the saucepan, adding the butter or oil and beaten egg and cook very slowly until the sauce coats the back of a wooden spoon. Remove from the heat and whisk in the vinegar. Pour at once into a screw topped bottle. This will keep for some days if stored in a cool place.

349   SLIMMING SALAD DRESSING

If you are a 'mayonnaise lover', to make a good substitute blend a little seasoning and lemon juice with plain yoghourt or with milk. Milk gives a thinner dressing.

350   SNAPPY CHEESE DRESSING

4 oz. cottage cheese	¼ teaspoon Worcestershire sauce
2 oz. blue cheese, crumbled	
1 teaspoon grated onion	3 tablespoons fresh or cultured cream or top of the milk
1 teaspoon made mustard	

Blend cheeses well together, beating with an electric mixer or by hand. Add the onion, mustard and Worcestershire sauce. Fold in the cream.

351   SWEET FRENCH DRESSING

1 teaspoon vinegar	3 dessertspoons olive oil
1 teaspoon salt	1 dessertspoon white wine or vinegar or 1½ dessertspoons lemon juice
pinch paprika	
1 — 2 teaspoons sugar	

Shake all well together and pour the dressing over the salad just before serving.

352   TARTARE SAUCE

A cold tartare sauce is made by blending chopped parsley, gherkins and capers with mayonnaise. The quantities depend very much on personal taste.

353   TOMATO MAYONNAISE

Add tomato purée or pulp and a few drops of Tabasco or Worcestershire sauce to mayonnaise.

354   VINAIGRETTE DRESSING

2 dessertspoons vinegar (wine vinegar, cider vinegar or Tarragon vinegar)	5 dessertspoons olive oil
	good pinch salt
	pepper to taste

Mix all ingredients in bowl.

355   FISH MAYONNAISE IN TOMATO CASES

1 lb. cooked flaked fish	1 gill mayonnaise (Recipe 337)
chopped spring onions or chives	
	parsley
large firm tomatoes (allow 2 each person)	chopped hard-boiled eggs

Remove pulp of tomato and sieve to remove pips. Mix gently with flaked fish, chopped chives and parsley and bind with the mayonnaise. Season well. Stuff the tomatoes with the mixture and top with chopped egg. Serve with mixed salad.
Illustrated in colour picture no. 15.

Salad Dressings and Mayonnaise

A good salad dressing adds not only flavouring but additional nourishment to a salad. If using French dressing toss the salad in this some little time before serving.

337 CLASSIC MAYONNAISE

1 egg yolk
good pinch salt, pepper and mustard

¼ — 1 gill olive oil
1 dessertspoon vinegar
1 dessertspoon warm water

Put the egg yolk and seasonings into a basin. Gradually beat in the oil, drop by drop, stirring all the time until the mixture is thick. When you find it creamy stop adding oil, for too much will make the mixture curdle. Beat in the vinegar gradually, then the warm water. Use when fresh. If using an electric blender, put egg, seasoning and vinegar into goblet. Switch on for a few seconds, then pour oil in steadily.

338 ATOCHA MAYONNAISE

6-oz. can evaporated milk
1 gill olive oil
1 gill vinegar or lemon juice

salt and pepper
about ⅓ teaspoon castor sugar

Pour the milk into a bowl and whisk in the oil gradually, then the vinegar or lemon juice. Season to taste with salt, pepper and sugar.

339 COCKTAIL DIP OR SALAD DRESSING

1 carton or bottle plain yoghourt
1 heaped tablespoon dried sliced onions

¼ level teaspoon salt
dash pepper

Mix all the ingredients together in a bowl. Leave in a cool place for a minimum of 6 hours. Serve with plain cocktail biscuits or potato crisps or as a low calorie dressing for salads.

340 CURRIED MAYONNAISE

Add a little curry powder and paste to mayonnaise.

341 ECONOMICAL SALAD DRESSING

1 small can full cream condensed milk
¼ teaspoon salt

¼ pint vinegar
1 teaspoon dry mustard

Mix all the ingredients and beat well. Chill or cool before serving.

342 FAMILY MAYONNAISE

3 tablespoons flour
1 teaspoon dry mustard
few grains cayenne or pepper
1 teaspoon salt

1 egg
¼ pint water
4 tablespoons vinegar
3 tablespoons olive oil
1 tablespoon sugar

Blend the flour, mustard and seasoning to a paste with the egg. Stir in the water gradually. Add the vinegar and cook over boiling water until thick and then allow to cook for a further 5 minutes. Cool and beat in the oil.

343 FRENCH DRESSING

1 dessertspoon vinegar
1 tablespoon salad oil
pinch sugar

1 tablespoon finely chopped parsley or chives
salt and pepper

Mix the ingredients for the dressing together in a basin.

344 GREEN MAYONNAISE

Add finely chopped parsley, chives, sage and thyme to mayonnaise.

330 BROWN SAUCE

(coating consistency)

1 oz. cooking fat or dripping	*1 oz. flour*
¼ pint brown stock	*salt and pepper*

Method of making as white sauce (Recipe 312). For a better flavour fry a little chopped onion and other vegetables in the dripping or fat first, using 2 oz. of this. Strain if wished.

331 HOLLANDAISE SAUCE

2 egg yolks	*1 — 2 tablespoons lemon juice*
2 — 4 oz. butter	*or white wine vinegar*
pinch cayenne pepper	*salt and pepper*

Try to use a double saucepan for hollandaise and similar sauces. Put the egg yolks, seasonings and vinegar into the top of the pan. Whisk over hot water until sauce begins to thicken. Add the butter in very small pieces, whisking in each pat and allowing it to melt before adding the next. DO NOT ALLOW TO BOIL otherwise it will curdle. If too thick, add a little cream.

Variations on Hollandaise Sauce

Variation	Method	To accompany
332 **Béarnaise sauce**	Add finely chopped shallot and extra pepper to ingredients for hollandaise sauce. Add little chopped parsley and tarragon vinegar	Steak
333 **Mousseline sauce**	Use only 1 oz. butter to the 2 egg yolks and add a little cream and grated nutmeg	Asparagus, broccoli and other vegetables

334 CHICORY AND HAM IN CHEESE SAUCE

8 small heads chicory	*8 thin slices cooked ham*
¼ pint water	*(approx. 8 oz.)*
few drops lemon juice	*¾ pint rich cheese sauce (see below)*

Butter a casserole, put in the washed heads of chicory, and pour over the water to which a few drops of lemon juice have been added. Cover with a buttered paper and the lid. Braise the chicory in a moderate oven (375° F. — Gas Mark 4) 50—60 minutes until tender. Drain well, then wrap each in a slice of cooked ham. Arrange neatly in a fireproof dish and coat with the cheese sauce. Reheat in a moderate oven (375° F. — Gas Mark 4) for 15—20 minutes, and serve with crisp toast.

335 RICH CHEESE SAUCE

1½ oz. butter	*6 oz. grated Cheddar cheese*
1½ oz. flour	*pinch salt and cayenne*
¾ pint milk	*pepper*

Heat the butter gently, remove from heat and stir in the flour. Return to the heat and cook gently for a few minutes so that the 'roux' does not brown. Again remove the pan and gradually blend in the cold milk. Bring to the boil and cook, stirring with a wooden spoon, until smooth. Add cheese and seasoning.

336 FRANKFURTERS WITH CHEESE SAUCE

¼ pint white sauce (Recipe 312)	*2 heaped tablespoons Swiss processed Gruyère cheese*
3 oz. cooked macaroni	*8 frankfurter sausages*
2 medium sized tomatoes	

Make up the sauce and add half the cheese with the macaroni. Season to taste. Pour a little of this mixture over the bottom of a fireproof dish. Slit the frankfurters lengthwise and stuff with the rest of the cheese macaroni. Place them crosswise down the length of the dish alternately with a chunky piece of tomato. Sprinkle with the rest of the cheese and grill until brown. *Illustrated in colour picture no. 13.*

Sauces

WHITE SAUCE

312

1 oz. butter or margarine   salt and pepper
1 oz. flour
¼ pint milk for coating consistency, i.e. sauce
¼ pint milk for panada or binding consistency
1 pint milk for thin white sauce for soups

Heat the butter gently, remove from the heat and stir in the flour. Return to the heat and cook gently for a few minutes, so that the 'roux', as the butter and flour mixture is called, does not brown. Again remove the pan from the heat and gradually blend in the cold milk. Bring to the boil and cook, stirring with a wooden spoon, until smooth. Season well. If any small lumps have formed whisk sharply.

Variations on basic White Sauce

Variation	Method	To accompany
313 Anchovy sauce	Add chopped anchovies or 1 teaspoon anchovy essence	Fish dishes
314 Cheese sauce	Stir in 3—6 oz. grated cheese when sauce has thickened, and add a little mustard	Vegetable, meat, fish and savoury dishes
315 Caper sauce	Use ¼ pint milk and ¼ pint stock. Add 2 teaspoons caper and little caper vinegar	Boiled lamb; can also be served with fish
316 Fish sauce	Use ¼ pint fish stock and ¼ pint milk	Fish
317 Egg sauce	Add chopped hard-boiled egg	Boiled chicken
318 Onion sauce	Boil 3 onions, chop or slice and add to sauce — use little onion stock	Lamb, mutton or sausages
319 Parsley sauce	Add 1—2 teaspoons chopped parsley and squeeze lemon juice if wished	Fish — broad beans
320 Creamed tomato sauce	Whisk a thick tomato purée (which should be hot but not boiling) into hot white sauce. Do not boil together	Fish, meat and savoury and vegetable dishes
321 Cucumber sauce	Whisk about ¼ pint thick cucumber purée into white sauce, add little lemon juice, green colouring and cream	Fish and vegetable dishes
322 Horseradish sauce (hot)	Whisk about 1 dessertspoon vinegar and 2 tablespoons grated horseradish into white sauce. Add small amount of cream and pinch sugar	Beef, hot trout
323 Mushroom sauce	Simmer 2—4 oz. chopped mushrooms in the milk until tender. Use this in the white sauce	All types of savoury dishes
324 Béchamel sauce	Simmer pieces of very finely chopped onion, carrot, celery in milk. Strain and make as white sauce	In place of white sauce as rich flavour
325 Economical hollandaise sauce	Make white sauce, remove from heat and whisk in 1 egg, 1 dessertspoon lemon juice or vinegar. Cook gently without boiling for a few minutes	Fish or with vegetable dish
326 Maître d'hôtel sauce	As white sauce, but use half fish stock. Add 2 teaspoons chopped parsley and 3 tablespoons thick cream just before serving	Fish
327 Oyster sauce	Make béchamel sauce, add about 12 oysters and little cream just before serving — do not over-cook	Fish
328 Prawn or shrimp sauce	Make white sauce, add about ¼ pint chopped prawns and a little anchovy essence just before serving. If using fresh prawns simmer shells and use ¼ pint stock instead of the same amount of milk	Fish
329 Tartare sauce (hot)	Make béchamel sauce, then whisk in 2 egg yolks, 1 tablespoon cream, 1 tablespoon capers, 1 teaspoon chopped gherkin, 1 teaspoon chopped parsley and a squeeze of lemon juice. Cook gently for a few minutes without boiling	Fish, vegetable and some meat dishes; excellent with veal

Milk and Butter

306   MILK IN DRINKS

One of the quickest ways of serving milk is in drinks and these can be varied for each and every case.

MILK SHAKES

Further suggestions will be found in Recipes 676—682 but generally speaking hot or cold milk shakes are a very acceptable way of serving milk.

A cold milk shake is made from flavouring, either the commercially prepared fruit syrups or fresh fruit juices, a little sugar, if desired, ice or ice cream and milk. They should be whisked together by hand or in the liquidiser or blender in an electric mixer.

With hot milk shakes care must be taken, if using rather sweet fruit syrups, to whisk the hot milk and the syrup very briskly together.

MILK TEA

Where it is important that a person has as much milk as possible tea can be made with boiling milk instead of boiling water.

COFFEE

Coffee can also be made with all milk if wished.

Other good ways of incorporating milk into a diet are in hot chocolate, cocoa and the many malted drinks.

307   WAYS OF SERVING MILK TO CHILDREN

From time to time a child will suddenly take a dislike to milk. Fortunately milk is still full of value when cooked so it can be served as jellies:

Dissolve a fruit flavoured jelly in ¼ pint boiling water, cool slightly and whisk in ¾ pint cold milk.

Adding milk to junkets, blancmanges, puddings and gravy are all ways to encourage a child to include milk in the diet.

308   PANCAKE BATTERS

Pancake batter is another way of giving milk to the family in a very pleasant form.

To make the batter sieve 4 oz. flour, plain or self-raising, with a pinch of salt. Beat in 1—2 eggs and ½ pint milk. Cook in a little hot fat until a golden brown on one side, turn and cook on the other.

The secret of a good pancake is to pour only enough batter into the pan at one time to cover it very thinly.

Fillings: Fruit (the picture shows sections of apple served with crisp sausages), savoury meat or fish fillings, vegetables etc.

Sauces on the opposite page are yet another good way of incorporating milk into the daily menu.

309   BUTTER
(Flavoured butters)

Butter can be flavoured for sandwiches and savouries in a variety of ways. Try adding:

Anchovy essence
Chutney
Curry powder
Chopped herbs
Grated lemon rind and a little lemon juice
Few drops of a rather sharp sauce like Worcestershire sauce.
Chopped watercress.

310   SEASONED BUTTER

Cream 4 oz. butter until fluffy. The bowl may be first rubbed with a cut clove of garlic. Beat into the butter 1 tablespoon mild mustard, 1 tablespoon finely chopped parsley, 1 teaspoon finely chopped onion or chives.

311   HOT BREAD FOR SALADS

Take a crusty long French loaf. Cut it diagonally in thick slices. Spread each slice with seasoned butter (Recipe 310), pack together and wrap in aluminium foil. Place in a moderately hot oven (400° F. — Gas Mark 5) and heat until piping hot, about 15 minutes. Transfer, still in loaf shape, to oblong board or serving platter.

301   HAWAIIAN FRIED RICE

3 tablespoons fat	8 oz. cooked rice
4 oz. chopped onions and green tops or chives	2 tablespoons soy sauce
8 oz. diced celery	1 egg
4 oz. sliced mushrooms	8 pineapple rings
8 rashers bacon	

Heat bacon fat in frying pan. Add onions and celery. Cook until almost tender. Add mushrooms, rice and soy sauce. Cook 10 minutes on low heat, stirring occasionally. Stir in beaten egg and cook only until egg is done. Meanwhile fry bacon until crisp and heat pineapple rings in bacon fat. Serve mounds of fried rice on pineapple rings with rashers of bacon.

302   EGG AND HAM CASSEROLE

4 hard-boiled eggs	¼ pint white sauce
4 oz. chopped ham	few breadcrumbs
2 oz. grated cheese	

Halve the eggs and put them cut side downwards into casserole. Add the chopped ham, and half the cheese to the sauce. Pour over the eggs. Add rest of the cheese and a few breadcrumbs and cook for approximately 20 minutes in a hot oven (425—450° F. — Gas Mark 6—7) until crisp and browned.

303   HAM AND APPLE SCALLOP

3 or 4 apples	brown sugar
2 slices ham (¼ inch thick)	1 tablespoon lemon juice

Peel, core and slice apples in rings. Trim off part of fat from ham and cut ham into small pieces. Put a layer of ham in baking dish, covering with apple rings and sprinkle lightly with brown sugar — 1 to 2 tablespoons for each layer. Repeat until all ingredients are used,

having apples and a piece of ham as top layer. Sprinkle lemon juice over top, cover, bake in a moderate oven (375° F. — Gas Mark 4) for about 25 minutes or until apples are tender, then remove cover and bake 20—25 minutes longer, until apples brown slightly and juice thickens somewhat.

304   HAM AND ORANGE COOKIES

7 oz. self-raising flour	1 level teaspoon finely grated orange rind
1 oz. semolina	
¼ level teaspoon salt	3 oz. lean ham
2 oz. margarine	1 medium egg
2 oz. cooking fat	1 gill milk

Sift dry ingredients into a bowl then rub in fats till mixture resembles fine breadcrumbs. Add orange rind and chopped ham then mix to a fairly soft consistency with the egg and milk. Beat thoroughly, then divide mixture equally between 14—15 well-greased bun tins. Bake towards the top of the oven at 400° F. — Gas Mark 6 for 15—20 minutes or till well risen and golden. Cool on wire tray. Serve warm or cold with butter and a mixed salad.

305   SPICED HAM BALLS

8 oz. boiled bacon or ham	1 oz. flour
2 oz. soft fairly fresh breadcrumbs	¼ pint milk
1 oz. butter	1—2 teaspoons tomato ketchup
seasoning	1 teaspoon Worcestershire sauce

For coating:

1 egg, crisp breadcrumbs, fat for frying OR
2—3 oz. rather dry finely grated cheese OR
toasted crumbs

Chop the ham very finely and mix with the crumbs. Make the thick sauce with the butter, flour, milk, add ketchup, Worcestershire sauce and plenty of seasoning. Add to the ham and crumbs while still hot, mix very thoroughly together then allow to cool and form into tiny balls. If you wish to fry these and give them a crisp coating then brush with beaten egg, roll in crumbs and fry. Or roll in the cheese or toasted crumbs and DO NOT cook. To carry for picnics put each ball into well drained lettuce leaves or halve and put into buttered rolls.

295 BACON PEASE PUDDING WITH PORK SAUSAGES

8 oz. chipolata (small) sausages	1 onion
6 oz. split yellow peas	1 bay leaf
1 shank bacon* or bacon pieces	salt and pepper
triangles of fried bread	

small end of big bone — very reasonable to buy

Soak the peas and shank overnight. Wash the peas, drain and put in a saucepan with the shank, onion, bay leaf, pepper and enough water to cover. Simmer gently and when tender remove shank and bay leaf. Rub the peas through a sieve. Skin and bone the shank and chop the bacon. Stir this into the pease pudding and season with salt if required. Put the pudding into a baking dish and place in a moderate oven (375° F. — Gas Mark 4) to heat through. Meanwhile fry chipolata sausages, halve them and fry triangles of bread in the fat. Garnish the pudding with these and serve piping hot.

296 BACON TWISTS

10 oz. short crust pastry	1 oz. margarine
(see Recipe 227)*	1 good sized onion
4—6 rashers streaky bacon	pinch sage seasoning

* or use cheese pastry

Roll out the pastry into a neat oblong shape. Cut into 2 equal sized pieces. Chop bacon very finely — fry until golden brown. Lift out of pan, add margarine and fry very finely chopped onion in this. Add to bacon with sage and seasoning. Spread over one half the pastry — cover with the second oblong of pastry. Cut into strips then twist these in centre. Lift on to baking tins and cook for about 25 minutes in hot oven (425° to 450° F. — Gas Mark 6—7).

297 BACON FINGERS

ingredients as Bacon Twists (Recipe 296)

Add 1 or 2 skinned chopped tomatoes to mixture. Lift one half of the pastry on to baking tin, cover with mixture then the second half of pastry. Seal edges. Bake for approximately 20 minutes in hot oven — then lower heat to moderate for rest of cooking time (approx. 20 minutes).

298 BACON PIE

Ingredients as Bacon Twists (Recipe 296.)

Line pie plate with half pastry. Fry bacon and onion mixture, add 8 oz. diced cooked potatoes, 2 or 3 chopped tomatoes and/or mushrooms. Put over bottom layer of pastry, cover with rest of pastry, decorate with leaves etc. of the dough and brush with egg or milk. Bake for approximately 20 minutes in hot oven then lower heat to moderate for further 20—25 minutes.

299 GAMMON AND BUTTER BEAN PLATTER

slice of gammon about	milk
¼ inch thick	¼ oz. margarine
1 small can butter beans	¼ oz. flour
little chopped parsley	4 tomatoes, halved

Grill the gammon slice, allowing approximately 10 minutes on each side. Meanwhile strain the liquor from the beans and make it up to ½ pint with milk. Use this to make a white sauce with the margarine and flour; when the sauce is cooked, add the butter beans and parsley and heat gently. Grill the tomato halves with the gammon for the last 10 minutes of cooking. To serve, place the gammon on a flat serving dish, coat half of it with the bean mixture and arrange the tomatoes along one side of the dish.

300 GAMMON AND GRILLED GRAPEFRUIT

For each serving take a slice of gammon about ½ inch thick and grill till golden brown. Turn and grill lightly on other side. Top with a round slice of grapefruit, ¼ inch thick, sprinkle with a little brown sugar, and grill again until sugar browns and bubbles.

Bacon and Ham

Bacon and ham are so much a part of traditional and farm cooking, and in this section you will find many new ways of serving them.

Many people are a little confused about the difference between ham and bacon. The hams of the pig are simply the legs which are cut off and are dry cured individually. Various hams are cured in different ways but they are (unlike bacon) generally unsmoked. It takes from 3—5 months to cure a ham. At the end of that time a perfect ham has a faint green mould, known as the 'bloom'. Never take this off until you are ready to cook it.

Gammon, on the other hand, is the leg of the pig but this is cured with the whole bacon side before being cut away. It is, on the whole, cheaper than ham and can be used in any recipe where ham is indicated.

Hams should be soaked for 24 hours before cooking, whereas bacon varies quite a bit. Green bacon, for example, is very lightly salted and needs little soaking at all. The other bacon can be soaked for up to 24 hours.

290   BACON AND EGG TART

5—6 oz. short crust pastry   ⅜ pint milk
   (see Recipe 227)   seasoning
5 rashers streaky bacon   4 eggs

Line a flan tin with the pastry but do not bake. Remove the rind from the bacon and chop up finely. Fry over a low heat until crisp. Drain on crushed tissue or absorbent paper and sprinkle half over the bottom of the pastry. Add eggs, beaten in seasoned milk, to cover the bacon. Top with the remaining cooked bacon. Bake in a moderately hot oven for 45 minutes (400° F. — Gas Mark 7) until golden brown. A delicious variation of this recipe is to sprinkle 2 oz. grated cheese over the mixture before placing in oven.

291   WILTSHIRE BACON AND PIG'S LIVER PIE

Short crust pastry:

8 oz. flour   1 egg
pinch salt   water to moisten
5 oz. lard

Filling:

6 oz. streaky bacon   1 pinch marjoram
6 oz. pig's liver   pepper
1 tablespoon tomato purée lard, flour
1 onion finely chopped   stock or water

Rub the lard well into the flour and salt sifted together. Work in the egg and moisten with only sufficient water to make a short crust. Dice the bacon and liver and brown in a frying pan with the onion in a little lard. Dredge with flour. Put the meat and onions into a pie-dish and add 1 or 2 cups of stock or water to the frying pan. Add the tomato purée and herbs and seasoning and mix well in. Pour over the meat. Cover with the short crust and bake in a moderate oven (375° F. — Gas Mark 4) for 45—55 minutes.

292   BACON AND SAUSAGE PIE

1 lb. short crust pastry
(see Recipe 227 — use double quantity)

Filling:

1 lb. pork sausage meat   2 tablespoons stock or water
1 pinch ginger   3 hard-boiled eggs
8—12 oz. streaky bacon   1 pinch cinnamon
1 teaspoon rubbed sage

Line a well greased loaf tin of suitable size with pastry. Chop the bacon finely. Mix all ingredients except the eggs. Place half the mixture in the pie and arrange the eggs in a line. Add the rest of the mixture. Cover with the paste, decorate, glaze and bake in the lower part of a moderate oven (375° F. — Gas Mark 4) for 1½ hours. *Illustrated in colour picture no. 27.*

293   BOILED BACON OR HAM

A piece of bacon, either hot or cold, makes a wonderful meal. To boil the bacon you should first soak overnight in cold water then simmer very gently, allowing 20—25 minutes per lb. and 20—25 minutes over. Do not cook too quickly. *See colour pictures nos. 6 and 10.*

294   BACON AND TOMATO KEBABS

Roll bacon rashers round segments of orange, and skewer them, alternating with tomato halves. Grill until nicely browned.

10   **FRIED CHEESE (Recipe 206)**

Custards and Sauces

282   EGGS IN CUSTARDS

It is a good idea to put a beaten egg into custard made with a custard powder. Draw the thickened custard to one side so it is no longer boiling, whisk in the beaten egg and cook gently for several minutes.

283   EGG CUSTARDS

For a pouring custard use 1 egg to ½ pint milk. For a thick custard that can be turned out use 4 eggs (or egg yolks) to 1 pint milk.

When making a thin custard beat the eggs with a little sugar, or seasoning for a savoury custard, pour on the warm milk, return to a basin or top of a double saucepan and cook over hot water until thick enough to coat the back of a wooden spoon.

For a thick custard you can either steam the custard in a buttered container in a steamer over hot water for approximately 1½ hours until firm or bake for approximately the same time, or even longer, in a very cool oven. It is advisable to stand the dish in another of cold water in the oven to prevent the possibility of curdling.

FLAVOURING CUSTARDS

Sweet custards can be flavoured with a caramel sauce, a little chocolate or coffee and savoury custards with grated cheese, flaked fish, chopped ham or crisply fried bacon.

284   CRÈME CARAMEL

4 eggs	4½ oz. sugar
1 pint milk	1 gill water

Put 4 oz. sugar and the water into a small pan. Stir until sugar has dissolved, then heat without stirring until it becomes a rich golden colour. Pour quickly into hot dariole moulds, and holding each with a cloth, coat the inside well; leave to set. Heat the milk, lightly beat the eggs and the remaining sugar and pour on the hot milk (not boiling). Strain into moulds or into one dish, stand in a pan of warm water, to prevent curdling, and cook in a slow oven (300° F. — Gas Mark 2) for 20—30 minutes. Allow approximately 2 hours. Turn out carefully on to warmed individual dishes. This can be served hot or cold.

285   RICH CHOCOLATE CUP CUSTARDS

1 gill evaporated milk	1 gill water
3 oz. plain chocolate	1 egg
1 egg yolk	

To decorate:

whipped evaporated milk

Grate the chocolate into a pan, add 2 tablespoons milk and water mixed. Melt chocolate over a gentle heat. Pour the chocolate and the rest of the milk over the eggs. Strain into a rinsed saucepan and stir over a very gentle heat until the mixture thickens and coats the back of the spoon. Do not over-beat, otherwise it will curdle. Cool. Pour into custard glasses. Leave to set. Decorated with whipped evaporated milk. *Illustrated in colour picture no. 29.*

286   EGGS IN SAUCES

When making a sauce which requires egg, draw the pan of thickened sauce to one side, add the beaten egg and cook again for a few minutes very slowly.

Hard-boiled eggs, however, can be served with a variety of sauces: cheese, tomato or a creamy curry sauce. To make this creamy curry sauce use a white or béchamel sauce recipe (Recipes 312, 324), add a little extra butter and when stirring in the flour stir in 1—2 teaspoons curry powder. Cook in the usual way.

287   USING LEFT-OVER EGG WHITES

Add stiffly beaten egg whites to half-set jellies or blancmanges to give lighter texture (like a mousse) or into thick fruit purée to make fruit snow (see Recipe 463).

Use them, too, to make the following.

288   MERINGUES

2 egg whites	2 oz. icing sugar (well
2 oz. castor	sieved) or
sugar	4 oz. castor sugar

Whisk egg whites until stiff, fold in the sugar gradually or beat in half the sugar and fold in rest. Then pipe or pile small spoonfuls on to a well oiled or buttered tin or oiled or buttered paper on a baking tin. Bake for 2—3 hours, depending on size, in a very low oven (225—250° F. — Gas Mark 0—½) until crisp, but still white. Lift from the tin with a warmed palette knife, cool, then store in airtight tins. Sandwich together with cream, ice cream or fruit and cream.

For savoury meringues omit sugar and add seasoning and little grated cheese. Serve hot.

289   USING LEFT-OVER EGG YOLKS

Add egg yolks to sauces, pancake batters, pastry (it makes it very crisp), biscuit dough or creamed vegetables.

Make up the soup mix as directed on the packet, or make mushroom sauce, but using HALF PINT WATER ONLY. When cooked add the cream, hard-boiled eggs and ham and heat through. Pour the sauce into the warmed flan case. Garnish with parsley and serve on a flat dish.

274   CREAMY QUICHE LORRAINE

2 — 3 oz. streaky bacon
2 eggs
pinch cayenne pepper
1 small can evaporated
   milk

4 oz. short crust pastry
   (see Recipe 227)
3 oz. Swiss processed
   Gruyère cheese

Line flan ring with short crust pastry and bake blind in a hot oven (425—450° F. — Gas Mark 6—7) for approximately 15 minutes. Cut up bacon and fry or grill. Arrange on base of flan case, cover with sieved cheese. Beat the eggs and seasoning together. Stir in evaporated milk and pour into flan case. Bake in moderate oven (375° F. — Gas Mark 4) for approximately 40 minutes or until set. Serve hot.

275   QUICHE LORRAINE

As Recipe 274, but use fresh milk and grated Cheddar or Parmesan cheese or mixture of these and rather more bacon. *Illustrated in colour picture no. 27.*

276   EGGS FOR COATING

To give a good coating on fish, savoury dishes etc., a beaten egg is invaluable. If you want a very delicate coating use the white only.

The Scotch eggs in colour picture No. 27 give you an idea of just how a good crisp brown coating improves the look of such a recipe.

277   EGGS IN PIES

Most savoury pies are improved by adding eggs — do not boil these for too long before putting into meat mixture as they will have prolonged cooking then.

278   EGGS IN VEGETABLES

Add an egg or egg yolk to vegetable purées, potatoes, turnips or swedes to give an extra richness of flavour.

279   EGGS ROYALE

5 hard-boiled eggs
1 can condensed chicken soup
1 onion
2 oz. butter
1 green pepper (or use
   cooked peas)

4 oz. grated cheese
little milk
1 small packet frozen
beans
olives

Heat the soup with just a little milk, add the cheese and the beans, which should be lightly cooked. Slice and fry the onion in the butter, then add the chopped pepper or cooked peas. When tender, stir into the soup mixture together with 4 of the chopped hard-boiled eggs. Arrange in a casserole and serve garnished with the last egg and sliced olives.

280   GOLDEN RING

5 hard-boiled eggs
1 small packet frozen peas
¼ oz. powder gelatine

1 pint tomato juice
seasoning
little grated cheese if desired

Shell and cut the eggs into halves across the centre. Cook and drain the peas, dissolve the powder gelatine in the heated tomato juice and add seasoning. Pour a little of this into a ring mould, which has been brushed with olive oil. When lightly set arrange the halved eggs, cut side downwards to the jelly, and the peas to form an attractive pattern. Spoon over a very little of the tomato gelatine mixture and when set add the rest of the tomato liquid. Turn out when quite firm and decorate as desired.

281   ULSTER EGGS

6 hard-boiled eggs
1½ lb. mashed potatoes
3 oz. grated cheese
fat for frying
pepper and salt

chopped spring onions or
chopped pickled vegetables
   (for flavouring)
egg and breadcrumbs
   (for coating)

Shell and chop the eggs into fairly small pieces. Mix together with the potato and cheese. Add seasonings and flavouring. Mix again. Mould into egg shapes or balls. Brush with beaten egg and roll in breadcrumbs. Fry in deep fat until golden brown.

For serving cold with salads:

Mould and cook as for serving hot (above). Allow to cool. Cut in halves and serve with a mixed salad and mayonnaise.

occasionally. When completely set turn out, without folding, on to a heated serving dish.

265 SOUFFLÉ

1 oz. butter	seasoning or sugar
1 oz. flour	(see below)
¼ pint milk	3 egg yolks
flavouring (see below)	4 egg whites

Make a thick sauce of the butter, flour and milk (or other liquid suggested in the recipes). Stir in the flavourings, the egg yolks and lastly the stiffly beaten egg whites. These should be always folded gently into the mixture. Pour into a greased soufflé dish and bake for approximately 35 minutes in the centre of a moderate oven (375° F. — Gas Mark 4).

266 CHEESE SOUFFLÉ

Season the sauce well with salt, pepper and a pinch mustard. Add 4 oz. grated cheese.

267 HAM SOUFFLÉ

Add 3 oz. finely chopped ham to the mixture. 1 oz. finely grated Parmesan cheese is an excellent addition to this.

268 SWEET SOUFFLÉ

As Recipe 265 but omit seasoning and flavour with vanilla, chocolate, coffee or rum, and add 1–2 oz. sugar. For fruit soufflés use a thick fruit purée istead of the white sauce made with butter, flour and milk.

264 TORTILLA ESPANOLA CON GUISANTES VERDES

(Spanish Omelette)

2 – 3 tablespoons salad oil or butter	1 small can peas, drained
1 medium onion, finely chopped	1 canned sweet red pepper, sliced
1 small potato, finely diced	4 eggs
1 clove garlic, crushed (optional)	seasoning

Heat the oil in a large frying pan and cook the onion, potato and garlic until tender, stirring frequently to prevent browning. Add the peas and red pepper and heat through. Meanwhile beat the eggs with a fork, season and pour into the pan. Cook slowly, stirring

Egg Pies and Flans

269 BACON, MUSHROOM AND EGG PIE

8 oz. short crust pastry (see Recipe 227)	2 – 4 oz. mushrooms (or mushroom stalks)
4 good-sized rashers of bacon	2 eggs
1 – 2 teaspoons chopped parsley	seasoning
	small knob butter or margarine

Roll out pastry. Use approximately half to line pie plate or tin. Using the extra butter or margarine, fry chopped bacon and mushrooms LIGHTLY, mix with the beaten eggs, parsley and seasoning and pour over pastry. Cover with rest of pastry, seal the edges and decorate the top. Brush with egg white — you will find a little left in the shell for this. Bake in centre of hot oven (450° F. — Gas Mark 7) for 15—20 minutes, then lower heat to moderate for further 20 minutes.

270 EGG AND SPINACH PIE

3 oz. short crust pastry (see Recipe 227)	1 oz. butter
1 lb. cooked spinach purée	seasoning
4 eggs	2 or 3 tablespoons cream

Use half the pastry to line a pie plate or flan ring (the

pastry should be very thin). Cover with the spinach purée and then make a slight 'well' in this for each of the 4 eggs. Break these in carefully, season, brush on the melted butter and cream with a pastry brush. Cover with the rest of the pastry, brush with a little milk and make air holes for the steam to escape. Bake for approximately 40 minutes in the centre of a moderately hot oven (400° F. — Gas Mark 5). Serve hot or cold.

271 EGG AND LEEK PIE

Use chopped leeks instead of spinach.

272 EGG AND CAULIFLOWER PIE

Use flowerets of cauliflower, which should be lightly cooked beforehand. Add grated cheese as well.

273 HAM, EGG AND MUSHROOM FLAN

1 packet mushroom soup or mushroom sauce (Recipe 323)	2 hard-boiled eggs, chopped
½ pint water	4 oz lean cooked ham — finely diced
3 tablespoons cream or top of milk	1 8-inch cooked pastry flan case (see Recipe 227)
parsley for garnish	

257 SAVOURY SCRAMBLED EGGS

Scrambled eggs can be given infinite variety. In the picture mushrooms are cooked first in the butter, the eggs added and scrambled in the usual way. They are topped with grilled bacon and mushrooms and served on ½ rolls or rounds of toast. There are many other ways in which scrambled eggs can be varied:

CHEESE SCRAMBLED EGGS. Half-cook the beaten eggs, add finely grated cheese and complete cooking.

CORN AND EGGS SCRAMBLE. Toss cooked corn in the hot butter, add the beaten eggs and cook in the usual way.

HAM SCRAMBLE. Add finely chopped ham to the beaten eggs and cook in the usual way.

VEGETABLE SCRAMBLE. Toss cooked diced vegetables in the hot butter, add the beaten eggs and cook.

Omelettes and Souffles

258 THE SECRET OF A GOOD OMELETTE

Use 2 eggs per omelette or per person for a really good result. Beat the eggs lightly for a plain omelette and season well. I like to add 1 tablespoon water to each 2 eggs. Heat a good knob of butter in the pan, pour in the eggs, allow to set lightly on the bottom, then work the omelette, lifting it and tilting the pan so that the liquid egg runs underneath. Serve at once, either rolled or folded. Fill with grated cheese, if desired, or finely chopped fried mushrooms, before folding.

OTHER FLAVOURINGS:

BACON. Fry bacon lightly, add a little mushroom, pour in the eggs and cook the omelette.

HAM. Add finely chopped cooked ham before cooking.

MIXED HERBS. Add finely chopped fresh or dried herbs to the eggs before cooking.

COOKED CHICKEN, FISH OR MEAT can all be heated gently in a sauce and put into the omelette before serving.

259 OMELETTE WITH CHICKEN AND HAM SAUCE

Omelette:

2 eggs
salt and pepper

¼ oz. butter

Filling:

1 can condensed cream of chicken soup

1 tablespoon milk
2 oz. chopped ham

Put cream of chicken soup into a saucepan. Add the milk and beat well. Heat, stirring gently for 1 minute, add ham. Season eggs and whisk. Cook as above. Put a little sauce on omelette, fold over and turn out quickly on to a hot plate. Serve with remaining sauce.

260 SOUFFLÉ OMELETTES

Separate the yolks from the whites. Beat the whites very stiffly, fold in the yolks and cook as before, but as this is very thick you may find it a good idea to cook for a few minutes in the usual way, then put under a low grill to finish the top.

261 JAM OMELETTE

Fill a soufflé omelette, to which you have added a little sugar to taste before cooking, with hot jam. Fold and dust with sieved icing sugar.

262 FRUIT OMELETTE

Fill with thick purée of fruit, or canned fruit; apricots are particularly good.

263 SAVOURY SOUFFLÉ OMELETTE

Savoury fillings can be used in soufflé omelettes but it is generally considered better to serve them as a sweet.

249   FRIED EGGS

First cook bacon so that you have bacon fat or if not cooking bacon first heat a good knob of fat in the pan. Break the eggs, one by one, into saucers, tilt the pan slightly, put in the egg and cook steadily until set. Repeat this with each egg, making sure the first one is lightly set before the second one goes in.

250   ECONOMICAL EGG FINGERS

Beat eggs well. Allow 1 for 2 people. Season. Dip fingers of bread into beaten egg, making sure it is thoroughly absorbed, and fry in hot fat.

251   FRIED DEVILLED EGGS

allow 2 eggs per person	little milk or mayonnaise
2 teaspoons made mustard	pinch curry powder
salt and pepper	1 extra egg
1 teaspoon Worcestershire	breadcrumbs
sauce	deep fat

Hard-boil and shell the eggs, then cut into halves lengthways. Remove the yolks, mash, adding the flavourings and mayonnaise to make a soft consistency. Press filling back into the white cases, and 'join' the 2 halves together again. Roll in the beaten egg, then the crumbs. Fry until crisp and golden brown and serve as a supper snack with diced vegetables and cheese sauce.

252   POACHED EGGS

Like all egg dishes poached eggs must be served the moment they are cooked, so it is advisable to toast the bread while they cook. Crack the shells and pour the eggs into a cup or saucer. If you have a proper egg-poacher put a piece of margarine or butter, about the size of a hazel nut, into each cup, wait until this is melted, then carefully slide the egg into the cup, adding a pinch of salt if wished. Put on the lid and allow the water in the pan underneath to boil steadily for about 3½—4 minutes. Slide the egg on to the buttered toast OR put a small piece of margarine or butter into an old cup and stand it in a pan of boiling water to melt. Pour in egg, put a lid on saucepan and cook as before. OR the following method is preferred by many people since it gives a lighter result. Bring a good ½ pint of water to the boil in either a saucepan or frying pan. Add 1 dessertspoon vinegar, if wished, for this prevents the egg whites from spreading. Put in a good pinch salt. Slide the eggs into the boiling water, leave for about 3 minutes, or until egg white is set. Insert spoon or fish slice, drain the eggs carefully and put on toast.

253   EGGS IN A NEST

8 oz. cooked rice	4 eggs
1 can condensed cream of	salt and pepper to taste
chicken soup	3 tablespoons milk
4 slices bacon	
6 oz. diced Cheddar cheese	

Fry and chop bacon. In a saucepan combine rice with 1 gill condensed cream of chicken soup, bacon and cheese. Heat through. Press into 6 individual ring moulds and turn on to serving plates. Place a poached egg in the centre of each. Season with salt and pepper.

Combine remaining soup with milk. Heat and serve as a sauce.

254   POACHED EGG AND SPINACH

Poached eggs and spinach are a perfect partnership. Cook spinach, drain well and top with poached egg. To make a more substantial meal coat with cheese sauce (Recipe 314) or cheese and onion sauce (recipe below).

CHEESE AND ONION SAUCE

1 oz. butter	salt, pepper and nutmeg
1 finely chopped	4 oz. grated Cheddar
onion	cheese
1 oz. plain flour	1½ gills milk

Toss onion in heated butter for a few minutes, taking care it does not brown. Stir in the flour and cook for 2 minutes then gradually add the milk. Bring to boil and cook until thicker. Add seasoning and cheese and heat without boiling again.

255   OEUFS POCHÉS OTÉRO

1½ pints prawns (fresh)	4 oz. cheese
4 large potatoes	tomato purée
2 oz. butter	salt
4 eggs	black pepper

Scrub potatoes well, and bake until floury. Meanwhile, peel prawns. When potatoes are cooked, cut a slice off each and scoop out flesh. Mash with salt and pepper, and replace in potato shell. Pat down thoroughly, leaving well in the centre. Fill with prawns which have been tossed in melted butter, thickened to taste with tomato purée. Place a poached egg on top of each potato, sprinkle with grated cheese and grill quickly until golden brown.

256   SCRAMBLED EGGS

Allow 1 egg per person or for more generous helping 3 eggs for 2 people. Beat the eggs lightly, adding a good pinch of salt and pepper. You can add 1 dessertspoon milk for each egg but some people prefer a firmer mixture with no milk added. Heat a piece of margarine or butter, the size of a small walnut in a saucepan, pour in the eggs and cook gently, stirring well from the bottom until the mixture starts to thicken. Turn the heat very low and continue cooking.

244   PEPPERPOT SHORTBREAD

4 oz. plain flour	2 oz. fine semolina
½ level teaspoon salt	good shake cayenne pepper
1 level teaspoon dry	good shake white pepper
mustard	about 2 tablespoons cold
4 oz. butter	water

Sift dry ingredients. Rub in butter until the mixture is like fine breadcrumbs. Mix to a dry dough with cold water. Turn on to a lightly floured board and knead quickly until smooth. Roll out into a round, about 8 inches across, keeping as neat a shape as possible. Pinch up edges with finger and thumb and cut into 8 equal triangles. Lift on to lightly greased trays and bake in a moderately hot oven (400° F. — Gas Mark 5) for about 15 minutes or until crisp and pale gold.

245   CURRIED MUSHROOM EGGS

5 hard-boiled eggs	¼ teaspoon curry powder
8 oz. fresh mushrooms	1 tablespoon chilli sauce or
¼ pint white sauce	Worcestershire sauce
2 oz. grated cheese	

Quarter the eggs. Chop and fry the mushrooms, then add the curry powder and fry this too. Combine all ingredients and heat very gently.

246   NURSERY BIRD'S NEST

Pipe a border of mashed potatoes on to fireproof dish. Fill centre with soft boiled or hard-boiled shelled eggs. Cover with a little white or cheese sauce and brown in oven or under grill.

247   SCOTCH EGGS

4 hard-boiled eggs	crumbs
12 oz. pork sausage meat	fat for frying
little milk or egg for	
coating	

Coat hard-boiled eggs with sausage meat, wrapping it around carefully so that the egg is completely covered. Brush with milk or egg and roll in crumbs. Fry steadily, until sausage meat is cooked and golden brown. Serve cold with green salad. *Illustrated in colour picture no. 27.*

248   TUNA AND EGGS INDIENNE

6 eggs	¼ teaspoon made mustard
1 raw egg yolk	salt and pepper
1 can (7 oz.) middle-cut tuna	

Curry sauce:

1½ oz. butter or margarine	2 medium onions
3 level tablespoons flour	1 level tablespoon curry
¾ pint stock or water	powder (or to taste)
1 large apple	8 oz. tomatoes, skinned and
1 tablespoon lemon juice	sliced
or more	1 or 2 tablespoons sultanas
salt and pepper	clove of garlic (optional)

To make sauce, melt the butter or margarine in a pan and fry chopped onion until soft. Add the flour and brown, stirring. Add the curry powder and stock or water. Bring to the boil, stirring, and simmer for 1 or 2 minutes. Add the peeled and chopped apple, tomatoes, lemon juice and pepper and salt to taste. Add, if liked, sultanas and finely chopped garlic and simmer gently about 7 minutes.

Hard-boil the eggs and shell. Slice them lengthwise and remove the yolks. Pound 4 of the yolks with the finely flaked tuna, raw egg yolk, mustard and other seasoning; warm over low heat. Sandwich the egg white cases in pairs with this fish mixture. Arrange the eggs in a warmed heat-proof dish and pour the hot sauce round them. Cover with foil or greased kitchen paper and slip into a moderately hot oven (400° F. — Gas Mark 5) for about 10 minutes. Serve with fluffy rice, sprinkled with the remaining 2 egg yolks, grated, and paprika; pass chutney and sliced bananas separately.

238 INDIVIDUAL BREAD BASKETS

3 servings

1 day-old sandwich loaf
mild mustard
2 oz. chopped ham
butter or margarine for
spreading and brushing
3 eggs

Cut 3 1½-inch thick slices from a day-old loaf. Remove crusts. Hollow out centre of each slice (leaving a base of at least ¼ inch in thickness) using a round biscuit cutter as a guide. Spread hollows with butter or margarine and mild mustard, then sprinkle with chopped ham. Transfer to a greased baking tray and brush slices all over with melted butter or margarine. Break 1 egg into each hollow, then bake in moderately hot oven (400° F. — Gas Mark 5) for 20—25 minutes or till eggs are set. Transfer baskets to a serving dish and sprinkle tops with chopped parsley.

239 BOILED EGGS

Most people like their eggs just set, in which case they will take 3½ minutes. Allow 4 minutes if you know the eggs are very fresh. An egg required to be rather under-set and liquid should have about 3 minutes. A very firm egg, i.e. hard-boiled, needs about 7—10 minutes. Put enough water into a small saucepan to cover the eggs. Bring this to the boil then lower the eggs into the boiling water. Time carefully and serve at once. If you find one of the egg shells cracking, immediately put about 1 tablespoon of vinegar into the water; this prevents the egg coming out of the shell and spoiling. You can adjust the cooking time according to personal taste. When hard-boiled eggs are cooked, crack shells and lower immediately into cold water. This prevents a dark ring round the yolk.

240 CURRIED HARD-BOILED EGGS

4—6 hard-boiled eggs
3—4 oz. cooked Patna rice

For the sauce:

1 oz. butter
1 small onion
tiny piece of apple
1 teaspoon curry powder
2 teaspoons coconut
1 teaspoon flour
½ pint white stock
1 teaspoon chutney
few sultanas
seasoning

Make the sauce first by frying the onion and apple in the butter. Work in the curry powder, flour and then add the stock. Bring to the boil and cook until smooth, then add the chutney, sultanas, coconut and seasoning and simmer the sauce for about 30 minutes. Add the

halved eggs, warm and serve in a border of rice and gherkins. Serve sliced tomatoes, grated carrots, and chutney in separate dishes.

241 CREAMED CURRY

Make the hard-boiled egg curry but instead of using stock use 1½ gills milk and ¼ gill cream in the sauce.

242 DEVILLED EGGS WITH CREOLE RICE

4 eggs

Creole rice:

1 small onion, peeled
1 stick celery
2 oz. mushrooms, sliced
½ pint stock
1 medium green pepper
1 oz. cooking fat
6 oz. rice
seasoning to taste

Devilled sauce:

1 oz. butter
¼ pint tomato juice
1 teaspoon Worcestershire sauce
1 oz. flour
1 rounded teaspoon made mustard
pinch brown sugar

Take seeds out of green pepper. Chop or coarsely mince onion, pepper and celery, fry 5 minutes in hot fat. Add mushrooms and rice. Fry 4 minutes. Add stock. Cover pan. Cook 20 minutes or till no moisture remains. Season. Meanwhile prepare sauce. Melt butter, stir in flour, cook 2 minutes. Remove from heat. Gradually add tomato juice. Reheat, stirring, till sauce thickens. Add remaining ingredients. Simmer 10 minutes. Add salt to taste. Hard-boil eggs. Put rice into bottom of serving dish. Arrange halved eggs on top. Coat with a little sauce. Hand rest of sauce separately.

243 EGGS DIABLE

6 eggs
1 tablespoon finely chopped spring onion
½ teaspoon made mustard
1 tablespoon chopped parsley
1 tablespoon cream
1¼ oz. butter
1¼ oz. flour
2 teaspoons curry powder
¾ pint milk
salt and pepper to taste
paprika

Boil the eggs for 15 minutes, rinse in cold water, shell and halve. Melt the butter, add the onion and gently cook until soft but not brown. Stir in the flour, curry powder and mustard. Stir in the milk and bring to the boil, stirring. Add parsley and salt and pepper to taste. Add the cream. Serve piping hot sprinkled with paprika, with Pepperpot Shortbread.

Eggs

232   TO BAKE EGGS

The simplest way of baking eggs is to put them into greased individual dishes, season, add a little cream or milk and bake for 10—15 minutes in a moderate oven. Serve with a spoon. They can be varied by topping with cheese, asparagus tips etc.

233   EASTER SUNDAY EGGS

4 eggs   1 oz. pure cooking fat
4 oz. mushrooms   salt and pepper

Peel and slice mushrooms. Divide fat between four small fireproof dishes (or use 1 large fireproof dish) placed on a baking tray. Place on the middle shelf of a moderate oven (375 °F. — Gas Mark 4) about 5 minutes to melt the fat. Add mushrooms, return to oven and cook for about 10 minutes. Break 1 egg into each dish on top of the mushrooms. Sprinkle with salt and pepper. Return to oven and cook for another 10 minutes until the eggs are set.

234   EGGS FLORENTINE OR EGGS IN SPINACH NESTS

3 servings

1 large size carton frozen   1 oz. margarine
  chopped spinach*   3 eggs
salt and pepper to taste
* If using fresh spinach then cook, drain and chop or sieve.

Cook the spinach according to the directions on the carton. Drain well, add seasoning to taste and ¾ oz. of the margarine and mix. Divide between three individual ovenproof dishes, which have been lightly greased, and make a hollow in the centre. Break an egg into each hollow, sprinkle with a little seasoning and put a dot of margarine on each. Place the dishes on a baking sheet, cover with a piece of greased paper to prevent the surface of the eggs from hardening, and bake in a moderate oven (375 °F. — Gas Mark 4) for about 15 minutes until the eggs are set. Serve at once.
Note. If desired the spinach can be arranged in an ovenproof dish, three hollows made and an egg broken into each hollow.

235   SWISS EGGS

4 eggs   little butter
4 oz. sliced Gruyère   seasoning
  cheese   little cream, if desired

Butter a shallow dish or 4 individual dishes and cover the bottom of the dish (or dishes) with thinly sliced cheese. Break the eggs carefully on to the cheese slices, season and cover with the rest of the cheese which should be finely grated. Bake for approximately 10 minutes in a moderately hot oven until the eggs are lightly set. A little butter can be put on top with the cheese and a small quantity of cream poured over the eggs before covering with the grated cheese.

236   TO PRESERVE EGGS IN WATERGLASS

You need a zinc pail or a crock for this and if buying a special pail you can obtain an inner container which allows you to lift out the eggs.

Directions for making up the waterglass solution are given on the tin and these should be followed most carefully. Put the eggs into the solution and it is quite a good idea to turn them gently from time to time.

When you preserve eggs choose eggs that are at least 24 hours old, although obviously it is not worth while preserving very stale eggs.

237   TO PRESERVE EGGS WITH A COATING

Select eggs that are uncracked — do not wash. Dip the eggs in Oteg solution as instructed on the box. Dry on wire sieve, then pack into boxes. There is no need to separate them, but do pierce holes in the boxes for air circulation. Keep in a cool dry place. Turn the eggs from time to time so the yolks do not get settled in one place.

Pure vaseline is often suggested as an alternative coating.

227   BACON AND CREAM CHEESE FLAN

6 oz. cream or demi-sel cheese   salt and pepper
2 egg yolks   ¼ pint thin cream or
1 whole egg   top of milk
4 oz. short crust pastry   4 oz. rashers streaky bacon
(see below)

Line 7- or 8-inch flan ring with the pastry. Cut bacon into strips and fry lightly. Mix the cheese with the egg yolks, egg and cream, season well. Arrange the bacon strips in circles on the pastry. Pour in the cream cheese mixture. Stand the tin on a baking sheet, place in the centre of a moderately hot oven (400 °F. — Gas Mark 5) for 30 minutes. If at this stage the filling is already golden put a buttered paper lightly over the top. Cook for another 10—15 minutes and serve quickly, before the filling sinks.

SHORT CRUST PASTRY

8 oz. flour   cold water to mix —
4 oz. fat   approx. 2 tablespoons
good pinch salt

Sieve flour and salt and rub in fat until mixture looks like fine breadcrumbs. Gradually add enough water to make dough into a rolling consistency. Lightly flour rolling pin and pastry board. Roll pastry to required thickness and shape, lifting and turning it to keep it light.

228   MACARONI CHEESE

3 oz. macaroni   2 oz. grated cheese
¼ pint cheese sauce   1 tablespoon crisp
(Recipe 314)*   breadcrumbs
seasoning   1 oz. margarine or butter

* If you like a more moist macaroni cheese, use ¾ pint cheese sauce to the same quantity of cooked macaroni

Put the macaroni into about 1½ pints boiling water, to which you have added a level teaspoon salt. Cook steadily until the macaroni is just tender. Do not over-cook; elbow-length quick-cooking macaroni takes only 7 minutes. Drain in a colander, arrange it in a hot dish and pour the cheese sauce over it. Sprinkle cheese and breadcrumbs on top and put the margarine or butter on in several small pieces. Either bake for about 25 minutes near the top of a moderately hot oven (400 °F. — Gas Mark 5) until crisp and brown, or put under a hot grill.

229   SUMMER CASSEROLE AU GRATIN

8 oz. cooked young carrots   about 12 spring onions
1 or 2 cooked diced turnips   2 or 3 tomatoes
4—6 cooked diced new   2 oz. butter
potatoes

Sauce:

1½ oz. butter   2 eggs
1½ oz. flour   3 oz. grated cheese
¼ pint milk   seasoning

Toss all the vegetables in the butter, except the tomatoes which should be sliced and added afterwards. Put into casserole. Make thick sauce of butter, flour, milk, add egg yolks and seasoning, the grated cheese and stiffly beaten egg whites. Put over vegetables and put into centre of moderately hot oven (400 °F. — Gas Mark 5) for about 25 minutes until well risen and firm.

230   TOMATO AND ONION PIE

4—5 oz. short crust pastry   4 oz. cream cheese
2 or 3 onions   2 eggs
3 or 4 skinned tomatoes   seasoning
paprika

Slice or chop onions and simmer gently in boiling salted water until soft. Drain, but keep just a little of the stock. Line pie plate with pastry, cover with thinly sliced tomatoes and the onions, season. Beat cream cheese and eggs and season well. Gradually beat in 1 tablespoon stock to make a smooth mixture. Season lightly, pour over onions and tomatoes and bake for approximately 40 minutes in the centre of a moderate oven (375 °F. — Gas Mark 4).

231   VEGETABLE PIE

¼ pint cheese sauce   1 lb. mixed cooked
(Recipe 314)   vegetables
1 lb. creamed potatoes   little grated cheese,
butter or margarine   if desired

Mix well-drained vegetables with the sauce. Put into a pie dish, cover with creamed potatoes. Pipe border of potato if wished. Put small pieces of butter or margarine on top, plus a little grated cheese if desired. Bake for approximately 25 minutes in moderately hot oven (400 °F. — Gas Mark 5). Serve with freshly cooked vegetables.

Cheese makes a meal

223   CHEESE AND VEGETABLE FLAN

cheese pastry (Recipe 226)   *¼ pint cheese sauce*
mixture of cooked, fresh or   *(Recipe 314)*
frozen vegetables

Line a flan ring with cheese pastry and bake in the centre of a moderately hot oven (425 °F. — Gas Mark 6) for 20—25 minutes. Cook and drain the vegetables, arrange in the flan and coat with the cheese sauce. Serve any sauce left over separately.

224   CHEESE AND VEGETABLE PLATTER

A mixture of vegetables, either fresh or frozen, provide a main meal if served with a good cheese sauce. Top with grated cheese if wished and brown under the grill or serve a selection of vegetables on a big dish, as shown in the picture, and hand the sauce separately.

225   COTTAGE CHEESE RING

1 lb. cottage cheese   *fruit, lettuce etc.*
thick mayonnaise

Blend a very small quantity of mayonnaise with the cottage cheese and press into a ring mould. Leave for a short time in a cool place and turn out carefully. Fill with either a fruit or vegetable salad, top with plenty of mayonnaise and serve on a bed of lettuce.

226   CORNISH CHEESE PIE

Cheese pastry:

8 oz. plain flour   *1 level teaspoon dry mustard*
4 oz. fat   *2 — 3 oz. finely grated*
cold water to mix   *Cheddar cheese*

Filling:

8 oz. potato   *2 oz. peas*
¼ level teaspoon mixed   *4 oz. carrot*
  herbs or thyme or 1 level   *1 medium onion (4 oz.)*
  dessertspoon chopped   *coarsely chopped*
  parsley   *salt and pepper to taste*

Cook and dice potato, carrot and cook peas. Mix all filling ingredients well together.

To make pastry, sieve flour and mustard. Rub in fat until mixture resembles fine breadcrumbs. Add cheese. Mix to a dry dough with water. Turn pastry out on to a lightly floured board and divide in two. Roll out one half and with it line an 8-inch well greased heatproof plate. Moisten edges of pastry with water, pile filling in the centre then cover with remaining pastry, rolled out into a circle slightly larger than the plate. Press edges well together to seal then knock up with the back of a knife. Brush top with beaten egg and/or milk and decorate with pastry leaves, rolled and cut from trimmings. Bake pie in the centre of a hot oven (425—450 °F. — Gas Mark 6—7) for approximately 20 minutes, lowering heat to moderate for further 20 minutes.

A QUICK LUNCHEON

219   CHEESE AND HAM ROLLS

8 thin slices cooked ham   *8 pineapple rings*
8 oz. Cheddar cheese cut   *lettuce*
   into fingers   *salad cream*
                      potato crisps

Wrap a neat slice of ham round each finger of cheese and slip a cut pineapple ring round it to hold the ham in position. Make 2 rolls per person and arrange them on a bed of crisp lettuce and serve chilled with salad cream and hot potato crisps.

220 PINEAPPLE AND CHEESE SALAD

thin slices of gherkin ⎫   *2 tablespoons lemon*
  and radish   ⎬*optional*   *juice*
¼ pint aspic jelly   ⎭   *4 oz. grated Cheddar*
1 small can crushed pineapple   *cheese*
pinch salt   *¼ pint double cream*
¼ oz. powdered gelatine *lettuce, cucumber, and*
2 tablespoons cold water   *tomatoes*
salad cream

If liked cover the bottom of each mould with thin slices of gherkin and radish set in aspic jelly. Heat the pineapple and add the salt. Soak the gelatine in the

cold water, add to the hot pineapple mixture and stir until well mixed and dissolved. Cool until the mixture begins to thicken then add the lemon juice and grated cheese, finally fold in the whipped cream and turn into the prepared moulds. Leave to set in a cool place. Turn out on to a bed of lettuce and serve with tomato slices, cucumber wedges and salad cream.

221   RAISIN AND CHEESE PYRAMIDS

4 oz. seedless raisins   *4 oz. rice*
6 oz. grated cheese   *salt and pepper*
1 small red pepper   *1 egg (lightly beaten)*
  (canned or fresh)   *salad*
hard-boiled eggs

Cook the rice and drain it carefully. Grease 8 dariole moulds and arrange a layer of seedless raisins in the bottom of each mould. Mix rice, cheese and remaining raisins together with seasoning. Remove seeds from pepper and chop. (If using fresh pepper blanch in boiling water for 5 minutes and drain well.) Stir into rice mixture with egg. Fill dariole moulds with this mixture, place on a baking sheet, cover well and bake in a moderate oven (375 °F. — Gas Mark 4) for 30—35 minutes until set. Allow to get cold, chilling if possible. Turn out on to a plate and serve with crisp salad and hardboiled eggs.

222   CHEESE TARTLETS

Cheese rough puff pastry:

4 oz. plain flour   *1 teaspoon lemon juice*
1 oz. butter or margarine *4 tablespoons cold water*
1 oz. vegetable fat   *2 oz. grated Cheddar cheese*
  shortening

Filling:

1¼ oz. raisins   *grated rind ¼ lemon*
2 oz. diced Cheddar cheese *2 teaspoons golden syrup*
¼ level teaspoon mixed spice

Sieve the flour and salt. Toss in the butter or margarine and vegetable fat shortening, cut into pieces the size of a walnut. Add the lemon juice and sufficient cold water to make a fairly soft dough using a knife. Gather the pastry together, pressing lightly, and leave to relax in a cool place for 10—15 minutes. Roll out to a strip keeping the ends square and sides even. Fold the strip into 3, seal the edges with the rolling pin, half turn the pastry, bringing the folded edges to the sides, and re-roll. Roll and fold 3 times, resting the pastry in a cool place when it becomes difficult to handle. Roll once more and put the grated cheese on two-thirds of the strip. Fold in 3 with the plain third inside. Seal the edges, half turn then roll and fold once more. Prepare the filling mixing the ingredients together. Roll out the pastry to approximately ¼ inch thick and cut out 8 rounds to fit the patty tins, cut out the remainder of the pastry into 8 rounds 1 size larger than the patty tins and line the tins with these rounds. Put in the filling, damp the pastry edges and seal on the 'tops'. Flake up the edges making a hole in the centre of each and bake in a hot oven (450 °F. — Gas Mark 7) for 20—30 minutes. Serve hot with cream or custard, or cold in a packed meal.

Sweet and Savoury

213   APPLE PIE AND CHEESE

In the North of England it is traditional to serve a finger of cheese with Apple Pie and this is a very good combination. If planning a cheese party have plenty of dessert apples and celery to serve with it. The cheese in the picture is Wensleydale.

214   BAKED APPLE AND CHEESE FLAN

Cheese pastry:

4 oz. flour	1½ oz. butter
pinch salt, cayenne pepper baking powder	2 oz. finely grated Cheddar cheese
cold water to bind	

Filling:

8 oz. cooking apples	2 oz. diced Cheddar cheese
½ oz. granulated sugar	¼ teaspoon nutmeg

Glaze:

¼ teaspoon finely grated Cheddar cheese	little egg white or milk

To make cheese pastry, sieve flour, salt, cayenne pepper and baking powder. Rub in the butter. Add the grated cheese and sufficient cold water to bind. Leave to stand in a cool place. Peel, core, quarter and slice the apples and mix with the diced cheese, sugar and nutmeg. Roll out the pastry approximately 8 × 8 inches. Cut 6½-inch strips off one side, with which to form the latticing. Spread the filling over the centre of the strip and fold over ¾ inch of pastry on each edge. Place diagonal strips of pastry ½ inch apart down the length of the flan. Glaze the pastry strips with egg white or milk and sprinkle with very finely grated cheese. Bake in a moderately hot oven (400 °F. — Gas Mark 5) for 25–30 minutes. Serve hot or cold.

215   CAKE AND CHEESE

A finger of cheese with really rich fruit cake is a very good combination of flavours. The cheese in the picture with this Dundee cake is Cheshire.

216   CHEESE CAKE

These cakes, filled with soft cream cheese, have become extremely popular.

The recipes are varied in a number of ways. You can either line your tin or dish with very thin pastry or an even better coating is to crumble biscuits very finely and to press these round the greased tin. The filling is given below: To fill an 8-inch pastry or biscuit crust, cream 3 oz. butter with 2 oz. castor sugar, add the yolks of 2 eggs and approximately 8–10 oz. of a soft cream cheese. A few sultanas could be added if wished. Fold in the stiffly beaten egg whites and put into the pastry or biscuit crust, being very careful not to break this.

Bake in the centre of a very moderate oven for approximately 1 hour.

217   FRUIT AND CHEESE

Most fruit blends very well with cheese, in salads or as a dessert. Spread rings of dessert apple with a soft cream cheese and nuts.

Dice melon and cheese and put on to cocktail sticks for an easy savoury. The cheese shown in the picture is Leicester.

218   MARMALADE AND CHEESE

In this picture Cheddar cheese is served for breakfast and while this may seem an unusual combination it is very good to eat. Cheese is an excellent beginning to the day. The famous Oslo breakfast, which is considered the finest breakfast of all, particularly for growing children, consists of brown bread, cheese, fruit and milk.

207   FONDUE

This famous Swiss delicacy has become very popular. There are quite a number of variations of it, but this is the classic way to make it:

1 lb. Gruyère cheese	*¼ pint dry white wine*
seasoning	*(Graves ideal)*

Butter the bottom and sides of an earthenware casserole, or fireproof dish. An unsalted butter is best for this. Add the grated Gruyère cheese, or for a milder flavour use a Dutch Gouda. Add seasoning and the white wine. Keep warm over a gentle heat and stir from time to time. If desired a little brandy or curaçao can be added. Some people use cornflour, which prevents the possibility of the mixture curdling. Blend a teaspoon cornflour with wine and add to mixture. Serve the fondue with toasted or untoasted bread. This is cut into squares and using a fork, or the fingers, dipped in the cheese mixture, and eaten at once. Under no circumstances let your cheese mixture boil quickly, or it becomes tough and is spoilt.

208   HAWAIIAN SANDWICHES

4 slices bread	*4 rings pineapple*
4 slices Gouda cheese	*4 slices ham*
parsley	*paprika pepper*
butter	

Toast bread, butter lavishly, then cover with ham, pineapple and lastly the cheese. Brown under the grill until the cheese begins to melt, then garnish with paprika, pepper and parsley. If more convenient heat in the oven.

209   POTATO CHEESE CAKES

1 lb. potatoes (after being peeled, cooked and mashed)	*salt and pepper to taste*
	flour or egg and crumbs for coating
4 oz. grated cheese	*fat or oil for shallow frying*
1 egg yolk	
1 teaspoon chopped chives or spring onions	*approx. 4 tablespoons tomato ketchup or tomato sauce*

Blend creamed and cooled potatoes with 3 oz. grated cheese and stir in egg yolk, chives and generous seasonings. Mix well and divide into small portions with floured hands. Use extra flour or egg and breadcrumbs for coating shapes, and shallow-fry in heated fat or oil until golden-brown on both sides. Keep hot. Serve hot tomato ketchup or tomato sauce over potato cakes and garnish with rest of the grated cheese.

210   STUFFED TOMATO CUPS

12 small tomatoes	*4 oz. seedless raisins*
8 oz. cottage cheese	*salt and pepper*
4 tablespoons chopped pineapple and juice from can	

Plump seedless raisins by covering with pineapple juice and leaving to stand for 2 hours, or bring to boil, cover and leave for 5 minutes. Mix pineapple and raisins with cheese. Halve tomatoes and scoop out inside, dry insides and fill with cheese and raisin mixture.

211   BUTTER BEAN RAREBIT

4 slices hot buttered toast	*1 small can butter beans*
½ oz. butter or margarine	*2 tablespoons milk*
1 level teaspoon dry mustard	*4 oz. grated cheese*
	salt and pepper

Make the rarebit topping as follows: melt the butter in a pan and add the milk and seasonings. When hot remove from the heat and add two-thirds of the grated cheese. Stir until melted. Lastly stir in the drained butter beans, then spread the mixture on to the slices of buttered toast. Sprinkle the remaining cheese on top, brown under the grill and serve at once.

212   APPLE WELSH RAREBIT

4 slices toast	*salt and freshly ground black pepper*
3 dessert apples	
8 oz. Cheddar cheese	*1 egg*
2 oz. butter	*corn oil for basting*
1 gill brown ale	

Grate the cheese. Put in a saucepan with the butter, ale, egg and seasoning and stir over a low flame until smooth and thick. Pile on to the toast. Core apples and slice, without peeling. Arrange on top of the cheese, brush with corn oil and place under the grill for a few minutes.

Stuffed Tomato Cups (Recipe 210)

Cake and Cheese

Quick Cheese Savouries

199 WELSH RAREBIT

4 — 6 large slices toast	butter for toast
8 oz. cheese	salt and pepper
1 teaspoon made mustard	1 oz. butter
1 tablespoon beer or ale or	1 oz. flour
Worcestershire sauce	¼ pint milk

Heat butter in a saucepan, stir in flour and cook steadily for several minutes, then gradually add the cold milk. Bring to the boil and cook until smooth and thick. Add the mustard, salt, pepper, most of the cheese and the beer. Heat steadily, without boiling too quickly, until the cheese has melted. Spread over the hot buttered toast, sprinkle with the remainder of the cheese and brown under a hot grill. Serve at once. A Dutch Gouda or Edam makes a soft creamy Welsh rarebit, or use Cheddar or Cheshire.

This Welsh rarebit mixture can be stored in covered jars for some days in a refrigerator.

200 CHEESE ON TOAST

If you do not want the bother of making Welsh Rarebit just place slices of cheese on top of hot buttered toast, and put under a hot grill. Do not over-cook or the cheese becomes tough.

For a more exciting version of cheese on toast try the following recipe.

201 CHEESE AND APPLE TOASTIES

1 large cooking apple	4 slices toast
a little ground nutmeg	4 cheese slices
4 rashers bacon	margarine

Peel and core the apple and cut into 4 rings. Fry the bacon rashers and keep hot. Fry the apple rings lightly in the hot bacon fat and lay 1 ring on each slice of toast. Sprinkle over a little nutmeg. Cover with a cheese slice and spread a little margarine over the slices. Place under the grill and brown the cheese lightly then top each with a bacon rasher and serve at once.

202 CHEESE PASTRY

By adding cheese to pastry you produce a very good flavour and texture that can be used in savoury dishes instead of short crust pastry. The ingredients are under Cornish cheese pie (Recipe 226) but the pastry can be varied by using different cheese, a little less or more. If you add much more cheese, though, you do produce a very rich short texture that is unsuitable for flans or pies as it breaks when sliced.

203 CHEESE RAFTS

12 slices hot buttered	1 small tin condensed milk
toast or crumpets or	2 oz. breadcrumbs
waffles	½ teaspoon salt
½ teaspoon paprika	¼ pint vinegar
3 oz. Swiss processed	¾ teaspoon mustard
Gruyère cheese	

Mix all the ingredients, reserving some of the cheese for garnish. Spread the mixture on the toast etc., sprinkle with sieved cheese, grill and serve hot for T. V. snacks or buffet meals with a cup of soup. In colour picture no. 22 they are served with tomato soup.

204 CHEDDAR SCOTCH EGGS

4 hard-boiled eggs	12 oz. sausage meat
3 oz. grated Cheddar cheese	little flour
tiny knob of butter	1 egg
little chopped chives or	breadcrumbs for coating
spring onions	fat for frying
seasoning	

Shell eggs and cut into halves very carefully. Remove yolk, put into basin, mash and add cheese, butter, chives and seasoning. Mix well and press back into white cases. Press the two halves together. Divide sausage meat into 4 portions. Flatten on lightly floured board. Put egg on to this then wrap round in sausage meat. Seal 'joins' very firmly. Coat with beaten egg, roll in crumbs. Fry *steadily* in deep fat until golden brown OR brush with a little melted fat, put on to hot greased tin and bake in moderately hot oven (400° F. — Gas Mark 5) for 25 minutes. Drain very well on kitchen paper.

205 CHEESE STUFFED POTATOES

4 really large potatoes	seasoning
margarine or butter	grated cheese

Bake the potatoes in the oven until tender. The time will depend on how quickly you wish to do them, but the best result is obtained by baking fairly steadily for about 1½ hours in the centre of a very moderate oven (350° F. — Gas Mark 3). Cut the potatoes in half, scoop out the pulp and put it into a basin. Mash well, add margarine or butter, seasoning and as much grated cheese as you like. Pile back again into the potato cases and return to the oven to brown. If wished a little grated cheese can be sprinkled on the top.

206 FRIED CHEESE

Small pieces of processed cheese can be fried. Add a piece of ham or bacon, if you wish, dip in beaten egg and crumbs and fry quickly. *Illustrated in colour picture no. 10.*

Cream cheese — Good for cooking — a soft and easily spread cheese. Sold in packets.

Cottage cheese — A low calorie crumbly cheese, excellent with salads.

Danish Blue — A blue veined cheese full of flavour, not unlike Gorganzola, although not as sharp.

Demi-Sel — Soft French pasteurised cheese with a fairly good 'bite'.

Derby — A close textured English cheese, not unlike Cheddar in appearance. Mild when young but a full flavour when mature — excellent for cocktail savouries if diced or served on biscuits.

Sage Derby — A Derby cheese delicately flavoured with sage.

Double Gloucester — This English cheese has an almost velvet texture and a likeness to Cheddar in flavour.

Dunlop — Scottish cheese, rather like Cheddar.

Edam — One of the Dutch cheeses — semi-hard and mild in flavour. Good for cooking as well as eating uncooked. Bright red skin.

Emmenthal — A firm Swiss cheese with large holes — not unlike Gruyère although milder in flavour. Not as good in cooking as Gruyère.

Gjetöst — A dark brown Norwegian goat's cheese — mild and rather sweet in flavour.

Gorganzola — A strongly flavoured blue-green veined cheese. Italian.

Gouda — A Dutch cheese slightly stronger in flavour than Edam. Good for cooking. Cream skin.

Gruyère — An excellent firm strongly flavoured Swiss cheese with holes in. Good for eating and excellent for cooking.

Lancashire — Although possessing a mild flavour when young this English cheese develops a full and rather pungent flavour as it matures. Its loose texture makes it ideal for crumbling over soups and hot-pots, and it is renowned for its toasting qualities. Also obtainable as 'Sage Lancashire' — this contains chopped sage leaves mixed in with the curd during cheesemaking.

Leicester — A rich russet coloured English cheese with a slightly flaky texture (moist when young). It has a mild flavour which specially recommends it as a dessert cheese.

Mozzarella — A soft Italian cheese, excellent for using with Italian Pizza pie. Sold in plastic covering.

St. Paulin — A soft French cheese covered with orange coloured rind, fairly strong.

Parmesan — The very hard Italian cheese for cooking. This is not suitable for dessert use. Parmesan grates easily because it is so hard.

Port Salut — A French cheese, round in shape with a fairly strong flavour.

Processed cheeses — These have been specially treated to make them store well; the flavour is generally mild.

Roquefort — French cheese. Similar in appearance to Danish blue cheese; good mild flavour.

Samsöe — A Danish cheese with holes like Gruyère. Good for cooking, mild in flavour.

Stilton — Blue Stilton has a close texture and is intermingled with blue veins which give it its special flavour. Fairly strong but a first class flavour.

Tome au Raisin — French cheese, rather soft in texture and fairly mild. Can be recognised by the covering of grape pips which add a distinctive flavour.

1
2
3
4

1 CAERPHILLY
2 DOUBLE GLOUCESTER
3 LANCASHIRE
4 STILTON

198   MAKING CHEESE

A number of people become very expert at making their own cheese and if you wish to do this proper equipment and instruction is important. Most housewives, however, can make their own soft milk or sour milk cheese.

Allow the milk to become sour, strain it through muslin, add seasonings, a little butter to give firmness if you wish, chopped chives etc. This now becomes your cream cheese.

Dairy Produce

The food value of dairy produce cannot be stressed too much.

MILK, the primary food for babies, is also an essential food for children and adults and the good thing about it is that the value is not lost in cooking, so when you add milk to dishes they provide extra food value.

Cream, of course, is another valuable dairy food with a very high fat content and by adding 1 or 2 tablespoons of cream to sauces etc., their food value and flavour are improved enormously.

Sour milk, in the form of yoghourt or soured cream, has the advantages of milk and is particularly easy to digest.

CHEESE, which of course contains a very high concentration of milk, is a good source of calcium and protein and the very wide variety of cheeses available means they need never become monotonous. Be careful, when cooking cheese, that it is not over-cooked otherwise it becomes stringy and rather indigestible.

BUTTER is again a very high concentration of milk fat and an excellent source of vitamin, so that adding butter to cooked vegetables, sauces etc. is adding food value.

EGGS are both an easily digested and economical source of protein; invaluable in cooking they can be added to many dishes such as sauces and custards made with powder to make them more nutritous.

Cheese

195 TO CHOOSE CHEESE

Experience of various cheeses is the best way to make your selection, for a cheese that some people will thoroughly enjoy will prove too mild or too strong for others. Generally speaking, to begin with, it is wise to take advice from the grocer as to the mildness, or otherwise, of the cheese and occasionally you will find one who will let you try them.

As you will see in Recipe 197, comment is made on the mildness etc. of most well known cheeses. For a well planned cheese party or interesting cheese board choose a Cheddar or Cheshire, a rather stronger cheese like Danish Blue, or Gorganzola, a very mild cheese and perhaps a cream type of cheese or soft cheese, like Camembert.

196 TO STORE CHEESE

English cheese will keep well if wrapped in a polythene bag to prevent drying and then stored in a cool larder or refrigerator. In the latter case the cheese should be lightly wrapped and brought to room temperature 30 minutes before serving.

Many grocers are now selling cheese in pre-packed portions, which means that the cheese reaches you in excellent condition. Cheese packed in this way will keep longer if stored in a refrigerator.

Camembert, Brie and other cheese are better not put into a refrigerator but left at room storage unless they are ripening too quickly.

Camembert, however, is delicious if put into the freezing part of the refrigerator 45 minutes before serving.

197 VARIETIES OF CHEESES

Below is given a description of some of the most popular cheeses together with their country of origin. Quite often other countries make these cheeses as well.

Bel Paese — Soft, rather sweet mild Italian cheese.

Bresse Bleu — A soft French cheese with faint blue veining. Medium strong.

Brie — A French cheese, not unlike Camembert in flavour, best when really ripe. As the cheese is wrapped it is quite permissible to press it, or ask your grocer to do so — if very firm and unyielding the cheese is NOT ripe.

Caerphilly — Creamy white Welsh cheese with semi-smooth texture. Mild flavour.

Camembert — French cheese; excellent Danish Camembert is also available. Rather similar to Brie and should be tested in same way.

Cheshire — A mellow, open-textured cheese. There is Cheshire Red and Cheshire White, both with the same flavour. There is also the famous Old Blue, rich and very rare. Cheshire is the oldest known English cheese — it has been produced in England for over seven centuries. Good for cooking.

Cheddar — The most popular English cheese. Its 'nutty' flavour becomes deeper as the cheese matures. Close and creamy texture. Excellent Cheddar cheeses come from Scotland, Canada, Australia and New Zealand. Good for cooking.

Cheshire

Cheddar

Double Gloucester

Stilton

Derby

Caerphilly

Wensleydale

Lancashire

Leicester

Fish Salads

187 BUTTER BEAN AND SARDINE SALAD

Toss butter beans in chopped chives and French dressing (made from sardine oil and vinegar) and serve with sardines. Garnish with tomato and potato crisps.

188 GERMAN HERRING SALAD

This typical German salad is usually made with filleted salt herrings, cooked potatoes, cold veal (cooked), mixture of pickled cucumbers (or gherkins) and Dutch (or greenhouse) cucumber, dessert apples and beetroot,

all diced small and dressed with salad cream to which has been added a little white wine, sugar and mustard.

A variation to please most tastes could be:

Rollmops (pickled herrings), chopped or left whole, with any of the ingredients mentioned above but particularly with thinly sliced spring onions, apples and beetroots. Heaped on to a dish lined with lettuce leaves they can be surrounded at the base with potato salad, sprinkling generously with chopped chives.

189 NIÇOISE SALAD

few cooked French or	black olives
runner beans	few capers (if desired)
tomatoes	anchovy fillets
cucumber	vinaigrette dressing
lettuce	(Recipe 354)
hard-boiled egg	

Toss beans, sliced cucumber, olives, lettuce in vinaigrette dressing. Arrange lettuce in bowl or dish and cover with sliced cucumber, tomatoes etc. Put anchovy fillets in centre. Serve with onion rings if desired. This salad can be made more substantial by using more beans and sliced potatoes. *Illustrated in colour picture no. 8.*

190 SALMON AND LETTUCE SHELLS

Wash and dry fairly big lettuce leaves. Mix flaked cooked or canned salmon with mayonnaise, a little horseradish, cream and chopped cucumber or gherkin. Pile into lettuce leaves.

191 SHELLFISH SALADS

All shellfish is excellent in salad. Remember it must be very fresh and it should not be covered too thickly with mayonnaise so that it loses the attractive colour.

192 SUMMER SALAD

4 cooked herrings	2 tablespoons horseradish
8 oz. cold cooked potato	sauce
8 oz. diced cooked beetroot	2 cups chopped peeled apples
1 hard-boiled egg	vinegar
1 tablespoon chopped	lettuce and cucumber for
parsley	garnish

Remove skin and bones from fish and break them up. Moisten with a little vinegar. Mix the vegetables and apples together and add the fish. Arrange in a salad bowl. Add the chopped parsley to the horseradish sauce and pour over the salad. Garnish with slices of hard-boiled egg, lettuce leaves and cucumber.

193 WHITE FISH SALADS

White fish makes both economical and interesting salads. The fish should be steamed or poached gently in seasoned water, taking care it does not over-cook. Flake rather coarsely and then mix with mayonnaise, gherkins, capers, diced cucumber etc. If pressed gently into a mould it can be turned out. See colour picture no. 6 for an attractive white fish salad.

Moulded Salads

181 CREAMED TOMATO SALAD RING

1 level tablespoon gelatine
1 large can cream of tomato soup
salt and pepper
¼ pint milk or evaporated milk
salad
shrimps
mayonnaise (Recipe 337)

Dissolve powdered gelatine in very hot cream of tomato soup. When cool, but not set, whisk in ¼ pint of milk, season well. Pour into ring mould and when set, turn out. Fill the centre with green salad, shrimps or a diced cheese salad and mayonnaise.

182 GREEN PEA SALAD

1 lb. cooked peas
½ pint liquid in which peas were cooked
1 envelope gelatine (to set 1 pint)
1 small cooked carrot
strips of red pepper
½ pint vinegar
2 tablespoons sugar
salt
2 tablespoons chopped mint

Dissolve gelatine in the hot liquid, add vinegar, sugar and salt to taste. Place a little in the bottom of a ring mould, and when it begins to thicken arrange a layer of peas and strips of red pepper, cover with a little more jelly mixture. Add mint to the balance of the jelly mixture. Cut shaped pieces of carrot, dip in the mixture and set round the top of the mould — this will have to be done a portion at a time. Fill the mould with the remainder of the peas and the jelly. When serving fill the centre of the mould with mashed potato. Decorate with sprigs of mint.

183 HAM AND RAISIN MOUSSE

½ oz. gelatine
3 tablespoons cold water
½ pint boiling stock (good measure)
8 oz. chopped ham
6 oz. seedless raisins
1 tablespoon chopped onion or chives
2 tablespoons mayonnaise (Recipe 337)
1 tablespoon sweet pickle
1 teaspoon Worcestershire sauce
seasoning

Soak gelatine in cold water. Pour on boiling stock and stir until gelatine is dissolved. Chill until nearly set, mix in rest of ingredients. Fill moulds with mixture, chill until set.

184 LOBSTER RELISH

2 teaspoons gelatine dissolved in 4 tablespoons hot water
lobster meat
¼ pint cream
small cucumber
green colouring

mayonnaise

2 teaspoons gelatine dissolved in 3 tablespoons hot water
¼ pint mayonnaise (Recipe 337)

Cut unpeeled cucumber into quarters, remove seeds, fork the pulp, add dissolved gelatine, salt and pepper to taste. When cool stir into the cream, leave for 10 minutes, strain, colour a delicate green. Pour carefully into the mould. When firm pack the lobster meat into the mould and add the clear jelly (if set stand in warm water to re-melt but wait till it is cold before placing in the mould).

Serve with jellied mayonnaise — add dissolved gelatine to mayonnaise, pour into small moulds. Decorate with salad.

185 MACARONI AND SAUSAGE MOULD

1 envelope gelatine (to set 1 pint)
6 sausages
¾ pint boiling water
1 tablespoon vinegar
2 cloves
2 slices onion
salt and pepper
3 tablespoons tomato sauce
3 oz. long macaroni (cooked)

Place sausages in boiling water and simmer till cooked. Leave till cold. Remove fat. Heat liquid with cloves, onion, salt and pepper for 5 minutes. Add gelatine moistened with 2 tablespoons cold water. Stir till dissolved. Stir in tomato sauce and vinegar. Strain. Pour a little into the bottom of a wet mould or basin. When thickening arrange sliced tomatoes round the mould, skin sausages, cut some lengthways and place on top of the macaroni. Slice the remainder and place in the mould. When all ingredients are in position pour in the jelly mixture. Serve with salads.

186 MOULDED CHICKEN SALAD

approx. 1 lb. cooked chicken or chicken and ham
1 pint chicken stock OR use can chicken soup and make up to 1 pint with milk or water
1 oz. gelatine
3 tablespoons mayonnaise
2 hard-boiled eggs
4 oz. diced vegetables (peas, carrots, diced cucumber)
seasoning

Chop chicken fairly finely, but do not mince. Heat most of the chicken stock, soften gelatine in remaining liquid, then add to hot stock and stir until thoroughly dissolved. COOL then stir in chicken, mayonnaise, chopped eggs, vegetables and seasoning. Pour into mould or basin and leave to set. Serve with lettuce and tomatoes.

Chicken and Meat Salads

176   CHICKEN ALMOND SALAD

12 oz. cooked chicken	1 tablespoon chopped parsley
4 oz. toasted almonds	1 teaspoon salt
6 oz. seedless raisins	pepper to taste
1 tablespoon grated onion	1 tablespoon lemon juice
2 tablespoons mayonnaise	¼ pint single cream or top of milk

Plump seedless raisins by covering with cold water, bring to boil, cover and leave to stand for 5 minutes. Cut chicken into long shreds, place all ingredients in mixing bowl and mix with mayonnaise and cream just before serving. Serve on bed of lettuce.

177   CHICKEN AND ASPARAGUS SALAD

1 7-oz. can asparagus tips or fresh asparagus	1 medium eating apple, peeled and diced
12 oz. cooked diced chicken	¼ pint mayonnaise
lettuce	(Recipe 337)

Strain asparagus and put few tips to one side for garnish. Chop remainder and mix with chicken, apple and mayonnaise. Serve on a bed of lettuce and garnish with a few asparagus tips. Alternatively the lettuce may be served separately.

178   CHICKEN PLATTER

This is a wonderful way of transforming cold chicken remains into a simple and exciting meal. Moisten the cubed chicken with creamy mayonnaise and pile into a shallow bowl. Set the bowl in the centre of a round breadboard or tray and surround with slices of salami or liver sausage, frankfurters or cold cooked sausages and a selection of salad vegetables — this photograph shows chicory, sliced cooked carrots and young French beans. Serve with crusty bread or rolls, and butter. Just perfect for a summer buffet style meal.

179   CORN AND HAM CORNETS

2 small size cartons frozen sweet corn off the cob*	1 level tablespoon chopped parsley
1 egg, hard-boiled and chopped	3 dessertspoons salad cream
lettuce	4 unbroken slices of lean ham
sliced cucumber	tomatoes
	little milk

* If using fresh corn cook and strip from cob

Cook the corn according to the directions on the carton or until tender, drain and allow to cool. When cold, add the egg, parsley, salad cream and milk and mix thoroughly. Roll each slice of ham into a cornet shape (this can be done round the outside of a cream horn tin) and place on a plate with the join underneath: Fill each with a little of the corn mixture and pile the remainder in the centre of the plate. Garnish with lettuce leaves and serve sliced cucumber and tomato.

180   MEAT SALADS

Left over-cold meat can be sliced, but makes a more interesting salad if diced and mixed with mayonnaise or French dressing and garnished with vegetables and/or fruits. For a beef salad add a little horseradish to mayonnaise. For a lamb salad add a little chopped mint. For a ham salad use diced apple or chopped pineapple with the dressing. For pork add orange.

Cheese and Egg Salads

167 TO PREPARE CHEESE SALADS

Use Dutch, Cheddar or other similar cheese, cream, cottage, processed cheese or a mixture of cheeses. The cheese can be sliced or grated or in the case of cottage cheese arrange neatly to one side or in the centre of the dish.

Toss in a salad dressing, if desired, and garnish with the salad. Chives, parsley or red pepper add colour to the cheese.

168 TO PREPARE EGG SALADS

The eggs can be hard-boiled or scrambled and mixed with chives, prawns etc. — hard-boiled egg should not be sliced until the last minute to prevent it becoming dry. If serving the eggs whole coat with mayonnaise and garnish with parsley or red pepper.

169 COTTAGE CHEESE AND PINEAPPLE PLATTER

1 lb. cottage cheese	*1 head chicory*
8 chilled pineapple slices	*4 medium tomatoes*
	sprigs of parsley

Pile the cottage cheese in the middle of a platter. Surround with a semi-circle of pineapple slices then with chicory leaves and whole tomatoes. Circle the cottage cheese with a ring of parsley sprigs.

170 DUTCH SUPPER SALAD

6 oz. Gouda cheese	*2 oranges*
2 heads chicory	*yoghourt or mayonnaise*
2 apples	*(Recipe 337 or 342)*

Dice all the ingredients. Mix with yoghourt or mayonnaise. Serve with crusty bread and butter or baked potatoes.

171 EGG SALAD

Hard-boil eggs. Shell then cut all but one into slices. Serve on crisp lettuce or endive. Garnish with chopped yolk and white of the remaining egg and mayonnaise.

172 GRAPE, CHEESE AND BANANA SALAD

8 oz. grapes	*12 oz. cottage cheese*
2 sliced bananas	*lettuce*
lemon juice	*mayonnaise (Recipe 337)*

Wash and seed the grapes if necessary and toss the banana in a little lemon juice to preserve the colour. Serve the fruit in the centre of a ring of chilled cottage cheese, garnished with lettuce, and hand mayonnaise separately.

173 COTTAGE CHEESE AND PEACH PLATTER

1 small head endive or lettuce	*8 oz. cottage cheese*
2 or 3 sliced olives	*4 canned peach halves*
1 oz. shelled walnuts	*2 clusters grapes*

Wash and dry lettuce or endive. Arrange on plate or wooden platter. Pile cottage cheese on one half and garnish with sliced olives. Place peach halves on other half and top with shelled walnuts. Arrange grapes on either side. Serve with thin slices of brown bread, lightly buttered.

174 NUTTY BANANA AND CHEESE SALAD

This makes a good high tea on its own but it is also delicious served with cold lamb. Try it when there seems hardly enough lamb to make a meal and see how the salad adds flavour to the meal.

For each serving

2 oz. cream cheese	*mayonnaise (Recipe 337)*
1 teaspoon sugar	*walnuts*
1 teaspoon cream	*lettuce*
1 banana	*strawberries (optional)*

Mash cream cheese with sugar and cream. Cut peeled banana into ½-inch pieces and sandwich together with the cheese mixture. Dip in mayonnaise, then into finely chopped walnuts. Arrange on a bed of lettuce, with strawberries when in season.

175 PIQUANT EGG SALAD

Chop hard-boiled eggs coarsely. Mix with diced cucumber, shredded mushrooms, chopped gherkins, capers and peppers. Arrange on a bed of crisp lettuce and serve with vinaigrette dressing (Recipe 354). To make a more substantial salad add anchovy fillets or thin strips of cooked ham.

161 ORANGE SALAD

lettuce   oranges

Arrange the crisp lettuce. Cut the oranges in sections. If you skin the orange with a very sharp knife and cut away the pith, you can then cut each section of orange without using the skin. Arrange on the lettuce. Serve with French dressing (Recipe 343) or vinaigrette dressing (Recipe 354).

162 ORANGE MAYONNAISE

Peel and remove the pith from several juicy oranges and cut across into thin slices. Serve on lettuce or watercress dressed with thick mayonnaise.

163 ORANGE AND PINEAPPLE SALAD

Add diced pineapple and finely chopped egg white to garnish. These salads are excellent with duck or rich meat.

164 ORANGE AND TOMATO SALAD

Have you ever eaten oranges and tomatoes together? They make a colourful combination that's delicious. To make the salad, simply alternate sections of well-peeled orange with slices of firm red tomatoes on a bed of lettuce and watercress. Sprinkle with fresh chopped mint and a slightly sweet, tangy French dressing (Recipe 343).

165 PEACH SALAD

4 half peaches   4 tablespoons thick mayonnaise
lettuce   chopped nuts

Cup the drained peaches in lettuces. Place a good tablespoon of thick mayonnaise in the centre of each and sprinkle over a few chopped nuts. Serve with cold meat.

166 EASY-TO-MAKE PEAR SALAD

Allow 1 pear per person. Peel, halve and core fresh pears or drain canned pears and serve, cut surface upwards, on a bed of lettuce. Put a good teaspoonful of thick mayonnaise in the centre of each half pear and garnish with a mint sprig.

Fruit Salads

156   FRUITS IN SALADS

APPLES. Leave the peel on if possible to give a touch of colour. Excellent added to cole slaw or mixed with nuts.

BANANAS. Blend very well with a cheese salad. Toss in mayonnaise or lemon juice to keep them a good colour.

DRIED FRUIT. Any dried fruit goes well in a salad particularly with cheese or ham and fruit.

GRAPEFRUIT. Excellent in a green salad or with rather rich ingredients.

MELON. Very pleasant to serve with ham or chicken. Cut into balls or cubes.

ORANGES. These are a perfect ingredient in a salad to serve with duck or goose to counteract the richness. See Recipes 161—164.

PEACHES. Canned or fresh peaches are excellent with ham.

PEARS. Fresh or canned pears can be filled with mayonnaise and served with a cheese or meat salad. An avocado pear, however, is best with the stone removed and tossed in French dressing or filled with shrimps or prawns in a mayonnaise. See colour picture no. 5.

157   APPLE AVOCADO SALAD

4 eating apples   *4 oz. salted mixed nuts*
1 avocado pear   *French dressing (Recipe 343)*
juice of 2 lemons   *watercress*

Core apples, but do not pare. Slice ⅛ inch thick. Pare avocado pear, cut in half, remove seed and cut into slices about ⅛ inch thick. Cover apple and avocado pear with lemon juice to prevent browning. Just before serving, drain, add salted nuts and watercress and toss with a good French dressing. Make the dressing with corn oil, some of the drained lemon juice, pepper, salt and a little sugar.

158   BANANA SALAD

Allow 1 banana for each person. Peel and split lengthwise then cut each piece across in half if large. Arrange fruit on a bed of crisp lettuce, top with thick mayonnaise and garnish with strawberries when in season or with chopped nuts. Serve with cheese etc.

159   FRUIT FLOWERS

Fruit flowers are just as luscious as they look. Versatile too, they are equally good served as hors-d'oeuvre with salad or as a sweet with a sprinkling of brown sugar and whipped cream. Simply halve ripe dessert pears (lengthwise), scoop out the core, fill with cream cheese and use halved, pipped, black grapes, matchstick slices of apple and thin segments of plums to make flower petal patterns on top.

160   GRAPEFRUIT SALAD

Arrange neatly on a flat dish, in concentric rings, sliced pineapple, orange, grapefruit segments, grapes and cherries. Then add firm lettuce hearts, shelled walnuts and sliced fresh tomatoes. Serve the salad with mayonnaise (Recipe 337 or 345) or French dressing (Recipe 343).

145 BEETROOT SALAD

Dice or slice the cooked beetroot and mix with French dressing (Recipe 343) or sugar and seasoning.

146 CORN SALAD

Use canned or frozen cooked corn or strip the cooked corn from the cob. Toss in French dressing or mayonnaise (Recipes 343, 337) and chopped parsley.

147 CUCUMBER SALAD

The cucumber should be mixed with either vinegar and seasoning or French dressing (Recipe 343) and left for an hour or so. Another way of preparing cucumber is to slice very thinly, add seasoning and leave for an hour or so, pouring away the surplus liquid.

148 GREEN PEA AND NEW CARROT SALAD

Prepare and cook the peas and carrots lightly, drain and cool — or use left-over peas and carrots. Arrange in tidy heaps on a large serving plate around thin slices of cold roast beef. Put a heaped teaspoon of thick mayonnaise on the piles of vegetables and serve as a delicious cold summer lunch.

149 GREEN SALAD

It is incorrect to mix hard-boiled eggs, tomatoes etc., with this. A green salad should just be lettuce, watercress or any other green vegetables. Toss in a French dressing (Recipe 343).

150 RAW MUSHROOMS

Good quality mushrooms can always be served raw. They make a delicious salad, if washed and thinly sliced, tossed in French dressing (Recipe 343) and left for a short time. They can be mixed with sliced tomatoes, red or green peppers, chicory or lettuce.

151 POTATO SALAD

1 lb. potatoes	1 gill mayonnaise or salad
2 teaspoons finely	dressing (Recipes
chopped onion	337, 348)
seasoning	3 teaspoons finely chopped
	parsley

The secret of a good potato salad is to mix it when hot, then eat it when very cold. Cook the potatoes in salted water until just cooked — be careful they do not become over-soft. Strain and leave until just cool enough to handle — BUT NOT COLD. Cut into neat dice and toss in the mayonnaise, adding onion, parsley and seasoning. Leave until cold, then if desired garnish with a little more chopped parsley. If preferred toss in oil and vinegar instead of mayonnaise.

152 POTATO AND CELERY SALAD

Make like potato salad, but include a good 4 oz. celery, which should be cut into very thin strips.

153 SPICED POTATO SALAD

Add capers, diced gherkins and good shake paprika pepper to potato salad.

154 RUSSIAN SALAD

8 oz. cooked potato	8 oz. cooked runner or
8 oz. cooked carrots*	French beans*
8 oz. cooked peas*	4 oz. cooked turnip*
2 tablespoons oil	mayonnaise (Recipe 337
seasoning	or 342)
	1 tablespoon vinegar

* or use cooked mixed frozen vegetables

Cut all the vegetables into neat dice. Put into a large bowl and pour over the oil and vinegar, then season well. Leave for several hours, turning round in the dressing from time to time. Do this gently so the vegetables are not broken. When ready to serve pile on to a dish — on lettuce if desired — and form into pyramid. Pour over just enough mayonnaise to coat.

155 TOMATO SALAD

Slice or prepare tomatoes as described in Recipe 138. Season well or toss in a little French dressing and chopped parsley. Garnish with raw onion rings.

Salads

137   TO MAKE GOOD SALADS

All the ingredients should be as fresh as possible for a salad since you lose both vitamin value and good appearance if they are limp. Salads vary a great deal in flavour. Today it is accepted that one can, for example, mix fruit and nuts in with green lettuce for a salad. In the same way it is perfectly correct, and very popular, to serve a cold salad with hot grilled or roasted dishes or as a contrast to hot pasta dishes (see colour picture no. 31).

138 TO PREPARE INGREDIENTS FOR SALADS

Lettuce, endive, cabbage and all other green vegetables should be well washed and dried. If shredding make sure you have a stainless silver knife so they are not discoloured. Do not shred too soon before serving the salad.

Cucumber can be peeled or not according to personal taste (see cucumber salad, Recipe 147). To give an attractive effect to peel, score the skin by dragging the point of a fork down very firmly.

Tomatoes can be skinned by lowering carefully into hot water for a minute and then into cold water. They can then be sliced or, if the skin is left on, cut into water lily shapes. To do this use a sharp knife.

Insert the point of the knife into the tomato and cut into the tomato in zigzags, each time feeling the point of the knife going through to the centre.

When you have completed doing this pull the tomato gently apart and you have two halves of a water lily.

Radishes should be washed, dried and either sliced or cut into water lilies as for tomatoes, or with practice you can make more elaborate shapes by cutting the actual skin away from the centre of the radish in petal shapes. If time permits the easiest way to make a flower is to cut the radish from the top into about 8 sections. Don't cut right down to the bottom. Put into very cold water for an hour or so and these will open up.

Celery should either be diced or cut into thin strips. Put into iced or cold water they will form celery curves.

Vegetable Salads

139   ASPARAGUS SALAD

1 bunch asparagus	*2 hard-boiled eggs*
lettuce	*little chopped parsley*
vinaigrette dressing	
(Recipe 354)	

Cook the asparagus as directed in Recipe 4, drain and allow to cool. Arrange on a bed of lettuce with quartered hard-boiled eggs. Pour over the dressing and garnish the eggs with the chopped parsley.

140   COLE SLAW

1 small Savoy cabbage	*salt and pepper*
2 dessertspoons olive oil	*1 — 2 tablespoons*
1 dessertspoon vinegar	*mayonnaise (Recipe 337)*

Shred the cabbage finely. Mix all the other ingredients in a bowl, pour over the cabbage, and toss. Stand a little before use.

141   APPLE COLE SLAW

Mix 2 grated dessert apples with cabbage.

142   APPLE AND CELERY COLE SLAW

Mix 1 grated dessert apple and 4 oz. finely chopped celery with cabbage.

143   SPICED COLE SLAW

Mix 1 grated apple and 4 oz. finely chopped celery with the cabbage. Soak 2 oz. seedless raisins in the oil and vinegar mixture with pinch mixed spice.

144   CHICORY SALAD

Wash, dry and fill the centres with diced vegetables in mayonnaise or chop and toss in mayonnaise.

6   **FISH SALAD (Recipe 193)**

7   **BOILED GAMMON WITH SALAD (Recipe 293)**

STRAWBERRY CREAM GATEAU

VICTORIA SANDWICH

4 oz butter
4 oz castor sugar

2 eggs
1 tablespoon water
4 oz S.R. flour

FILLING, etc.

3 tablespoons strawberry jam
5 fluid oz fresh double cream

desiccated coconut

Make sponge by beating the sugar and butter together until light and creamy, add the eggs a little at a time, beating well. Fold in the sieved flour, add the water to make a dropping consistency. Divide into two 7" greased sandwich tins and bake at Mark 5 or 350°F for approximately 20 minutes.

Cool, fill with jam and cream—coat sides with cream and roll in coconut—pile whipped cream on the top. Serve.

Fresh strawberries or other fresh fruits may be used instead of the jam

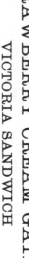

brush with a little beaten egg or milk to glaze. Bake for 10 minutes i̲n̲ h̲o̲t̲ o̲v̲e̲n̲, 450-475°F, Mark 7/8. Pull out metal horns carefully. Leave cases to cool. Fill with whipped cream.

CREAM SWISS ROLL

3 eggs   4 oz castor sugar   3 oz flour
½ tablespoonful hot water
1 gill whipped cream
½ tablespoonful warm jam

Grease a swiss roll tin and line with greased paper. Warm and sieve the flour. Beat eggs and sugar till thick and creamy. Fold in flour. Add sufficient tepid water to make a pouring consistency. Turn into prepared tin and spread out to corners. Bake in a hot oven 7/10 minutes. Mark 7/8 or 450-475°F. Turn on to a sugared paper. Roll with paper and leave to cool. Unroll, spread with warm jam and whipped cream. Roll up.

CREAM SLICES

1 pkt Frozen puff pastry
raspberry jam
¼ pint double dairy cream

Roll out pastry to fit baking sheet 10" x 12". Using back of a knife, cut into 15 squares. Brush with water and sprinkle with castor sugar. Place in centre of oven at Mark 7/8 or 450-475° F and bake for about 10 minutes. Split and fill with jam and whipped cream.

Makes 15 cakes. Cost approx. 2½d each

MPC 353/10

Issued by the National Dairy Council

SCONES

2 oz butter   2 oz sugar
8 oz S.R. flour
½ teaspoon cream of tartar
¼ teaspoon bicarbonate of soda
pinch of salt   1 egg   strawberry jam
¼ pint double dairy cream

Sift flour with salt, cream of tartar and bi-carbonate of soda. Add sugar. Rub in fat (add dried fruit if desired). Add egg and a little milk if necessary. Roll out to good ½ inch thickness. Bake at Mark 7 or 450°F for 10/15 minutes. Serve with strawberry jam and whipped cream.

Makes 12 scones. Cost approx 3d. each

BRANDY SNAPS

1 pkt brandy snaps
¼ pint double dairy cream

Pipe a little whipped cream into each end of brandy snap.

Makes about 30 cakes. Cost approx. 1½d. each

CREAM HORNS—Frozen puff pastry

real dairy cream recipes

CHOCOLATE ECLAIRS

7½ oz water
pinch of salt
4 small eggs
½ pint double dairy cream

2 oz butter
4 oz plain flour
chocolate icing

Add salt and fat to water and bring to boil. Add flour, stirring over heat until mixture leaves sides of the pan. Leave to cool, then beat in eggs gradually. Pipe mixture with a forcing bag and ¾" plain tube on to a greased tray. Bake about 25 minutes at Mark 8 or 475°F. Split whilst hot, leave to cool and fill with whipped cream and coat with chocolate icing.

Makes 18 Eclairs

MERINGUES

4 egg whites
4 oz granulated sugar
glacé cherries
½ pint double dairy cream

4 oz castor sugar

Place the egg whites in a basin and whisk until very stiff. Fold in the sugar. Place greaseproof paper, on to a baking sheet and either pipe in shapes or place on to the tin in table-spoonfuls. Sprinkle with castor sugar. Put immediately into oven and bake for 2½ to 3 hours at Mark ¼ or 250° F. The meringues are "dry," when they can be lifted off the paper. Sandwich together with whipped cream and decorate with glacé cherries.

5 QUICK SUPPER DISHES
CREAMED AND FRIED MUSHROOMS (Recipes 58 and 60);
CANNED GINGER PUDDING GARNISHED WITH GINGER;
STUFFED AVOCADO PEARS (Recipe 156)

130   BAKED YAMS

4 whole yams   butter
salt and pepper

Wash the outside well and prick. Bake for approximately 35 minutes for each lb. in a moderately hot oven (400° F. — Gas Mark 5). Remove top skin, lift out pulp, mash with butter and seasoning and return to the skin.

131   PURÉE OF YAM

Peel yam, cut into dice with sharp knife. Put into boiling salted water, adding squeeze of lemon juice if wished. Cook steadily for approximately 1 hour until tender then mash, adding margarine or butter and a little top of milk. Season well.

Quick Vegetable Dishes

132   FROZEN VEGETABLES

Frozen vegetables have become extremely popular during recent years and for a very good reason: their flavour is excellent and there is a very large variety to be obtained. Take care not to over-cook frozen vegetables. Cooking times are given and should be followed carefully. In this chapter no particular reference is made to frozen vegetables, but they can be used in suitable recipes in place of fresh vegetables. The following dish for instance, is very good made with frozen beans.

132   BEANS AND MACARONI
A quickly prepared supper dish

3 oz. quick cooking   4 oz. grated cheese
*   macaroni   seasoning*
1 oz. butter   1 large carton frozen
3 tomatoes   sliced green beans*
* or use fresh sliced runner beans

Skin and roughly chop the tomatoes. Cook the macaroni according to the directions on the carton. Melt half the butter and sauté the tomatoes for a few minutes until piping hot. Add the cooked macaroni, reheat and lastly stir in the cheese and seasoning to taste. Meanwhile cook the beans according to the directions on the carton. Strain, toss in butter and season with pepper. Serve the beans down the centre of a flat dish with the macaroni mixture on either side.

133   CANNED VEGETABLES

It is always wise to have a selection of canned vegetables in the cupboard for an emergency. Do not overcook them, for in processing they have become softened and generally need heating only.

134   MIXED VEGETABLE GRILL

1 packet thick onion soup   1 lb. cooked diced,
2 oz. grated cheese   vegetables, either fresh,
*   canned or frozen*

Make up soup mix according to the directions on the packet, but use only ½ pint water. Add the vegetables and heat through. Turn into a shallow greased dish, sprinkle with grated cheese, and brown under the grill.

135   DE-HYDRATED VEGETABLES

Mixed vegetables, onions etc. are now obtainable in dried form. They are an excellent stand-by in the cupboard. Illustrated opposite is a de-hydrated vegetable curry which provides a complete meal.

136   VEGETABLES IN CASSEROLES AND STEWS

Vegetables add flavour to most meat casseroles and stews; include plenty of carrots, onions, shallots or celery, but add only a small amount of turnip or swede since this gives too strong a flavour. Colour picture no. 32 shows an attractive meat and vegetable casserole.

118 SPINACH SOUFFLÉ

1 lb. cooked spinach   seasoning
1 oz. butter   4 eggs
1 oz. flour   2 oz. grated Parmesan
¼ gill milk   cheese (can be omitted)

Chop spinach finely or sieve. Heat butter, stir in flour, cook for several minutes then add milk, spinach purée and seasoning. Beat in egg yolks and cheese and stiffly beaten egg whites. Pour into soufflé dish and bake for approximately 30 minutes in centre of moderate oven (375° F. — Gas Mark 4).

Tomatoes

119 BAKED TOMATOES

Halve the tomatoes, top with a little butter and seasoning and bake for about 15 minutes in a moderately hot oven. There are many fillings for baked whole tomatoes. The centre pulp is generally taken out and mixed with the filling: minced meat, creamed fish, cheese and crumbs etc. Before returning to the oven season the tomato case well and then put in the filling.

120 FRIED TOMATOES

Slice tomatoes and fry in a little hot fat; a pinch of sugar as well as seasoning improves the flavour.

121 GRILLED TOMATOES

Top with a little butter and seasoning and grill steadily under moderate heat.

122 RICE-STUFFED TOMATOES

6 firm, ripe, good-sized   few buttered breadcrumbs
   tomatoes   salt, pepper and thyme
4 oz. cooked rice   2 tablespoons chopped
2 tablespoons olive oil   chives

Cut top off tomatoes, scoop out pulp and chop. Sauté cooked rice in olive oil for 5 minutes, or until oil is absorbed; season with salt, pepper and thyme; add chopped chives, stuff into scooped-out tomatoes. Place filled tomatoes in a greased baking dish; sprinkle with buttered crumbs and bake in a moderately hot oven (400° F. — Gas Mark 5) for 20 minutes. Serve with cheese sauce (see Recipe 314).
Illustrated in colour picture no. 2.

123 GLAZED TURNIPS

Choose very small turnips. Cook in boiling salted water until just tender, drain then cover with little sugar blended with vegetable water. Heat until turnips are just golden brown and have absorbed liquid.

124 MASHED TURNIPS

Cook the turnips as in Recipe 4. Strain and mash very well indeed. Add a knob of butter, a little grated nutmeg and milk or cream. Beat very well.

125 FRIED MARROW

Peel and cut the marrow into rings, removing the seeds. Fry steadily in shallow fat.

126 ROAST MARROW

Peel the marrow and cut into fairly large pieces, removing the seeds. Put into hot fat and roast for about 40 minutes in a moderately hot oven.

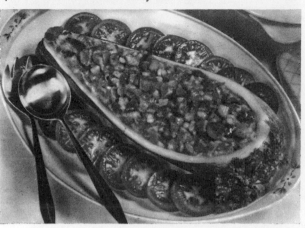

127 STUFFED VEGETABLE MARROW

1 medium sized marrow   ¼ small green pepper
1 can condensed Scotch   1 teaspoon
   broth   Worcestershire sauce
salt and pepper   4 tomatoes (sliced)
6—8 oz. cooked mutton   parsley
   (diced)

Put green pepper into boiling salted water for 2—3 minutes, lift out and drain. Skin marrow if wished, but when young the skin can be left on. Slice off top to give boat shape, and then remove the seeds. Mix the condensed Scotch broth with seasoning, mutton, chopped green pepper and Worcestershire sauce. Stuff the marrow with this mixture and replace top. Wrap in foil, place in roasting tin and bake in a moderately hot oven (400° F. — Gas Mark 5) for 1½—1¾ hours. Serve marrow with or without top, garnished with parsley and lightly grilled tomato slices.

128 STUFFING MARROW AND COURGETTES

There are many other ways in which marrows and courgettes can be stuffed, e.g.:
1. Fried onion, tomatoes and cooked rice.
2. Left-over cooked meat, minced and blended with a thick sauce, fried onion, tomatoes and capers.
3. A vegetarian stuffing of a thick cheese sauce with diced cooked vegetables.
4. Grilled bacon rashers either whole or minced with sausage meat.

129 MARROW (COURGETTES) PORTUGUESE

Young marrows are delicious if cooked in this way. Fry thinly sliced onion and a crushed clove of garlic in hot oil or oil and butter. Add several peeled and sliced tomatoes and when the mixture is soft add the diced marrow (with the skin on if very young) and cook until tender.

Parsnips

108 PARSNIP CROQUETTES

Peel, dice the parsnips and cook until tender in boiling salted water, sieve or mash very thoroughly. Allow to each lb. parsnip purée an egg yolk, knob of butter, seasoning and a dessertspoon cream or milk. Form into croquette shapes, roll in the egg white and crumbs and fry until crisp and golden brown.

109 FRIED PARSNIPS

Parsnips are better if they are partially boiled before frying. Peel, cut into fingers or slices and cook steadily for about 15 minutes in boiling salted water. Drain well, then coat with batter if wished or toss in seasoned flour. Lower into hot fat and cook until golden brown.

110 ROAST PARSNIPS

These can be roasted in hot fat raw or to give a better flavour boil for 15—20 minutes in salted water, drain, pat dry in a cloth or kitchen paper and then put into hot fat. They will take approximately 1¼—1½ hours if raw and about 1 hour if partially boiled, in a hot oven.

111 RATATOUILLE

2 onions	1 red or green pepper
1 lb. tomatoes	little bacon fat or rind
1 medium marrow	from gammon
4 small aubergines	1 or 2 cloves garlic
little chopped parsley	seasoning

Chop the onions. Skin the tomatoes, then cut them in half, sprinkle with salt and leave upturned to drain. Peel the marrow, cut in large chunks, remove the stalks from the aubergines, cut in half, scoop out slightly and cut into chunks. Seed and slice the pepper. Heat the fat or rind in a strong pan and gently fry the onions and the crushed garlic. Add the aubergines, marrow, tomatoes and pepper. Season well and simmer slowly, with well-fitting lid on the pan, until the vegetables are tender. Serve, sprinkled with parsley, if wished.

112 SAUSAGE RATATOUILLE

1 oz. fat	1 medium marrow
1 lb. pork sausages	½ cucumber
4 oz. mushrooms	12 oz. tomatoes

Peel marrow, remove seeds. Peel cucumber and cut both marrow and cucumber into ½-inch dice. Skin and chop tomatoes. Melt the fat in a large frying pan and fry the sausages quickly turning continuously for about 2—3 minutes until golden brown. Add the mushrooms to the pan, turning them quickly in the fat, then add the marrow and the cucumber and fry gently for about 5 minutes. Add the tomatoes, bring to simmering point and simmer gently, covered, for 30 minutes. Check the seasoning and then arrange the marrow mixture in a serving dish and lay the sausages on top.

113 SAUERKRAUT

12 lb. cabbage	vinegar
8 oz. salt	

Rub a clean wooden tub with vinegar and cover the bottom with outside leaves of large white cabbage. Shred remainder of cabbage, mix with the salt and pack into tub until it is filled. Cover with more cabbage leaves, sprinkle freely again with salt, then spread with a damp cloth. Cover with a lid slightly smaller than top of tub and weight it down. Leave for 3 weeks. From time to time it will be necessary to stir the cabbage with a clean wooden stick in order to allow gas to escape. When cabbage has fermented the tub must be put in a cooler place. Great care should be taken that air does not reach the cabbage.
To cook. Drain the sauerkraut, put into a pan with boiling water and cook slowly for 1—2 hours. Season and flavour with ¼ teaspoon caraway seeds.

114 APPLE SAUERKRAUT

1 lb. sauerkraut	2 onions, sliced
2 oz. pork fat or butter	4 frankfurter sausages
3 tart eating apples	2 slices bacon
2 bay leaves	caraway seeds (optional)
	salt and pepper to taste

Put sauerkraut in an ovenproof casserole with pork fat or dripping. Core and quarter apples, but do not peel, and add them to sauerkraut, together with onions, sausages, bacon, bay leaves and a little water. Cook in a moderately hot over (400° F. — Gas Mark 5), then add a little salt, pepper and a sprinkling of caraway seed. Cook in a moderate oven for a few minutes longer.

115 CHOUCROUTE GARNIE

Toss choucroute (sauerkraut) in melted bacon fat or butter, to which should be added a little made mustard. Arrange on flat dish and serve with bacon and sausages.

Spinach

116 CHOPPED SPINACH

Cook the spinach with a little salt but no water until tender. Strain, tip on to board, chop quickly and re-heat with pepper and butter.

117 CREAMED SPINACH

Cook the spinach with salt but no water and when tender rub through a sieve. To each lb. of spinach make a very thick white sauce with 1 oz. butter, 1 oz. flour and 1 gill milk. Add the spinach purée and seasoning. Heat together and serve at once.

103 HERRING STUFFED POTATOES
To serve 6

6 large potatoes	1 dessertspoon finely
3 fresh herrings	chopped parsley
1 oz. butter or margarine	seasoning
1 tablespoon milk	6 grilled tomato halves
1 level teaspoon sage	6 grilled mushrooms
halved lemon slices	parsley

Scrub and wash the potatoes and lightly prick all over.
Brush with cooking oil or melted margarine or lard and
bake in a moderately hot oven (400° F. — Gas Mark 5)
for 1—1½ hours or until they feel soft to the touch.
Meanwhile gently poach the fish in water (salted, if
fresh herrings are used) and when tender drain, remove
all skin and bones and flake up the flesh with a fork.
When the potatoes are ready, cut a slice off the top of
each one, carefully scoop out the centres and mash.
Add the butter or margarine, milk, the flaked fish, sage,
parsley and seasoning to taste. Whip with a fork till light
and fluffy, then pile back into the potato cases.

Reheat and brown in a hot oven (425—450° F. — Gas
Mark 6—7) for 25—30 minutes. Transfer to a platter
and garnish each with ½ lemon slice and a small spring of
parsley. Serve with grilled mushrooms and tomatoes.

104 BACON BARBECUED POTATOES
To serve 6

12 rashers streaky or back	1 onion, thinly sliced
bacon	3 large tomatoes
6 large potatoes	4 oz. grated cheese
knob butter	dash Worcestershire sauce
1 oz. butter	mustard, pepper, salt

Cook the potatoes in their jackets until soft. Halve carefully. Remove the potato pulp. Mash this with seasoning, knob butter and nearly all the cheese. Pile or pipe
back into potato cases, leaving a large well in the middle.
Sprinkle with rest of cheese. Make six rashers into
twelve small bacon rolls and put on a skewer. Put the
bacon rolls and potato cases in a moderately hot oven
for about 10 minutes until crisp and brown. Meanwhile heat butter in pan and fry sliced onion until
nearly tender, add rest of bacon cut in thin strips, fry
until cooked. Stir in sliced tomatoes, seasonings, includ-

ing mustard and Worcestershire sauce. Cook gently
until a soft moist mixture. Pile into each potato case.
Top with bacon rolls as illustrated in colour picture
no 23. Garnish with parsley and serve as supper snack.

105 BAKED STUFFED POTATOES

To bake potatoes. Scrub large potatoes, wipe them dry
and rub with a little melted fat or oil. This makes the
skin thin, shiny and delicious to eat. Place on a baking
tray or on the oven shelves. Test with a fork to see if
they are cooked and then make a small cross on top and,
holding the potato in both hands, squeeze gently until
the cross opens in four points and allows the steam to
escape. The cooking time varies from 45 minutes to
1 hour (400°—425° F. — Gas Mark 6—7). The stuffings
shown in the photograph are:

1. Strips of anchovy topped with an olive.
2. A frankfurter or chipolata sausage stuck through a
   hole in raw potato made by an apple corer.
3. Bacon skewered round potato with cocktail stick.
4. Fried egg with tomato slices and chopped chives.
5. Chopped fried mushrooms garnished with a strip of
   bacon rolled up and secured with a cocktail stick.
6. Peas mixed with potato flesh, garnished with butter.
7. A grilled kidney garnished with fried onion rings.
8. Cooked chopped meat, garnished with parsley.
9. For a sweet tooth, sultanas and cubes of cheese.

106 SOUFFLÉ POTATOES

Slice the potatoes, dry and fry as for chips (Recipe 77)
until cooked and a good golden brown. Take out of the
deep fat and allow the fat to get very hot and return the
golden potatoes to the very hot fat. The type of potato
makes a great deal of difference to the way in which
they puff. On the whole a really good matured King
Edward is the best for this.

107 POTATOES VICHY

Scrub medium size potatoes and prick the skins. Bake
in a moderate oven (375° F. — Gas Mark 4) for 2 hours.
When cooked slice off a piece of the potato lengthwise.
Scoop out potato and mix with cream, chopped chives
and salt. Replace in the potato skins.

91   POTATOES MACAIN

1½ lb. mashed potato   *1 chopped onion*
6 rashers bacon   *1 tablespoon chopped*
1 oz. butter   *parsley*
1 gill milk   *salt and pepper*

Fry the bacon rashers and put them to drain. Then fry the onion in the bacon fat. Combine the mashed potato, butter, milk, seasoning and parsley with the onion, form into cakes and brown on both sides. Serve with the bacon rashers, garnished with quartered tomatoes.

92   MATCHSTICKS

Cut potatoes into very thin chip shapes. Cook like chips, but since potatoes are very much more thinly cut they need shorter cooking time.

93   NEW POTATO BITES

A delicious snack is made by frying new potatoes (do not skin — just wash and dry). Drain and serve with hot tomato sauce or a cream cheese dip made by blending cream cheese, cream or milk and chopped chives until very soft.

94   POTATOES AND MUSHROOMS

Bake potatoes in their jackets, then halve and mix pulp with fried chopped mushrooms. Season well and return to potato cases. Top with grated cheese and brown under grill or in the oven. Garnish with parsley or dill and serve with tomatoes.

95   POTATO PANCAKES

1 lb. potatoes   *1 small onion*
(weight when peeled)   *seasoning*
2 oz. flour   *2 eggs*
¼ gill milk   *oil or fat for frying*

Grate potatoes into a bowl. Add flour, grated onion and beaten eggs. Gradually beat in milk and seasoning. Heat fat or oil in a pan and drop in spoonfuls of the mixture — smaller pancakes are easier to turn, so make them the size of a Scotch pancake, i. e. about 2 inches across. Brown on both sides, and keep hot in the oven or on a plate over boiling water.

96   POTATOES PARISIENNE

These are small balls of raw potato, roasted in hot fat or oil in the oven. Buy a vegetable scoop (the one illustrated is a vegetable or fruit scoop or 'baller' on

the left hand end and butter curler on the right). To get a real ball of potato insert the scoop into the potato and push firmly, turning the scoop to get a ball shape. Dry and roast for about 40 minutes.

97   ROAST POTATOES

Prepare the potatoes, dry them well in a cloth. Put into hot fat, turning them so that they are evenly coated. Cook for about 1 hour in a hot oven, or roast in the fat round the joint.

98   RIBBON POTATOES

Peel long strips from potatoes and fry like game chips (see Recipe 87).

99   SCALLOPED POTATOES

approx. 1½ lb. potatoes   *chopped chives or little*
1 can condensed   *onion*
mushroom soup   *seasoning*
½ pint milk   *little butter*

Slice potatoes very thinly. Arrange in casserole or dish, seasoning well. Mix soup and milk. Pour over potatoes, add a little butter to the top of the dish. Bake for approximately 2 hours in centre of very moderate oven (350° F. — Gas Mark 3). Garnish with chopped chives.

100   ST. MARTIN'S BOATS

4 large potatoes   *3 oz. grated cheese*
2 eggs   *butter or margarine*
8 small bacon rolls   *seasoning*

Bake the potatoes in their jackets until tender. Halve, remove all centre pulp. Mash well, adding butter, seasoning, egg yolks and cheese. Whisk egg whites until very stiff, fold into potato mixture. Pile back in cases and cook for approximately 20 minutes in centre of moderately hot oven (400° F. — Gas Mark 5). Meanwhile grill bacon rolls and serve on top of potatoes.

101   SHALLOW FRIED POTATOES

Peel and slice the potatoes. Heat enough fat to cover the bottom of the pan and cook the potatoes steadily on one side until golden brown; turn and cook on the other side. Drain well on kitchen or absorbent paper.
It is possible to 'fry' potatoes in the oven with little or no fat. Grease a baking tin and get it very hot. Put on the well dried peeled and sliced potatoes, brush with a little melted fat and put into the oven for about 45 minutes until crisp and golden brown.

102   POTATOES SAVOYARDE

1 lb. potatoes   *4 oz. grated cheese or*
(weight when peeled)   *thinly sliced cheese*
1 chopped onion   *2 — 3 oz. butter or*
little stock or water   *margarine*
seasoning

Fry the chopped onion in butter until just soft. Slice the potatoes as for potatoes Anna (Recipe 75) then arrange sliced potatoes, onion and cheese in the dish, ending with a good layer of cheese. Season well. Pour over enough water or stock to half cover the potatoes and bake for approximately 1 hour in the centre of a moderately hot oven (400° F. — Gas Mark 5).

83 BAKED CORN POTATOES

4 large potatoes
1 can corn or corn off the
  cob mixed with red pepper

butter
grated cheese

Scrub potatoes and bake in hot oven until soft. Slice in half, scoop out all the insides and mash very thoroughly adding butter, hot milk, salt and pepper to taste. Add the drained corn. Replace mixture in potato shells and top with grated cheese. Return to oven until mixture is heated through and cheese is melted and golden brown.

84 CURRIED POTATOES

4 large potatoes
small slice bread
few raisins

2 oz. butter
curry powder
1 apple
seasoning

Bake the potatoes in their jackets, and cut off the tops, serrating these if wished. Scoop out centre pulp and mash well, adding butter and seasoning. Press into potato cases leaving a nest shape. Add a good pinch of curry powder to the butter in the pan. Dice bread and apple, and toss in this curry mixture, add raisins. Pile hot apple mixture into potato cases.

85 DUCHESSE POTATOES

1¼ lb. mashed potatoes
parsley to garnish

1 or 2 eggs or yolks
2 oz. butter

Sieve the potatoes then mix the beaten egg and butter with the potatoes, pipe in rosette shapes on to greased baking tins and bake for about 25 minutes in a moderately hot oven, (400°F. — Gas Mark 5).

86 DAUPHINE POTATOES

To 1 lb. of a very smooth potato purée (with no margarine, butter OR milk added) allow the following:

1 oz. margarine or butter
  (for richer choux paste
  allow 2 oz.)
3 oz. flour

¼ pint water
good pinch salt
2 whole eggs and the yolk
  of a third

Heat the butter, water and salt together until butter melts. Stir in ALL the flour then return to the heat, stirring well until the mixture forms a dry ball. THIS IS VERY IMPORTANT. Cool, then GRADUALLY beat in the eggs until a smooth mixture. Gradually add the potato purée to the choux paste, then taste, and add more salt, pepper and a little grated nutmeg if wished. You can also add a little grated Parmesan cheese if wished. Put into a forcing bag with a plain pipe and force small amounts (about the size of a nut) into a pan of boiling fat; cook until golden brown. Drain well. Pile on hot dish. Dauphine potatoes 'swell' during cooking, so do not cook too many at one time.

87 GAME CHIPS

Cut wafer-thin slices of potatoes — an electric slicer is ideal for this. Dry well and fry in hot deep fat for about 1 minute. Lift out; get fat very hot and fry again for ¼ minute. Drain on absorbent paper.

88 HASHED BROWN POTATOES

1 — 1½ lb. potatoes
3 oz. butter

1 — 2 onions
salt and pepper

Peel and cook diced potatoes and onion together in boiling salted water until tender. Mash well, adding half the butter and seasoning. Heat butter in pan and add potato mixture; cook steadily until golden brown underneath. The pan can then be put under grill or in oven to brown top, or if preferred the potatoes can be spread on buttered baking tin and brushed with melted butter on top then cooked in a moderate oven (375° — 400°F. — Gas Mark 4—5) for about 30—40 minutes.

89 LIMOUSINE POTATOES

Grate some uncooked potatoes after peeling them. Add a few pieces of bacon and some thin rounds of sausage. Cook in a frying pan in hot fat and shake frequently. Add salt and pepper to taste. When one side is cooked turn over so that both sides are browned. The layer should not be too thick as this dish is more delicious when really light and crispy.

90 LYONNAISE POTATOES

1½ lb. potatoes
8 — 12 oz. onions
butter or fat

seasoning
parsley or bacon
  for garnish

Boil the potatoes steadily in salted water until nearly cooked. Meanwhile chop or slice the onions thinly and fry in fat. Slice the nearly cooked potatoes and add to the onion mixture, seasoning well. Cover the frying pan and cook very gently until tender. Garnish with chopped parsley or crisply fried bacon.

Potatoes

75   POTATOES ANNA

1 lb. potatoes   *dripping, butter or*
seasoning   *margarine*

Grease a tin liberally with well-clarified dripping and heat this until the dripping begins to smoke slightly. Arrange well-dried slices of potatoes — the thickness of a shilling — in the tin, just letting them overlap, and seasoning each layer and brushing with butter or margarine. Cook for about 45 minutes to 1 hour on the bottom shelf of a hot oven (425—450°F. — Gas Mark 6—7) until the potatoes are tender, and the top layer brown. Serve in the dish, garnished with parsley, or turn out on to a serving dish.

76   BAKED POTATOES IN THEIR JACKETS

Scrub good sized potatoes, prick a little and if you want a crisp skin rub with margarine or butter. Bake for 1—2 hours in a moderate to hot oven. When cooked the best flavour is produced if they are cut through the centre and left covered for a minute or so. Serve with butter and seasoning.

77   CHIPPED POTATOES

Peel potatoes, then cut into long fingers. Wash these, then dry well. Heat and test the fat, using one chip. When you think the fat is hot enough drop this in. If the potato sinks to the bottom and there is no movement of the fat it is not sufficiently hot. If, however, the fat bubbles immediately the chip is put in, and the chip stays at the top of the fat, then the fat is the right heat. Put enough chips into the frying basket to about a quarter fill it. Lower carefully into the fat, watching to see there is no danger of overflowing. Cook the potatoes for about 3 minutes. Remove the potatoes with the basket and stand on a plate. Just before serving the chips, re-heat the fat, test to make sure it is hot enough, and fry rapidly for about 2 minutes until crisp and brown. Drain on crumpled tissue paper or absorbent kitchen roll.

78   POTATO CREAM

1 — 1¼ lb. potatoes   *milk*
2 oz. margarine   *seasoning*

Put the potatoes into boiling salted water and cook for about 10 minutes — until half cooked. Strain off the water, then just cover with milk. Continue cooking slowly until the potatoes are so soft that they begin to break, then add margarine and seasoning, and beat to smooth cream. This is an excellent way of introducing more milk into the diet. Other vegetables can be cooked in the same way — especially carrots, swedes, peas and turnips. The cream must be perfectly smooth and soft.

79   CREAMED POTATOES

1¼ — 1½ lb. potatoes   *seasoning*
1 — 2 oz. margarine   *1 gill milk*

Put the potatoes into boiling salted water and cook until just tender. Strain and mash with fork, then beat with wooden spoon; try to do this near an open window or door, for you will then whiten the potatoes. Heat margarine and milk together and then gradually add to the potatoes, beating as you do so. Season. Pile or pipe into dish, garnishing with sprig of parsley. To make a change from the familiar white of the potatoes put them for a few seconds under very hot grill to lightly brown the top.

80   POTATO CRISPS

Potato crisps are just a popular name for game chips (see Recipe 87).

81   POTATO CROQUETTES

mashed potatoes   *egg*
deep fat for frying   *fine breadcrumbs*
                       flour

Form mashed potatoes — which should be smooth, but firm — into desired shapes. Coat with little flour, then with beaten egg and crumbs. Heat fat until a faint haze is seen (see instructions for chipped potatoes — Recipe 77) and put the croquettes carefully into frying basket. Fry for several minutes and drain well.

82   POTATO AND CABBAGE CASSEROLE

2 lb. potatoes   *2 oz. unsalted butter*
1 lb. cabbage*   *4 oz. Gouda cheese*
8 oz. tomatoes   *salt and pepper*
* Use crisp white cabbage if possible

Peel the potatoes, cut into small pieces and boil with a little water. Strain when cooked but unbroken. Meanwhile chop the cabbage finely and fry lightly in butter in a frying pan. Add chopped tomato and cook with the cabbage for about 5 minutes. Add the cabbage and tomatoes to the potatoes, as well as the diced cheese, and season. Serve immediately to prevent the cheese from melting too much.

70   MUTTER CURRY

8 oz. potatoes finely diced
3 level teaspoons curry
  powder
1¼ oz. margarine
1 large can peas
2 tomatoes chopped
2 oz. sultanas

2 heaped tablespoons dried
  sliced onions or
  2 medium onions
1 teaspoon lemon juice
1 level teaspoon
  redcurrant jelly or jam

In a saucepan sauté the potato and the curry powder in the margarine until the potato begins to soften. Drain the peas and make the liquor up to ¼ pint with water. Stir this into the saucepan and add the onion, tomato, sultanas, lemon juice and redcurrant jelly. Cover and simmer for about 15 minutes or until the onion is cooked. Add the peas and stir gently until heated through. Serve hot with rice or as an accompaniment to sausages, hamburgers, hard-boiled eggs etc.

Peppers

71   PEPPERS AU GRATIN

slices of toast
grated cheese

slices of ham (if desired)
slices of red pepper
butter

Toss sliced red pepper in a little hot butter. Toast bread, cut into neat squares and butter lavishly. Cover with slices of ham, red pepper and grated cheese, and brown under grill.

72   CHEESE STUFFED PEPPERS

4 large green peppers
6 oz. bread
4 tablespoons milk
1 tablespoon chopped
  parsley
salt and pepper to taste

2 tablespoons tomato
  chutney
4 oz. cream cheese or
  jar soft cheese spread
tomato sauce
  (Recipe 320)

Cut off the tops of the peppers, scoop out core and seeds and wash carefully. Drop into boiling water and cook for 3 minutes. Crumble the bread and soften with milk, mix in the parsley, tomato chutney, seasoning and warmed cream cheese or cheese spread. Fill peppers with this mixture, replace the caps and put into a baking tin with a little water. Bake in a moderately hot oven (375° F. — Gas Mark 5) 30—35 minutes until soft. Serve hot with tomato sauce.

73   RICE STUFFED PEPPERS

4 green peppers
3 oz. cooked rice
2 onions

3 tomatoes
2 oz. margarine
seasoning

Halve the peppers lengthwise, remove the seeds and the hard centre. Put into boiling salted water and cook for about 5 minutes only. Take out and drain. Meanwhile, fry the chopped onions and tomatoes in the margarine, add to the rice, season well and put into the centre of the peppers. Cover with greased paper, put into a well-greased dish and bake for approximately

25 minutes in the centre of a moderate oven (375° F. — Gas Mark 4).
Variation: Add plenty of grated cheese to the above. Use minced meat as well as the onions and tomatoes and only 1 or 2 oz. rice.

74 PORK STUFFED GREEN PEPPERS

4 large green peppers
8 oz. cold boiled rice
12 oz. pork sausage meat
4 tomatoes skinned and
  chopped

4 mushrooms chopped
salt
pepper
lard

Cut the tops off the peppers and remove core. Take care to get rid of all the white seeds as these are very 'hot' to taste. Mix all the other ingredients thoroughly and fill peppers with them. Replace tops, brush with melted lard and bake in centre of a moderate oven (375° F. — Gas Mark 4) for 30—40 minutes.

3 POTATOES

2   HOPPING JOHN (Recipe 68);
RICE-STUFFED TOMATOES (Recipe 122)

Recipe 61

62   STUFFED MUSHROOMS

12 large mushrooms	*seasoning to taste*
2 oz. quick cooking	*2 teaspoons mixed herbs*
rolled oats	*4 tablespoons stock*
2 oz. breadcrumbs	*3 large tomatoes*
2 oz. margarine	*triangles of toast*

Peel the mushrooms, remove and reserve the stalks. Fry the breadcrumbs in the margarine until golden-brown, add the oats and the seasoning and mixed herbs. Moisten with stock or water. Place this mixture on to the mushrooms, stand the stalks in the centre and bake in a moderately hot oven (400° F. — Gas Mark 5) for about 20 minutes until the mushrooms are tender. Meanwhile, slice the tomatoes and grill. Serve the mushrooms piping hot on top of tomatoes and decorate with triangles of toast.

Onions

63   BRAISED ONIONS

8 small or 4 good-sized	*2 oz. fat*
onions	*1 oz. flour*
¼ pint brown stock	*seasoning*

Dry onions well and cook in the hot fat until pale golden brown. Lift out, add the flour and cook for several minutes in the fat. Stir in the stock, bring to the boil and cook until thickened. Season well. The onions can either be added to the thick sauce and cooked very gently with a lid on the saucepan or they can be transferred with the sauce to a casserole, covered tightly and baked for 1—2 hours in a very moderate oven (350°F. — Gas Mark 3).

64   BAKED ONIONS

To bake onions put into a dish with a little butter, milk and seasoning and cook in the centre of a moderate oven until tender. This will take approximately 1½ hours. Cover with buttered paper if desired.

65   FRIED ONIONS

Peel and cut the onions into slices then separate into rings. Dry well then coat with a little seasoned flour or to give a thicker coating dip first in milk and then in seasoned flour. Shake away the surplus flour and put into deep fat and fry until crisp and golden brown.

66   ROAST ONIONS

Dry the onions well, roll in hot fat and cook for approximately 1—1½ hours in a moderately hot oven.

67   STUFFED ONIONS

4 large onions weighing	*½ oz. grated stale blue*
about 8 oz. each	*vein cheese such as*
2 oz. finely chopped bacon,	*Danish blue,*
about 3 rashers	*Gorgonzola, etc.*
1½ oz. quick cooking	*pinch mixed herbs*
rolled oats	*1 — 2 oz. grated*
1 teaspoon	*Cheshire or Cheddar*
Worcestershire sauce	*cheese*
salt and pepper	*2 — 4 tablespoons stock**

* or water flavoured with meat extract

Peel the onions then make 2 cross cuts about ¼ inch deep over top of each one. Cook in boiling salted water for about 20—25 minutes, then drain and leave until cold; with very sharp knife, cut slice from top of each onion about ½ inch down. Prise out onion centres and the trimmings from the top (these can be used in soup or a sauce). Chop remaining centre very small. Remove rind from bacon and chop bacon finely. Put in small saucepan and cook until bacon is crisp. Remove from heat and stir in oats followed by chopped onion, Worcestershire sauce, cheese, herbs and seasoning to taste. Mix thoroughly then pack stuffing into onions. Put onions in greased casserole. Pour in just enough liquid to cover the bottom of the dish. Put lid on and bake for 1½ hours in oven (350° F. — Gas Mark 3) until onions are tender.

Peas

68   HOPPING JOHN
(Rice and Peas)

4 oz. dried peas	*6 oz. cooked rice*
water to cover	*1 red pepper*
4 oz. smoked bacon or salt	*salt and pepper to taste*
pork, cut in pieces	

Soak peas overnight, cook with pork and chopped red pepper until peas are good and tender (not over-done — keep the peas whole). Add cooked rice, season with salt and pepper to taste. Place in covered casserole and cook until liquid is absorbed and dish is hot through. Illustrated in colour picture opposite.

69   PEAS À LA FRANÇAISE

Take the peas from the shells, wash but do not dry. Wash several good sized lettuce leaves and do not dry these. Put a layer of lettuce leaves at the bottom of a strong saucepan, add the peas, a few spring onions or shallots, seasoning, a knob of butter and another layer of damp lettuce leaves. Put a tightly fitting lid on the pan and cook steadily for about 40 minutes, until tender. If wished this can be cooked for 1—1½ hours in a covered casserole in a moderate oven. The peas will darken in colour but their flavour is delicious.

oven (375°F. — Gas Mark 4) for 35—40 minutes. Baste from time to time. Serve with new or creamed potatoes, spinach and the brown sauce.

Leeks

54   BRAISED LEEKS

Prepare like braised onions (Recipe 63), taking care the leeks remain a very good shape.

55   LEEK, BEAN AND BACON SAVOURY

4 medium-sized leeks	*2 (or more) hard-boiled*
1 medium can baked	*eggs*
beans	*2 oz. butter*
6 rashers bacon	

Cut bacon rashers in halves. Roll up pieces and thread on thin skewers. Fry in a large pan until lightly crisped. Remove bacon to a dish and keep hot. Cut well washed and drained leeks into ½-inch slices. Add butter to bacon fat in pan and when hot put in sliced leeks and sauté until tender, keeping slices as whole as possible. Take up slices with a draining spoon and put on dish with bacon. Stir baked beans into residual fat in pan and make piping hot. To serve, heap beans into middle of serving dish and top with the bacon rolls, with slices of leeks around. Garnish with slices or wedges of hot freshly boiled eggs.

Lettuce

56   LETTUCE AS A COOKED VEGETABLE

Wash the lettuce and divide into about 6—8 portions. Put into boiling salt water together with few spring onions, shallots, chopped chives and cook until JUST tender. Strain and toss in melted butter.

57   BRAISED LETTUCE

1 large lettuce or	*1 oz. flour*
2 medium ones	*¾ pint brown stock*
1 sliced onion	*little chopped bacon*
1 oz. fat	*seasoning*

Wash and dry lettuce and divide into neat pieces. Fry sliced onion in fat, add flour and cook for several minutes then add stock. Bring to boil and cook until thickened, add chopped bacon, seasoning and lettuce. Simmer gently in covered pan (or casserole in the oven) for about 35 minutes.

Mushrooms

58   CREAMED MUSHROOMS

Simmer mushrooms in milk until just tender. Blend a little cornflour or flour with cold milk, add to the milk and cook until thickened, put in a good knob of butter and a little cream, season well and add a squeeze of lemon. Serve with toast or bread and butter.

59   MUSHROOMS WITH CHEESE FILLING

8 oz. medium-sized	*1 teaspoon finely*
mushrooms, skinned and	*chopped parsley*
with stalks removed	*2 oz. finely grated*
approx. ¼ pint milk	*Cheddar or Parmesan*
1 tablespoon fried onion	*cheese*
4 rashers streaky	*1 tablespoon fresh*
bacon, roughly	*breadcrumbs*
chopped and fried	*egg yolk*
salt and pepper	*¼ teaspoon mustard*
	thick slices fried tomato

Mix mustard with little water and blend with egg yolk. Lightly poach the mushrooms and trimmed stalks in the milk. Remove and drain. Mix together the onion, bacon, breadcrumbs, chopped parsley, grated cheese and seasoning to taste. Bind with the beaten egg and mustard then put the mixture, in teaspoons, on to the poached mushrooms. Top each with a stalk and grill for 3 to 5 minutes and place on the tomato slices. Transfer to a serving dish and garnish with parsley.

60   MUSHROOMS, GRILLED OR FRIED

Mushrooms are not only an excellent accompaniment to many dishes, but can in themselves form a savoury dish. Either grill or fry and serve on hot buttered toast with egg, meat, fish or cheese dishes.

61   MUSHROOM RICE

1 lb. fresh mushrooms	*6 oz. rice*
2 tablespoons chopped	*2 oz. butter*
green pepper	*or margarine*
2 tablespoons minced	*¼ teaspoon salt*
onions	

Cook the rice in salted water, or preferably chicken stock, until tender. Strain. In a heavy pan sauté chopped mushrooms, green pepper and onions lightly in butter or margarine. Combine with rice and salt. Place in an earthenware casserole and bake for about 15 minutes in a very moderate oven (350°F. — Gas Mark 3) or under the grill. This makes a good accompaniment to fried chicken.

Corn on the Cob or Sweet Corn

47   CORN BAKE

1 can corn or corn	*milk*
mixed with red pepper	*1 oz. butter*
1 tablespoon flour	*2 eggs*

Drain can of corn, reserving liquid. Make the liquid up to ½ pint with milk. Melt the butter, add the flour and make a sauce with the liquid stirring well all the time. Add the corn and stir until the mixture boils. Cool slightly and then add well beaten egg yolks. Season and cook until it thickens slightly. Cool. Fold in the stiffly beaten egg whites. Bake in a moderate oven.

48   SWEET CORN PIE

1 packet frozen corn-	*3 oz. grated cheese*
off-the-cob	*2 oz. butter*
or 1 can sweet corn*	*salt and pepper*
2 eggs	*½ pint milk*

* Fresh corn-on-the-cob can be used. Cook the corn and remove from the cob when tender

If using frozen corn cook this until just tender, then mix with the milk. Season well and bring just to the boil. Beat the eggs, pour over the milk, whisking well. Add the butter and cheese and mix thoroughly. Turn into a pie dish and bake until golden-brown, i. e. approximately 1 hour in the centre of a very moderate oven (350° F. — Gas Mark 3).

49   HARLEQUIN CORN PIE

2 corn on the cob	*seasoning*
½ red pepper	*4 tomatoes*
½ green pepper	*1 grated carrot*
1 onion or 6 spring onions	*2 oz. butter*

Cook the corn on the cob until just tender. Remember NOT to add salt until about end of cooking time as this helps to make it tender. Strip corn from cob. Chop all vegetables and fry with carrot in hot butter. Add corn and serve with crisp bacon rolls, or roast or creamed chicken, or plenty of grated cheese.

50   CORN TOASTIES

1 can corn or corn	*5 oz. butter*
mixed with red pepper	*½ onion*
2 tomatoes	*2 oz. ham*
1 oz. grated cheese	*2 oz. mushrooms*

Heat butter in pan and gently sauté finely chopped onion, chopped tomatoes and mushrooms. Drain can of corn and add to mixture in pan. Heat gently and stir in chopped ham. Serve with or on slices of toast, sprinkled with grated cheese and grilled until golden brown.

Cucumber

51   COOKED CUCUMBER

First peel cucumber then cut into 1—1½ inch slices. Put into small quantity of boiling salted water and cook until tender (about 10 minutes). Drain and serve with white or cheese sauce (see Recipes 312, 314) or toss in hot margarine or butter. Garnish with chopped parsley or chives and paprika pepper.

52   FRIED CUCUMBER

Cut into slices of about ¼ inch and fry in shallow or deep fat until tender. Cucumber does not brown a great deal.

53   CUCUMBER STUFFED WITH MUSHROOMS AND BEEF

1 large cucumber	*fat for roasting*
4 oz. chopped mushrooms	*1 oz. margarine or*
8 oz. minced beef	*dripping*
seasoning	*½ pint good brown sauce*
	(Recipe 330)

Skin the cucumber and cut into 3-inch lengths, then cut lengthways through each piece. Take out the centre and chop this finely. Heat the margarine in a saucepan and toss in the chopped mushrooms for a few minutes. Stir in the meat and season well. Put the pieces of cucumber into boiling salted water and cook for 5 minutes only. Drain carefully and fill with the meat mixture. Heat a small knob of fat in a baking tin, put in the cucumber covered with greased greaseproof paper and bake in the middle of a moderate

38 CAULIFLOWER AND MUSHROOMS AU GRATIN

1 good-sized cauliflower	*2 — 3 oz. grated cheese*
6 oz. mushrooms	*2 — 3 tablespoons*
½ pint milk	*breadcrumbs*
1 oz. flour	*seasoning*
2 oz. butter	*parsley*

Divide cauliflower into flowerets and cook in boiling salted water until just soft. Meanwhile simmer chopped mushrooms in milk until tender. Blend flour and 1 oz. butter, stir into mushroom mixture together with seasoning and cook until smooth. Pour into shallow dish. Arrange cauliflower on top. Sprinkle cheese and crumbs on top with melted butter and brown under grill or in oven. Garnish with chopped parsley.

39 CAULIFLOWER NOISETTE

1 large cauliflower	*salt and pepper*
4 oz. grated Cheddar	*nutmeg*
cheese	*chopped parsley*
2 oz. butter	*tomato wedges*

Cook the prepared cauliflower in boiling salted water until just tender. Drain well. Butter a fireproof dish and cover the bottom with a layer of grated cheese. Break up the cauliflower carefully and distribute over the dish. Season well and sprinkle over the remainder of the cheese. Heat the butter until it browns and pour over the cauliflower. Brown in a hot oven (425—450°F. — Gas Mark 6—7) or under a grill. Sprinkle with chopped parsley, garnish with tomato.

40 CAULIFLOWER POLONAISE

Cook cauliflower as in Recipe 4. Garnish with fried breadcrumbs etc. as for Asparagus Polonaise (Recipe 10).

41 PURÉE OF CAULIFLOWER

Cook the cauliflower as directed in Recipe 4 and mash very well, adding butter and a little nutmeg and seasoning. Put into a dish and cover with a layer of fried breadcrumbs or grated cheese and crisp under grill.

42 SAUTÉED CAULIFLOWER

cauliflower	*butter*
seasoning	*parsley*

Wash the cauliflower and divide into small flowerets. Heat the butter in a pan, and fry cauliflower carefully until golden brown and tender — but not too soft. Toss in chopped parsley and seasoning.

Celery

43 BRAISED CELERY

1 head of celery or	*1 oz. butter*
can celery hearts	*1 oz. flour*
½ pint water or stock	*seasoning*
from can	*meat extract*

If using fresh celery, cut into 3-inch pieces. Heat butter, toss celery in this for several minutes until slightly brown on the outside. Stir the flour into the fat and cook well for a few minutes. It is advisable to remove the celery on to a plate while doing this. Gradually stir in the cold water or stock from can, bring the sauce to the boil and cook for about 5 minutes, until thick, add salt and pepper to taste and a little meat extract, if using water. Put in the celery and either cook over a very low heat covered for just over 1 hour, or 15 minutes with canned celery, or transfer to a covered casserole and cook in a very moderate oven (350° F. — Gas Mark 3), for just over 1 hour, or 25 minutes with canned celery.

44 CELERY AND LEEK CASSEROLE

large head celery	*4 leeks*
4 oz. bacon	*1 oz. flour*
2 oz. butter	*¾ pint stock or water*
parsley	*seasoning*

Prepare the leeks (see Recipe 4) and cut into inch lengths. Wash and cut the celery into the same sized pieces. Heat the butter and fry the diced leeks with the chopped bacon until just golden brown. Work in the flour, stirring well, and cook for several minutes. Add the stock or water, bring to the boil and cook until you have a smooth sauce. Put in the celery, seasoning, transfer to casserole and cook for approximately 45 minutes in a moderate oven (375° F. — Gas Mark 4).

45 CELERY PURÉE

1 head celery	*1 oz. butter*
8 oz. potatoes	*little milk or cream*
seasoning	*nutmeg*

Cook diced celery and potatoes in boiling salted water until tender. Rub through a sieve and return to the saucepan, adding butter and a little milk. Heat until smooth, seasoning well. Top with grated nutmeg.

46 CHESTNUT PURÉE

A smooth purée of chestnuts is excellent to serve with poultry or game. Prepare the chestnuts as in Recipe 4 then cook until tender enough to shell easily. Return the shelled chestnuts to the pan, adding milk to half cover. Simmer gently until very tender. Rub through a sieve, then re-heat with butter and seasoning.

29 STUFFED WHOLE CABBAGE (2)

1 large cabbage	*4 oz. sausage meat*
8 oz. cooked meat	*1 oz. breadcrumbs*
2 oz. cooked rice	*1 egg*
2 oz. butter	*seasoning*
1 onion	*3 or 4 rashers streaky*
¼ — 1 clove of garlic	*bacon*

For the sauce

1 small can tomatoes or	*1 gill stock or water*
fresh tomatoes	*seasoning*
1 onion	

Cut off any tough or bruised leaves and cut the bottom of the cabbage quite flat. Scoop out the centre — this can be cooked separately and served as a second vegetable. Put the cabbage for about 5 minutes into boiling salted water, then drain carefully. Fry the chopped onion and crushed clove of garlic in the butter, add the rest of the ingredients, except the bacon, blending well. Pile into the cavity of the softened cabbage, wrapping the leaves round the stuffing. Roll the rashers of bacon round the outside of the stuffed cabbage and secure with string or small skewers. Put the tomatoes (skinned and sliced if fresh), the sliced onion, stock and seasoning into a deep casserole and arrange the stuffed cabbage on top. Baste once with the tomato mixture then put a lid on the casserole and bake for approximately 1¼ hours in the centre of a very moderate oven (350°F. — Gas Mark 3). Baste once or twice with the tomato mixture during cooking if possible. Serve with the liquid as a sauce — this can be thickened if desired.

30 RED CABBAGE

Red cabbage can be cooked in exactly the same way as green cabbage. It does, however, lend itself rather better to pickling. Special ways in which red cabbage are particularly good served hot are *Russian Cabbage* (Recipe 31) and *Red Cabbage with caraway seeds* (Recipe 32).

31 RUSSIAN CABBAGE

1 cabbage — preferably a	*1 onion*
red cabbage	*2 oz. butter*
1 apple	*few drops vinegar*
seasoning	

Shred the cabbage finely, and cook in boiling salted water until just tender, but still crisp. Meanwhile chop the onion and apple in small pieces. Strain the cabbage, heat the butter in the pan, fry onion and apple until soft, add the cabbage, vinegar and seasoning and heat thoroughly.

32 RED CABBAGE WITH CARAWAY SEEDS

Caraway seeds can be added to all cabbage but they are particularly good with red cabbage. Add 1 or 2 teaspoons when cooking the cabbage. When cooked strain carefully so they are not lost, and toss in butter.

Carrots

33 CARROT SOUFFLÉ

Prepare like spinach soufflé (Recipe 118) but use 8 — 10 oz. carrots which can be cooked and sieved but are delicious if used raw and grated with pinch nutmeg.

34 CARROTS VICHY

1 lb. young carrots	*2 tablespoons cream or*
2 oz. margarine	*milk*
salt and pepper	*chopped parsley*

Slice the carrots thinly, toss in hot margarine until well coated, put into a covered dish with plenty of seasoning and cream or milk. Cook for 30 minutes in hot oven (425—450°F. — Gas Mark 6—7), or for 1 hour in moderate oven (375°F. — Gas Mark 4).

35 CREAMED CARROTS

1¼ lb. carrots	*salt, pepper, nutmeg,*
1 oz. margarine	*¼ gill milk*

Scrape the carrots then cook in boiling salted water until just tender. Rub through a sieve. Melt the margarine in the saucepan, then add the milk and carrot purée and re-heat gently, adding a little additional salt, very small pinch of pepper and a pinch of nutmeg. Pile into neat pyramids or pipe into rose shapes.

Cauliflower

36 CAULIFLOWER AU GRATIN WITH MUSHROOM SAUCE

1 cauliflower	*1 oz. browned bread-*
1 can condensed	*crumbs*
mushroom soup	*chives or parsley*
1 oz. grated cheese	

Cook the cauliflower whole in boiling salted water. While the cauliflower is cooking, mix the soup and the cheese together in a saucepan, and then heat, stirring constantly, until the cheese has melted and the sauce is very hot. Pour sauce over cauliflower, then sprinkle with the breadcrumbs. Brown under a grill or in an oven. Garnish with chopped chives.

37 CAULIFLOWER CHEESE

1 medium-sized	*1 oz. grated Cheddar*
cauliflower	*cheese*
*½ pint cheese sauce**	*1 tablespoon crisp*
(Recipe 314)	*breadcrumbs*

* *If desired use half milk and half cauliflower stock for this.*

Soak the cauliflower in cold water for about 15 minutes, then break into flowerets. Cook in a little boiling salt water in a covered pan until tender and arrange neatly in buttered scallop shells or a fireproof dish. Make the cheese sauce. Coat the cauliflower with the cheese sauce. Sprinkle with the mixed grated cheese and crisp breadcrumbs, brown under a hot grill or in a fairly hot oven (425°F. — Gas Mark 6). Serve hot.

Brussels Sprouts and Cabbage

22 BRUSSELS SPROUTS AU GRATIN

1 — 1¼ lb. Brussels sprouts	½ pint cheese sauce
1 lb. mashed potatoes	(Recipe 314)
2 — 3 oz. grated cheese	little butter

Cook the Brussels sprouts as directed in Recipe 4, then drain. Meanwhile pipe a border of mashed potato on an ovenproof dish. Arrange the sprouts in the centre. Cover the sprouts — but NOT the potato — with the cheese sauce, grated cheese and a little melted butter then brown under the grill or in the oven.

23 WINTER CASSEROLE

2 lb. Brussels sprouts	1 gill double cream
1 lb. chestnuts	salt and pepper
4 oz. raw gammon	a little butter

Cook the chestnuts in salted water for about 10 minutes. Remove the skins while hot and return to fresh salted water and cook for further 10 minutes. Boil the sprouts in a little salted water for 10 minutes, drain. Meanwhile, cut the gammon strips ¼ inch wide and fry gently in a little butter. Mix this with the sprouts and chestnuts in a hot casserole and keep hot. Pour the cream into the frying pan, add some pepper to taste and bring to the boil. Stir as it thickens and pour over the other ingredients. Serve very hot.

24 'BUBBLE AND SQUEAK' or CABBAGE AND POTATO HASH

Mash potatoes and mix with finely chopped cooked cabbage until you have a smooth cake; season well. Heat a little fat in a pan, brown the underside of the mixture. Turn out, brown on the other side. Serve very hot.

25 BRAISED CABBAGE

1 good sized cabbage	1 pint stock or water
2 or 3 rashers rather salt fat bacon	little chopped thyme or pinch dried herbs

1 oz. flour	seasoning
1 oz. butter or dripping	parsley

Chop the onion and bacon and fry in butter. Make sure the onion does not become too brown. Stir in the flour and cook gently for a few minutes, then gradually add stock. Bring to the boil and cook until you have a smooth sauce. Meanwhile quarter the cabbage, remove any hard core. If the cabbage is young it can be put into the sauce at once, but for older vegetables boil for about 5 minutes in boiling salted water and strain. Put the cabbage in the sauce, adding seasoning, thyme or herbs. Cover with a lid and cook steadily for approximately 1 hour. Garnish with chopped parsley.

26 CABBAGE WITH MUSTARD DRESSING

1 medium sized cabbage	2 teaspoon mustard
1 oz. butter	made with vinegar

Cut the cabbage in strips and cook it in as little salted water as possible without letting it burn. Drain it well and then toss it with two forks while it is still hot in a dressing made by mixing the melted butter with the mustard. If you mix the cabbage and dressing quickly, it should keep hot enough for serving right away.

27 STUFFED CABBAGE LEAVES

5 — 6 large cabbage leaves	1 dessertspoon Worcestershire sauce
8 oz. minced beef	little milk
1 small onion	little stock or water
1 egg	seasoning to taste
1¼ oz. quick-cooking oats	tomato sauce (Recipe 320)

Wash the cabbage leaves and drain. Chop onion finely and mix together all the other ingredients, except the tomato sauce, moistening if necessary with a little milk. Place this filling on the cabbage leaves and roll up. Arrange in a greased ovenproof dish and pour on a little stock. Cover dish. Bake in centre of a very moderate oven (350°F. — Gas Mark 3) for 50 — 60 minutes until tender. Drain and serve with tomato sauce.

28 STUFFED WHOLE CABBAGE (1)

1 medium-sized cabbage	salt and pepper
½ pint stock	3 tablespoons
8 oz. pork sausage meat	breadcrumbs

Cut off any bruised leaves and trim the base of the cabbage flat. Scoop out the centre and cook this cabbage as a separate vegetable. Fill the cavity with sausage meat. Place in casserole, pour over stock, sprinkle with breadcrumbs and bake with the lid on in a very moderate oven (350° F — Gas Mark 3) for 1¼ hours. Remove the lid of the casserole for the last 15 minutes. Thicken stock if wished.

15   *BROCCOLI*

Use in all ways suggested for asparagus. Frozen broccoli heads are particularly good and are shown in the picture with a variety of frozen vegetables.

Beans

16   HAWAIIAN BAKED BEANS   ▶

1 level teaspoon dry mustard	*1 tablespoon vinegar*
1 tablespoon pineapple juice	*1 large can baked beans*
1 small can chopped pork	*4 pineapple rings*
and ham or 4 slices ham	*8 cloves*

Blend the mustard with the vinegar and pineapple juice and mix with the baked beans. Spread at the bottom of an oblong ovenproof dish. Cut the chopped pork with ham into 4 slices of equal thickness and arrange on top of the beans. Place a pineapple ring on top of each and stud each ring with 2 cloves. Cover and bake in a moderately hot oven (400°F. — Gas Mark 5) for about 30 minutes.

17   SAVOURY BEAN BAKE

2 large cans baked beans	*1 or 2 tomatoes (skinned)*
2 hard-boiled eggs	*salt and pepper to taste*
1 medium-sized	*4 oz. grated Cheddar*
Spanish onion	*cheese*
1 oz. butter (or olive	*few breadcrumbs*
oil)	*little extra butter*

Turn baked beans into a buttered fireproof dish and fold in 1 chopped hard-boiled egg. Peel and slice onion and fry in fat or oil until soft. Set aside some of the onion rings, keeping them warm. Fold remainder into bean mixture together with seasoning to taste and half the grated cheese. Sprinkle remaining cheese over surface, adding a few breadcrumbs and pieces of butter. Set dish in a moderately hot oven to heat through and brown appetisingly on top. Garnish with wedges of remaining egg, onion rings and tomatoes.

18   FRENCH BEANS LYONNAISE

1 or 2 onions	*1 lb. French beans*
2 oz. butter	*seasoning*

Prepare the French beans and cook in boiling salted water until just tender. Meanwhile chop the onion very finely and fry in the butter until golden brown. Add the strained beans and toss gently in the onion mixture. Season well, and serve with chopped parsley.

19   FRENCH BEANS PAYSANNE

1 lb. French beans	*2 oz. butter*
small piece of boiled	*1 onion or shallot*
fat bacon or ham	*8 oz. tomatoes*
2 medium sized potatoes	*seasoning*
1 gill water	

Prepare the beans and cut into halves. Chop the onion or shallot and fry in the butter, until soft, but not browned. Dice the bacon or ham and brown gently in the pan, then add the beans, skinned and if possible de-seeded tomatoes, diced potatoes, seasoning and water. Bring just to boiling point, lower the heat and cook steadily for about 40 minutes until tender. Either strain or serve in the liquid in which cooked. Excellent with grilled sausages, gammon or pork.

BEETROOT

20   BEETROOT CUPS

Scoop centre out of small cooked beetroot. Fill with mixed vegetables and diced cheese or meat and French dressing (Recipe 343) for a cold supper dish.

21   HOT BEETROOT

Toss sliced beetroot in melted butter, add seasoning, chopped chives and squeeze lemon juice OR grate beetroot coarsely and mix with creamy white sauce.

Artichokes

5 ARTICHOKE FRITTERS

Cook globe artichokes as directed in Recipe 4 but be careful they do not become over-cooked; they should be slightly firm. Allow to cool until able to handle and cut into fairly thick slices. Coat in a thin batter and fry until golden brown.

6 STUFFED ARTICHOKES

4 globe artichokes	seasoning
1 small onion or shallot	1 or 2 teaspoons chopped
2 oz. chopped ham	parsley
2 oz. butter	4 bacon rashers
4 chopped mushroom	

For the sauce

¼ gill white wine	1 sliced carrot
1 sliced onion	seasoning

Trim the outer leaves from the artichokes, put into boiling salted water and cook steadily for 15 minutes. Meanwhile heat the butter and fry the chopped onion and mushroom in this; add the rest of the ingredients except the rashers of bacon. Allow the artichokes to become cool enough to handle, then remove the chokes from the centre of each artichoke. Fill with the ham and onion mixture. Wrap a rasher of bacon round each artichoke, and secure with fine string or a small skewer. Put into a casserole, and cover with the sauce ingredients. Cover the casserole, and cook for approximately 1 hour in the centre of a moderate oven (350—375°F. — Gas Mark 3—4). Remove the string or skewer and serve with the sauce, which can be thickened slightly if desired.

Asparagus

7 ASPARAGUS AS AN ACCOMPANIMENT

While asparagus is served quite often as a separate course it is an excellent accompaniment to meat, fish or poultry. The coloured picture no. 14 shows cooked asparagus garnished with a ring of red pepper, banana fritters (Recipe 371,) and meat balls.

8 ASPARAGUS NORMANDE

Cook the asparagus as directed in Recipe 4. Heat a good knob of butter and about 1 gill cream very gently together. Pour over the asparagus and dust with a little red pepper.

9 ASPARAGUS PARMESAN

Cook the asparagus as directed in Recipe 4, until a light golden brown. Carefully put into a rather shallow large dish, cover with melted butter, and finely grated Parmesan cheese and brown for just a few minutes under a heated grill.

10 ASPARAGUS POLONAISE

Cook the asparagus as directed in Recipe 4 and while cooking brown fine breadcrumbs in hot butter. Add 1 or 2 chopped hard-boiled eggs, and 2—3 teaspoons chopped parsley. Put this mixture over asparagus just before serving. Heat more butter to serve separately.

Aubergines (Egg Plant)

11 FRIED AUBERGINES OR EGGPLANT

Halve aubergines. Scoop out the hard centre core and fry the aubergine cases until just tender. Fill the cases with a cooked 'sage and onion stuffing. Serve with bacon and sliced carrots.

12 FRIED AUBERGINE SLICES

Cut aubergines across in thin slices. Coat lightly with seasoned flour, fry until crisp and pale golden brown.

13 STUFFED AUBERGINES

(4 small or 2 large servings)

2 medium-sized	1 skinned chopped tomato
aubergines	2 oz. fresh breadcrumbs
¼ teaspoon salt	seasoning
2 teaspoons olive oil	4 oz. grated Cheddar
2 oz. diced cooked bacon	cheese and 1 oz. extra
1 tablespoon chopped	1 tablespoon finely
parsley	chopped cooked onion

Wash aubergines, remove stalk, and cut in half lengthwise. Cut round each half aubergine ¼ inch from the skin and then score the surface lightly to ensure even cooking. Sprinkle with salt and olive oil. Put on a greased baking tin in a moderately hot even (400° F. — Gas Mark 5) until the centre is nearly cooked (15—20 minutes). Make stuffing by mixing all the ingredients together. Scoop out half flesh from centre of cooked aubergine, chop up and add to stuffing. Fill aubergine cases with stuffing, sprinkle with grated cheese and return to oven for 15 minutes. Serve hot with tomato or cheese sauce (Recipes 320 and 314).

14 AUBERGINES PROVENÇALE

2 aubergines	4 large tomatoes
1 shallot or onion	clove of garlic — more if
2 oz. butter or	desired
2 tablespoons oil	seasoning
parsley	little flour

Wash aubergines and cut into thin slices, removing any seeds. They can be peeled if wished. Coat with seasoned flour. Heat the butter or oil and fry the finely chopped shallot and crushed clove of garlic, then fry the aubergine until tender. Meanwhile skin and quarter the tomatoes and fry separately in a little extra butter or oil. Toss tomatoes and aubergines together and garnish with chopped parsley.

NETTLES	When young can be cooked like spinach — when preparing grasp firmly in gloved hands.	717
OKRA (Gumbo)	Pea-like vegetable in pod, obtainable canned if not fresh; slice, boil and serve with butter.	
ONIONS	Put into soups and stews, fried with meat or savoury dishes. As a separate vegetable boil for a good hour in salted water and serve with white sauce (see Recipe 312).	63—67, 230, 529—530
PARSLEY	Eat raw, use as garnish or fry.	703, 722
PARSNIPS	Boil, steam or put into soups and stews, but do not have too large a proportion of parsnips as their flavour is very strong and will dominate the dish. Very good baked round the meat.	108—110
PEAS	Shell and cook steadily in boiling salted water for 10 to 15 minutes. Serve with a little melted butter. Mint and a teaspoon of sugar improve the flavour.	68—70, 148, 182, 510, 513
PEPPERS, SWEET RED OR GREEN (Capsicums)	Shredded and used raw or fried, added to sauces, egg dishes, casserole or as main dish stuffed whole.	71—74, 556
PEPPERS, HOT RED OR GREEN (Chilis)	Very pungent. Use sparingly for flavouring.	
POTATOES	Always put into *boiling* salted water and cook steadily until soft. Can also be fried, roasted, baked in their jackets or steamed.	24, 70, 73—107, 151—3, 205, 209, 510, 515, 705
PUMPKIN	Use as vegetable marrow.	
RADISHES	Serve in salads or cook in place of turnips.	138
RUTABAGA	Swedish turnip, yellow or white fleshed. Cook like turnip.	
SALSIFY (sometimes called Oysterplant)	Wash or scrape well, then cook like Jerusalem artichokes. Serve with a little melted butter and chopped parsley.	
SAUERKRAUT	Made by fermenting cabbage: Recipe 113. Can be obtained ready prepared; heat with butter and flavourings.	113—115
SEAKALE	Cook like celery — rather bitter if served raw.	
SHALLOTS	Use like onions.	
SORREL	Generally used in soup but can be cooked like spinach.	
SPINACH	Wash leaves in several waters. There is no need to add water to spinach, so just put into a strong pan with a little salt and boil rapidly until tender — about 15 minutes. Turn on to a board and chop finely, then return to the pan with a little milk and butter and re-heat.	116—118, 254, 270
SPRING GREENS	Cook like cabbage.	
SQUASH	Cook like vegetable marrow.	
SWEDES	Cook like potatoes.	
SWEET POTATOES OR YAMS	Cook like turnips.	
TOMATOES	Delicious raw, or can be used in every way cooked; they add flavour to all savoury dishes.	119—122, 138, 155, 164, 210, 230, 294, 558—561, 567, 614, 635, 665, 673
TURNIPS	Put into soups and stews. When young they are very good cooked in boiled salted water, then mashed.	123, 124, 706
TURNIP TOPS	Cook like cabbage.	
VEGETABLE MARROW (when small known as courgettes)	Peel, cut into neat pieces and either steam over boiling water, adding a little salt, or bake stuffed, or boil in salted water until tender. Serve with cheese or white sauce (see Recipes 314, 312). Also used in sweet dishes and jam. Courgettes (baby marrows) are delicious cooked with garlic in butter and oil (see Recipe 129).	111, 112, 125—129, 524, 550, 715

CABBAGE, SPRING, SUMMER or SAVOY	Shred finely with sharp knife and boil rapidly for about 10 minutes in salted water. Serve raw in salads.	24—29, 82, 138, 140—3
CABBAGE, RED	Cook like green cabbage, or pickle.	30—32, 531
CARDOONS	Looks like tall celery. Cut away outer stem. Cut inner stems into short pieces, but leave heart whole. Put into boiling salted water with 1 tablespoon lemon juice or vinegar, cook steadily for 1½—2 hours until tender. Serve with melted butter or a white or hollandaise sauce (see Recipes 312, 331).	
CARROTS	Scrub well, cook in boiling salted water until soft.	33—35, 148, 510
CAULIFLOWER	Cut off thick stalks and outer leaves, divide head into small sprigs, cook rapidly in boiling salted water. Serve with white, parsley or cheese sauce (see Recipes 312, 319, 314).	36—42, 272
CELERIAC (turnip-rooted celery)	Large ugly root needs peeling and dicing. Cook like celery — tastes delicious.	
CELERY	Generally eaten raw and in salads, but very good cooked. Divide into neat pieces and cook in boiling salted water for about 20 minutes. Serve with white, parsley or cheese sauce or braise (see Recipes 312, 319, 314).	43—45, 138, 142—3, 510
CHARD	Cook like cabbage.	
CHESTNUTS	Slit skins, boil for 10 minutes then remove outer and inner skins. Finish cooking in boiling salted water. Serve as purée, with melted butter or mixed with Brussels sprouts (see Recipe 23).	23, 46
CHICORY	Cook like celery. In France and America this is called endive.	144, 334
CHIVES	Used chopped in flavouring as mild onion.	
CORN ON THE COB or SWEET CORN	Wash corn cob, strip off outer green leaves, and boil in salted water for about 20 minutes, until the corn feels soft. Serve with melted butter. Do not boil too quickly or for too long otherwise the corn becomes tough again.	47—50, 83, 146, 510
CUCUMBER	Generally served with vinegar, but can be boiled in pieces in salted water or braised like celery.	51—53, 138, 147, 523, 619
DANDELION LEAVES	Wash well. Cook like spinach or serve in salads.	701, 711
ENDIVE	Known as chicory in France and America. Cook like lettuce or serve in salads.	138
FENNEL	A little, cut finely, flavours a salad, but it can be cooked like other vegetables in boiling salted water and served with a white sauce. Particularly good served with fish.	
GARLIC	Use very sparingly — a clove is one small portion.	
KALE	Cook like cabbage or spinach.	
KOHL-RABI	Cook root like turnip; stems can be cooked separately.	
LEEKS	Cut off roots and outer leaves, split down the middle and wash thoroughly. Use in place of onions in soups and stews, or boil for 30 minutes in salted water. Serve with white or cheese sauce (see Recipes 312, 314).	44, 54, 55, 271
LENTILS	Dried pulse — soak and cook in main dishes.	
LETTUCE	Although normally served in salads, lettuce can be cooked like cabbage or in a little butter in a covered pan until soft, or braised.	56, 57 (see SALAD section, Recipes 138—193)
MUSHROOMS	Can be fried or grilled in butter or baked in a covered casserole for about 30 minutes. Mushrooms can also be stewed in milk, then remaining liquid thickened with a little flour or cornflour. Champignons or button mushrooms are the small round type, cèpes the larger flat type of mushroom.	53, 58—62, 94, 150, 513, 526, 566

Vegetable Cookery

3   CORRECT COOKING OF VEGETABLES

In order to retain both colour and vitamin content in vegetables it is important to cook them with care. Unless stated to the contrary vegetables should go into a small quantity of boiling salted water and in the case of a large amount of vegetable, like cabbage, should be added steadily rather than all at once. By putting into the water in this way the liquid keeps boiling.

Put a lid on to the pan and try to serve the vegetables immediately they are cooked, for keeping hot, even for a short time, causes a loss of vitamins. When cooking root vegetables, particularly potatoes, steady cooking, rather than too rapid, is considered advisable.

Most vegetables can be cooked with great success in a pressure cooker (see Recipe 1).

4   HOW TO PREPARE AND SERVE VEGETABLES

Vegetable	Basic method of cooking	Other Recipes
ARTICHOKES, GLOBE	Cook steadily in boiling salted water for about 30 minutes. Serve with a little melted butter, or white, cheese or hollandaise sauce (see Recipes 312, 314, 331)	5, 6
ARTICHOKES, JERUSALEM	Scrub well and peel or scrape. Soak in a little cold water, adding a few drops of vinegar. Cook for about 30 minutes in boiling salted water, adding a few drops of vinegar. Serve with melted butter, white, cheese or hollandaise sauce (see Recipes 312, 314, 331)	
ASPARAGUS	Wash carefully, then cut off a little of the thick white base of stalks. Either steam or boil the bunch in salted water in a tall pan for 20—25 minutes. Serve with melted butter or mousseline sauce (see Recipe 333)	7—10, 139, 177, 510, 723
AUBERGINES	Wash and remove any hard stalk. Bake in a casserole with knob of margarine and little milk for 30 minutes. Can be stuffed or fried like potatoes.	11—14, 111
BEANS, BROAD	Shell and wash, unless very young, when they can be cooked whole. Cook in boiling salted water for 20 minutes. Serve with melted butter and chopped parsley.	510
BEANS, BUTTER	Generally purchased dried. Soak overnight in cold, or better still, boiling water. Drain, cover with cold salted water and simmer gently for 2—3 hours. Drain and toss in butter and chopped parsley or serve with white sauce. Excellent pressure cooked (see Recipe 1).	187, 211, 299
BEANS, FRENCH or RUNNER	Wash and string. French beans can be left whole, but runner beans are better thinly sliced. Cook steadily in boiling salted water for about 15 minutes.	18, 19, 133, 510, 513, 514
BEANS, HARICOT, and FLAGEOLETS (Green Haricot Beans)	Prepare and cook like butter beans.	
BEANS, LIMA	Prepare and cook like butter beans. Add to casserole.	16, 17
BEETROOT	Wash carefully and cook in boiling salted water until soft; test by pressing gently. Generally served cold with salads, but delicious hot with parsley or hollandaise sauce (see Recipe 319, 331).	20, 21, 145, 510, 522, 544, 704
BROCCOLI	Cook large broccoli heads and sprouting broccoli like cauliflower and serve with melted butter or white sauce. Broccoli spears are cooked carefully like asparagus to retain firmness of stem; serve with melted butter or hollandaise sauce (see Recipe 331).	15
BRUSSELS SPROUTS	Mark cross with sharp knife at base of each sprout. Boil rapidly like cabbage.	22, 23

Basic Methods of Cooking

Baking — Cooking in dry heat in the oven.

Boiling — Cooking by immersing the food in a pan of liquid, which must be kept boiling gently — all the time.

Braising — Almost a combination of stewing and roasting. Meat is placed on a bed of vegetables with a little liquid surrounding, in a covered vessel, and cooked slowly in the oven.

Casserole — Cooking slowly in the oven in a covered casserole dish — usually meat, rabbit, etc.

Frying — Cooking in a little hot fat in an open pan. Deep frying is cooking by immersion in a deep pan of smoking hot fat.

Grilling — Cooking quickly under a red-hot grill: used for small tender pieces of meat, fish, etc.

Poaching — Cooking gently in water which is just below boiling point: usually eggs or fish.

Pressure Cooking — Cooking at higher temperatures than usual, so that food is cooked much more quickly.

Roasting — Cooking with a little fat in a hot oven. Fat is poured from the baking tin over the meat or poultry from time to time, using a long-handled spoon: this is known as basting.

Simmering — The rate of cooking used for stews — just below boiling point, so that the liquid bubbles gently at the side of the pan.

Steaming — Cooking either in a steamer over a pan of boiling water, or in a basin standing in (but not covered by) boiling water.

Stewing — Cooking slowly until the food is tender. It is done in just enough liquid to cover the food, as the liquid is served with it and should be rich. Stews may be cooked in covered saucepans or casseroles, either on a hotplate or in the oven — but always at a low temperature.

1   PRESSURE COOKING OF VEGETABLES

The importance of cooking vegetables correctly, so that they lose as little as possible of their value, has been stressed more and more during recent years. The correct way to cook vegetables is to put them into the smallest quantity of water, in a covered container, and cook them for the shortest possible time — in this way they retain not only their vitamin content but their colour and flavour. When vegetables are cooked in a pressure cooker this procedure is carried out, and in consequence vegetables are cooked to perfection.

1. Remember that every minute of pressure cooking time is equivalent to many minutes in an ordinary saucepan, so time the cooking very accurately.

2. It is important to see that pieces of vegetable are much of the same size; obviously if care is not taken smaller pieces or sprigs of cauliflower, for example, will be badly over-cooked by the time the larger pieces are ready.

3. Pressure should be lowered immediately by putting the cookers under the cold water tap for 10—15 seconds. The exception to this rule is when cooking potatoes — they will be more 'floury' if pressure is allowed to drop gradually.

4. Since only a small quantity of water is used in cooking vegetables, less than the usual amount of salt is needed.

5. Unless vegetables are being cooked as part of a meat dish — such as braised or stewed dishes — they will be better if put on the racks.

Times at 15 lb. pressure

While the time for cooking the various vegetables is given as accurately as possible, it might vary very slightly, due to larger vegetables being used. At the end of the season when vegetables are getting older they will naturally take a little longer to cook, so to counteract this they should be cut rather smaller.

Artichokes (Globe) 10 minutes; (Jerusalem) 10 minutes
Asparagus 2 minutes
Aubergine or Egg-plant 3 minutes; (Stuffed) 4 minutes
Beans (Haricot) 30 minutes (after soaking)
Beans (Broad) 3 minutes   Beans (Runner) 2 minutes
Beetroot 10—25 minutes   Brussels Sprouts 2 minutes
Cabbage 2—3 minutes   Carrots 3—8 minutes
Cauliflower 2—5 minutes   Celery 3 minutes
Chicory 3 minutes   Corn on the Cob 4 minutes
Leeks 3 minutes   Mushrooms 2—3 minutes
Onions 6 minutes
Peas (Fresh) ½—1½ minutes; (Dried or Split) 15 minutes
Peppers (Red or Green, Stuffed) 3—4 minutes
Potatoes 8—15 minutes   Salsify 10 minutes
Spinach 1 minute   Turnips 3—8 minutes
Vegetable Marrow 2 minutes

2   TO PRESSURE COOK FRUIT

Although soft fruits like raspberries or redcurrants do not require the rapid cooking of a pressure cooker, there are many others where cooking time can be saved with improved results. In particular, dried fruits and hard cooking pears, which normally are stewed for a very long period, can now be cooked in a pressure saucepan within minutes. As well as saving time, the flavour of pressure cooked fruit is always excellent, because such small quantities of liquid are used in cooking that the juice is never watery but full of fruit flavour. Allow ¼ pint water to 1 lb. fruit. Never have the pressure cooker more than half full when cooking fruit pulp, and allow pressure to drop gradually.

Apples 2 minutes   *Purée 3 minutes*
Gooseberries 2 minutes   *Purée 4 minutes*
Plums 3 minutes   *Rhubarb Purée 4 minutes*

Weights and Measures

English weights and measures·have been used throughout this book. 3 teaspoonfuls equal 1 tablespoon. The average English teacup is ¼ pint or 1 gill. The average English breakfast cup is ½ pint or 2 gills.

When cups are mentioned in recipes they refer to a B.S.I. measuring cup which holds ½ pint or 10 fluid ounces. The B.S.I. standard tablespoon measures 1 fluid ounce.

In case it is wished to translate any of the weights and measures into their American, Canadian or French counterparts, the following tables give a comparison:

Liquid Measure

The most important difference to be noted is that the American and Canadian pint is 16 fluid ounces, as opposed to the British Imperial pint, which is 20 fluid ounces. The American ½-pint measuring cup is therefore actually equivalent to two-fifths of a British pint.

French Weights and Measures

It is difficult to convert to French measurements with absolute accuracy, since 1 oz. is equivalent to 28.352 grammes. The table below is therefore very approximate.

Solid Measure

ENGLISH		AMERICAN
1 pound	Butter or other fat	2 cups
1 pound	Flour	4 cups
1 pound	Granulated or Castor Sugar	2 cups
1 pound	Icing or Confectioners' Sugar	3 cups
1 pound	Brown (moist) Sugar	2½ cups
1 pound	Golden Syrup or Treacle	1 cup
1 pound	Rice	2 cups
1 pound	Dried Fruit	2 cups
1 pound	Chopped Meat (finely packed)	2 cups
1 pound	Lentils or Split Peas	2 cups
1 pound	Coffee (unground)	2½ cups
1 pound	Soft breadcrumbs	4 cups
½ ounce	Flour	1 level tablespoon (must be proper measuring tablespoon)
1 ounce	Flour	1 heaped tablespoon
1 ounce	Sugar	1 level tablespoon
½ ounce	Butter	1 tablespoon smoothed off
1 ounce	Golden Syrup or Treacle	1 level tablespoon
1 ounce	Jam or Jelly	1 level tablespoon

Liquid Measure. Approximately 1¾ pints may be regarded as equal to 1 litre. 1 demilitre is half a litre, and 1 décilitre is one-tenth of a litre.
Solid Measure. 1 oz. is equal to approximately 30 grammes.
Approximately 2 lb. 3 oz, is equal to 1 kilogramme.

Oven Temperatures

In most recipes in this book reference has been given to the oven temperature or the gas setting. This is an approximate guide only. Different makes of cooker vary and it is a fact that even the same make of cooker can give slightly different individual results at the same temperature or setting.

If in doubt as to whether the temperature given is EXACTLY right for your particular cooker, then do at all times refer to your own manufacturer's temperature chart. It is impossible in a general book to be exact for every cooker, but you will find that the following are a good average in every case.

	Electricity °F.	Gas Regulo.	°C.
COOL oven	225—250	0—½	107—121
VERY SLOW oven	250—275	½—1	121—135
SLOW oven	275—300	1—2	135—149
VERY MODERATE oven	300—350	2—3	149—177
MODERATE oven	375	4	190
MODERATELY HOT oven	400	5	204
HOT oven	425—450	6—7	218—133
VERY HOT oven	475—500	8—9	246—260

Introduction

In this book you will find more than 700 helpful recipes on the foods which are either home grown or considered basic natural foods: fruits, vegetables, cheese, eggs, milk, butter, ham and bacon.

I have given you a large selection of recipes for cooking vegetables, either to serve as part of a meal or, in many cases, as a complete dish — and you will find new and interesting salads and ways of serving and preserving all the fruits that are now available.

Most housewives feel proud of a well-stocked store cupboard. Jams, pickles, chutneys and bottles of fruit are neither difficult nor expensive to prepare when the ingredients are home-grown or in season, yet what a difference they make to winter catering! There is also a large section on home-made drinks and wines, many of them old traditional recipes which have been handed down through several generations.

In these days of home freezers many people like to freeze their own produce and you will find help on this, as well as on canning. I hope that this book will give you as much pleasure to use as it did me to compile for I feel it enables modern housewives to retain the pride in home cooking made so famous by our grandmothers.

The recipes will serve four people unless otherwise stated. Once again my thanks are due to the many Home Economists who worked so hard to produce the splendid pictures.

Marguerite Patten.

Contents

Weights and measures etc.

Pressure cooking of vegetables and fruit — Recipes 1—2

Vegetable cookery — 3—136

Salads — 137—193

Dairy Produce: Cheese, eggs, milk, butter, ham and bacon — 194—312

Sauces and dressings — 312—355

Fruit — 356—496

To crystallise fruit — 477—482

Using spices and herbs — 483—489

Dried fruits — 490—494

Bottling and preserving fruit and vegetables — 497—517

Pickles, chutneys and relishes — 518—569

Jams, jellies and marmalade — 570—664

Canning — 665—666

Home made drinks and wines — 667—722

Freezing of foods — 723

Index and acknowledgements follow last recipe

© Paul Hamlyn Limited 1962

PAUL HAMLYN LIMITED

WESTBOOK HOUSE · FULHAM BROADWAY · LONDON

Printed in Czechoslovakia

MARGUERITE PATTEN'S
BOOK OF

FRUIT AND VEGETABLE COOKERY

— and eggs, cheese, bacon, pickles, chutneys, jams, home-made wines

PAUL HAMLYN · LONDON